GW00580231

A Market Town
and its Surrounding Villages

Cranbrook, Kent in the Later Seventeenth Century

A Market Town
and its Surrounding Villages

Cranbrook, Kent in the Later Seventeenth Century

ANTHONY POOLE

Phillimore

2005

Published by
PHILLIMORE & CO. LTD
Shopwyke Manor Barn, Chichester, West Sussex, England
www.phillimore.co.uk

© Anthony Poole, 2005

ISBN 1 86077 345 1

Printed and bound in Great Britain by
ANTONY ROWE
Chippenham, Wiltshire

Contents

List of Illustrations, Figures, Maps and Tables

Illustrations

Figures and Maps

Tables

Acknowledgements

I owe a debt of gratitude to the late Professor Kevin Keohane, then Chairman of Governors at Wimbledon College, for facilitating my retirement three years early, and to Paul Hodges, then head of the department of Humanities at Roehampton, for having the faith to take on one apparently so ill-equipped to tackle the seventeenth century. Since then several kind people have helped and encouraged me in one way or another: they include Elizabeth Parkinson, by her infectious enthusiasm and expertise on the hearth tax, Joanna Mackinder for maps of nonconformists in the Weald, Susan Rose and Sarah Pearson by their help with the Kent hearth tax returns, Cliff Webb by his ideas on apprenticeship, and the staff of the Society of Genealogists and the Centre for Kentish Studies for their cheerful forbearance.

To my academic supervisors I owe an incalculable debt: to Peter Edwards for his unflagging willingness and determination, and to Margaret Spufford for her courteous encouragement and consideration, and her fund of knowledge and common sense. In this I also associate her husband, Peter, who has been cheerfully helpful at every turn, and Joan Thirsk and David Hey who encouraged me to make my findings more public.

I should also like to thank Mrs Betty Carman and Tony Allison, archivists respectively at the Cranbrook Museum and St Dunstan's Church, Cranbrook, and Richard Harris at the Weald and Downland Open Air Museum, for their ready cooperation and advice when I was in search of appropriate illustrations. I should like further to acknowledge with thanks the following for permission to reproduce illustrations: the Centre for Kentish Studies for nos. 1-3, 5, 7, 21-2, 24-8; Lord Cornwallis for no. 19; Rev. Martin Burrell, vicar of Cranbrook, for nos. 17, 18, 26 and 28; Rev. A.E. Norris, rector of Frittenden, for nos. 24 and 25; Rev. Canon Christopher Smith, vicar of Benenden, for nos. 3 and 21; Rev. Canon Paul Cox, rector of Biddenden, for nos. 2, 22 and 27; Bridget and David Connell for their photographs of exhibits at the Weald and Downland Museum reproduced as nos. 10-16; Dr Douglas Moss for his photographs nos. 17 and 18; the Cranbrook Museum for permission to reproduce nos. 6, 8, 9, 20 and 29; The National Portrait Gallery, London, for no. 23; and Margaret and Peter Spufford for no. 4. Finally my thanks go out to Phillimore, especially to Noel Osborne, Sarah Kiddle and Nicola Willmot, for guiding this work to fruition, and to my wife Patricia, who has lived with my distractions with unqualified support and understanding.

ANTHONY POOLE

September 2005

Foreword

It is a very long time since I wrote a plea in *Contrasting Communities*, which appeared in 1974, for studies by local historians based not on individual communities, as I had then just done, but on 'social areas' based on a contiguous group of parishes, ideally focused on a market town. I had found yeomen in all of 'my' parishes buying land for their sons in adjacent parishes, finding the daughters of other yeomen in neighbouring parishes suitably well dowered as brides for the same sons, and even purchasing manors elsewhere for themselves. The poorer people hired themselves out as servants over an extensive area round their own parishes. I did not then realise that the overseers of the poor habitually apprenticed poor children out well beyond the parish boundaries, nor had I become aware of the range of shops which drew 17th-century people well beyond even their own local market towns. Dr Susan Mee, who is now (2005) completing with me a book on *The Clothing of the Common Sort*, has compiled a voluminous list of all the retailers she has found from the probate accounts in Kent, which is quite startling in its length and variety. People in Cranbrook and around commonly went to Maidstone (p.22).

All that a group of my then research students and I have done since 1974 towards this goal of covering an extended area, is a study of heterodox belief, which we centred on the market town of Amersham in Buckinghamshire, a focus of late Lollardy. That showed that later Lollards and Quakers were so eager for contact with each other that they would travel well beyond the ten-mile limit around Amersham, which we thought reasonable (*The World of Rural Dissenters*, 1995, Maps 2 & 3, pp.112 and 137). Even this relatively small piece of work based on a marketing region was enough to demonstrate how enormously time-consuming such a study would be.

Now Anthony Poole has done it. The area round the market town of Cranbrook in the well-wooded area of the High Weald in Kent is of particular interest, not only because of its lengthy puritan history, but also because a detailed study of a market town and its adjacent parishes has never previously been completed, to my knowledge.

Dr Poole has very good source material, and he is meticulous in his use of evidence, checking one source very carefully against another for accuracy. His work is grounded in a reconstruction of families from the registers, limited to the period 1660-1700, although he pursues individual families both forward and backward from those time limits. He finds a tenth of his children un-baptised: something like 27 per cent of nonconformist children are missing from the record. This is not surprising, considering that, in 1676, Cranbrook with 31 per cent and two adjacent parishes with 35 per cent and 39 per cent of nonconformists were not unfaithful to their puritan past. He also found relevant baptisms quite often in the parish of the bride's parents – which could not have been found in any single parish study. Because it is rooted in the parish registers his major emphasis is on the formation and maintenance of the family and provision for its orphans. His world of kin and neighbourliness, spreading as it does between parishes, is set against an excellent chapter outlining the economy of this pastoral and clothing area. Clothing continued to dominate Cranbrook until the 18th century (Fig. 2.4, p.33). Despite this the connection between cloth-production and dissent which has so often puzzled historians is not environmentally determined. The Weald of Sussex immediately touching on the borders of these Kentish parishes only had a median of three per cent of nonconformists (Fig. 2.7, p.43). The particular determinism which ran 'forest = weavers = nonconformity' can be dropped. Because partible inheritance was the norm in Kent, most farms or fragments of land were too small to support a household by themselves, so the world of these parishes was a world of multiple occupations. Even multiple occupations did not always make ends meet and he has an innovative chapter on the rampant use of credit in these seven parishes. This new realisation of endemic debt has never been adopted and examined in a local study before.

Dr Poole has splendidly conveyed the close working and family connections of the 'chiefer inhabitants', the office-holders who actually ran these parishes. He shows schematically their relationships to each other in a series of diagrams which illustrate their inter-marriages, their services to each other as overseers, executors and guardians after death, and will-witnessing before death. In this he follows Professor Takahashi, who mapped the relationships between villagers to illustrate them in a very telling way in 1996 (*Albion*, 28, Figs. 3-7, pp.410-14), yet these close-knit vestrymen of the Cranbrook area were not totally exclusive: just as on the much more egalitarian fen-edge of Willingham they also used many poorer will-witnesses to perform these services for them. There was no rigid social divide.

When he reaches the 'other inhabitants' an ironic point emerges. We know a great deal about the office-holders. We also know a great deal about the poor, thanks to his splendid analysis of the careful work of the churchwardens and the overseers of the poor which gives much insight into the world of the poverty stricken. These made up between a third and a half of the inhabitants. But ironically we know least about the husbandmen and craftsmen who made up the ordinary people in the population, those who lived in houses with one or two hearths. These people in the middle, who neither held office, nor were exempt from rates or taxation, the 'common sort', are least visible to us, unless they happen to be owed wages on the death of an inhabitant whose probate account survives. Can any historian suggest a means of throwing a searchlight on the doings of these most illusive of our ancestors, in most places the silent majority?

Good microscopic studies are of national importance. It has been a long time since mining *Whickham* appeared, and although we have had dairying *Myddle* for even longer, we have never had a study of a group of parishes around a market town before, let alone one on the wooded-heavy clays where oxen were still the normal draught animals. This study of Cranbrook fills a gap on our shelves. Dr Poole is to be congratulated.

MARGARET SPUFFORD

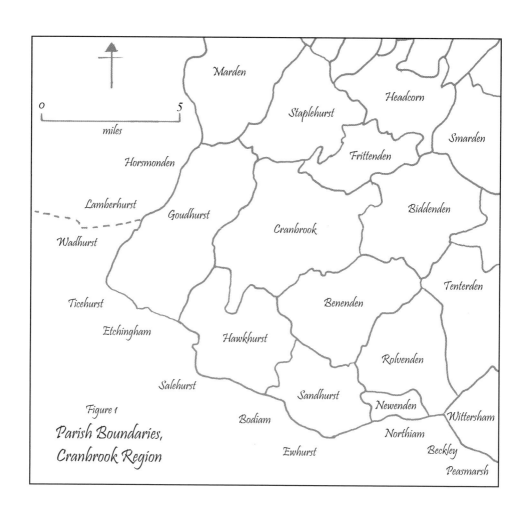

Figure 1

Parish Boundaries, Cranbrook Region

Introduction

It is nearly forty years since Margaret Spufford, doyenne of 16th- and 17th-century local history, expressed the need for someone to undertake the study of a '"neighbourhood" or contingent group of communities', ideally centred on a market town.[1] She saw this as important because, although the activities of most people at that time were short-distance, they crossed individual parish boundaries. This book is based on a study which attempted to fulfil that need,[2] and to satisfy another of her pleas, more recently expressed: that all work on local history should be seen against a background by which the typicality of the area of study might be judged. This, she suggested, is 'increasingly ... the central problem with which micro-historians have to wrestle.'[3]

The neighbourhood chosen is Cranbrook and its six contiguous parishes in the Weald of Kent. The period centres on the 40 years between the Restoration of the monarchy in 1660 and the close of the 17th century. The following pages are increasingly filled, not with the great men whose actions influenced politics and national events, but with local people. Their concerns were with their households and their families, their lands, their livestock and their living, and their local churches or non-conformist conventicles.

The main reason for choosing Cranbrook as the central market town was that its registers are substantially complete for the period in question, as are the registers of each of the six parishes which border it. The period itself coincides with the Hearth Tax returns, recently published for Kent,[4] and benefits from some remarkably full contemporary accounts by Churchwardens and Overseers of the Poor, as well as from a wealth of probate records.

Any worthwhile attempt to understand 17th-century village societies requires as thorough a knowledge as possible of the men, women and children who peopled those villages. The first task, therefore, was to construct a comprehensive picture of the inhabitants of the seven parishes. In 1966, E.A. Wrigley introduced to England the technique used by Louis Henry in France of reconstituting the families of a given parish by using its parish registers; Alan Macfarlane later explored how this basic information might be enhanced to provide a more thorough picture.[5] He recommended use of every document relating to a selected area and those living there to build up a profile of a parish or parishes.

Wrigley and Macfarlane stressed the time-consuming nature of such work, and Pamela Sharpe subsequently argued that even to link documentary sources to an existing family reconstitution is 'simply not cost-effective for the single researcher to

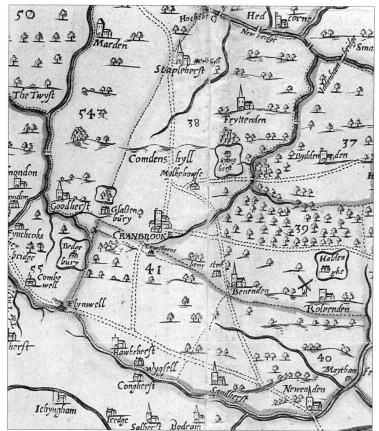

1. Detail from 'A new description of Kent', by Philip Symondson. He first published his map of the County of Kent in 1596; the third edition, shown here, is dated 1659. (CKS 16/1203)

undertake'.[6] What makes the present task so accessible is that it concerns a period of just forty years; it sets out to provide a snapshot of village societies rather than to trace their development over time. The resulting window may be small but the view is panoramic.

The first chapter looks at the sources used and suggests some caveats when interpreting them, and the second chapter sketches in the background essential to understanding post-restoration Kent. In the pages which follow there are constant references to parents, children, family groups and kinship links. Most of these relationships are secure, and have been confirmed by probate or other evidence. Nevertheless, one should take note of the cautionary words of David Hey, in his analysis of Richard Gough's contemporary account of the parishioners of Myddle, when he says 'time after time [Gough] explains a relationship that cannot be worked out from other sources; so much so, in fact, that one wonders how other demographers manage without a Gough. Far too many of the most obvious guesses about relationships are found to be completely wrong when checked with Gough'.[7]

All dates are new style.

Chapter 1

The Sources

Parish Registers

The most important source for the names of the people who lived in any English village in the latter half of the 17th century is likely to be the record of baptisms, marriages and burials provided by the Anglican parish registers of the period. This registration process, however, suffered change. In many English parishes it was greatly disrupted in the 1640s by the Civil War, and from 1653 to 1660 a civil registration system was imposed by Parliament.[1] A parish 'Register' was now elected by parishioners and sworn in by one of the local Justices of the Peace; he was to record births (not baptisms), marriages and burials, and local justices presided over the marriage ceremonies until at least 1657.[2] The registers of all but one of the Cranbrook area parishes benefited from this requirement, and in three parishes the entries during the 1650s are particularly detailed.

The Restoration of the Monarchy in 1660 heralded a reversion to traditional recording by Anglican clergy. Then from 1 August 1678 a new Act of Parliament required that all persons had to be buried in woollen cloth, and that fact recorded in the register. Finally, the so-called Marriage Duty Act, which came into force in May 1695, could have affected the coverage of registration. It required commissioners to break down the population of a given area by status groups for the purpose of taxation, and to widen the scope of parochial registration of births and deaths so that they could be taxed as well.[3]

Reconstitution of the family groups which lived in the Cranbrook area in the latter half of the 17th century naturally began with the marriage registers, recording the creation of a new family in embryo. To these couples were added their children as indicated by the baptismal registers, while a constant check on the survival or otherwise of family members was provided by the registers of burial. From the start this reconstitution process encompassed everyone, recording every entry of baptism, marriage and burial unless the individual concerned was clearly a stranger. Spinsters, bachelors and otherwise apparently unconnected individuals were recorded, thereby taking note of concerns that earlier reconstitutions dealt only with families.[4]

Frequently marriages took place, and were therefore recorded, in a different parish from the one in which the couple settled, but baptismal entries invariably give the name of the father and usually of the mother. Some families were therefore built up with the date of marriage and details of the antecedents of the parents unknown.

Subsequently many of these details, and the circumstances of apparently unconnected individuals, could be added from other sources, fully justifying Macfarlane's preferred approach and ensuring that the reconstitution was not restricted to a small subset of a parish.[5] Inevitably, however, families do dominate the reconstitution.

Families do not, of course, fit neatly into a 40-year period, so those which were half-formed in the 1650s were pursued back in time (sometimes without success because of lack of registration in the 1640s and 1650s), and those incomplete in 1700 were pursued into the 18th century, so that a more complete picture could be formed. Peripheral parishes were also looked at, with useful results in terms of dates of marriages and, occasionally, burials or baptisms in adjacent parishes.

Because parish registers are at the heart of the reconstitution process, we need a clear idea of their accuracy and their coverage if we are to gauge their reliability, and therefore the validity of any conclusions. This is probably best achieved by looking, in turn, at the twin problems of defective registration and under-registration.[6]

Defective Registration

Some 17th-century parish registers were diligently and regularly compiled, but many are in fact secondary texts, copied up monthly, or maybe quarterly or even annually, by a clerk, a curate or the incumbent. In practice a rough-book was often kept in which events were jotted down more or less as they happened; such a note-book survives from the parish of Mitcham in Surrey. Comparison between the notebook and the final register reveals omissions, additions and discrepancies over forenames, surnames and relationships. Some clerks did not even maintain a rough book but made notes on scraps of paper; the reference in the register of St Peter's, Dorchester, under the year 1645, to 52 persons who had died within the year but whose names had not been inserted because of the death of the old clerk who had the notes, probably does not reflect a unique situation![7]

Incumbents had to send copies of their registers to the diocesan registry every year, and these returns are known as Bishop's, or Archdeacon's, Transcripts (BTs or ATs); there were no transcripts during the Commonwealth. In the Canterbury Archdiocese the BTs went to the consistory court at Michaelmas, the ATs to the archdeacon's court at Easter. Because they should be an exact copy of the original, these returns are invaluable in supplying details where parish registers have been lost. Anyone who has worked with them, however, knows that copies were rarely exactly accurate. In a detailed comparison of a South Yorkshire parish register with copies in the BTs, for instance, Dennis Ashurst found typical discrepancies.[8] Mostly these consist of variations in the spelling of surnames, which causes neither surprise (at a period when an individual could spell his own name in different ways within the course of one page) nor concern (since it is a normal hazard of research). More seriously, copies sometimes contain entries which are not in the originals, and some register entries do not appear in the copies.

Identification of occupations occasionally differs between one version of the register and another, with the definition of husbandman, labourer and farmer clearly resting in the eye of respective scribes. Again such findings should not cause concern; rather they reinforce the need for flexibility in approaching such definitions, especially as a person's status could change over time, and not a few had multiple occupations. Of more concern are actual changes in surname and forename, which do happen, though usually on a relatively insignificant scale.

The extent to which any register is defective can largely be gauged from an internal audit of the documents themselves. Five of the seven parishes being considered here actually contributed to the statistics which formed the basis of Wrigley and Schofield's monumental work on the population history of England; such a fact might encourage one to think that their registers must be reliable.[9] On the other hand, of the three tests imposed by Wrigley and Schofield in choosing their parishes, the first concerned the accuracy of aggregative totals as presented by workers in the field, and the second simply required that registers were extant from at least January 1662. Neither of these tests related to the quality of the registers as such. Only the third test, that a parish should be rejected if in any consecutive run of 40 years of baptisms there were 20 years without a recorded baptism (and similarly for burials), imposed any limitation on the quality of the registers, and this 20-year rule was hardly stringent; it was inserted to allow the use of those many registers which had failed to cover the Commonwealth period.[10] It follows, therefore, that inclusion of our parishes among the 404 used by Wrigley and Schofield does not establish their quality.

The marriage registers of Benenden, Cranbrook and Hawkhurst are very full for the period 1653 to 1662, and at Cranbrook the baptism and burial records are full for the same period. It is probably no exaggeration to suggest that the records from these parishes for this period are as comprehensive as those of Colyton in Devon which Wrigley famously used for the first family reconstitution.[11] For this very restricted period, therefore, these registers provide us with a wealth of information on the occupation and parish of origin of those about to be married, and therefore clarifies contacts across parish borders.

All the parishes except Frittenden have adequate marriage registers for the period 1660 to 1700, and even for Frittenden a record can be reconstructed satisfactorily from surviving BTs and ATs back to 1661. Marriage registers frequently provide the parish of origin of the bride and groom. Some marriages escaped record altogether, especially after 1660, and others took place outside the parishes of the Cranbrook area, but baptismal information mitigates the effects of that lack by invariably naming the father and usually the mother. With minor breaks, and those usually in the early 1660s, all seven registers appear to provide a consistent coverage of baptisms. Canterbury marriage licences help to fill in dates and details, and reference to peripheral parishes and to Boyd's marriage indexes has added to the picture.

The burial registers have provided most difficulty because at Cranbrook (from 1662), Goudhurst (from 1680), Hawkhurst (especially from 1691) and Staplehurst (from 1693) the returns are minimal. When the deceased person is given a name but no further ascription it is sometimes impossible to be sure who has died. It is impossible adequately to identify a 'widow Sharpe' or 'Thomas Munn', and the formula 'child of ...', so commonplace in the Cranbrook burial register, makes precision impossible, whilst the Goudhurst register even fails to distinguish between adult and child.

The extant Frittenden record is full from 24 June 1696 onwards. Prior to that date, the BTs and ATs, in single unbound sheets each of which contains baptisms, marriages and burials, combine to provide a thorough coverage every year from 1661 onwards. What makes the Frittenden record so useful, however, is the preservation of the 'register of the parish of Frittenden since the Act was in force for buriing in woolen: viz from August 1st 1678.'[12] The relatives of the deceased person had to lodge an affidavit with the appropriate incumbent, at a cost of 1s, stating that burial had been in woollen.[13] If they failed to do so they were liable to a penalty of 50 shillings.[14] Each of the Frittenden depositions records the names of those who swore the oath, the name of the person before whom the oath was taken, and the names of the witnesses to the oath. Among Cranbrook area parishes the information contained in this register is unique, but it reflects what was also happening in the other parishes; it provides a vivid illustration of constant interplay across parish boundaries, and relationships between people of all walks of life (page 154).

Under-registration
Parish registers do not set out to provide the dates of vital events; what they record are the dates of baptisms, marriages and burials, a fact to which some commentators merely pay lip service, and which others fail even to recognise. On the other hand, burials and marriages do provide a close approximation to the vital events required for reconstitution. A delay between death and burial of more than a week was so exceptional as to allow use of the date of burial as an accurate indication of the date of death (Figure 1.1). Marriage dates directly relate to a life-changing moment. Failing them, banns of marriage give a potential date for a possible ceremony, and marriage licences provide an approximate date, often, but not always, within days of the ceremony. Baptisms are the least reliable indicator of vital events for two reasons: the delay between birth and baptism could vary greatly according to parish and period; and some children were simply omitted from the register. Baptismal delay and omission are best dealt with in turn.

For most periods, and in most parishes, registers recorded baptisms not births. If baptism had always taken place within a few days of birth, the close association of baptism and birth would render them interchangeable. Recent work, however, has shown that the commonly accepted view that post-Restoration baptisms took place within a few days of birth is based on a false premise.[15] Accumulated evidence over the last 30 years has shown a wide variation in baptismal delay between one parish and another at this time.[16] The evidence from Cranbrook and some of its neighbouring parishes is that baptism within days or weeks of birth was far from the norm in the two decades after 1660.

Figure 1.1 *Interval between death and burial, Hawkhurst, 1663-91*

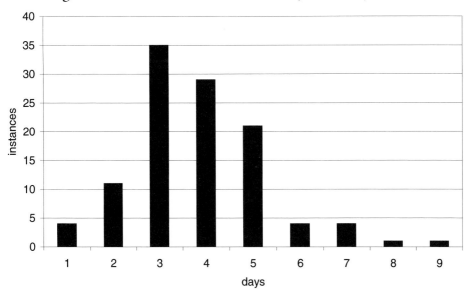

There is clear evidence that baptisms frequently did not follow closely on births during the late 17th century. The Acts of 1660-62, which brought back the established church and reinstated Anglican clergy, made orthodox public baptism mandatory again but could not enforce it. This was especially true where there was a strong nonconformist element within the parish. Ecclesiastical court records of the 1660s list page after page of laymen 'refusing baptizement' for their children. The churchwardens of Great Parndon, Essex, regretted in 1664, 'many children as yet unbaptized which were born in that notorious rebel's time'. As late as 1699 Robert Barrett, a medical writer, refers to bringing children to baptism as 'a duty nowadays too much neglected and slighted'. Cressy refers to some parishes where there was much rejoicing at whole families returning to the fold, with several children being baptised at the same time; in some Cranbrook parishes examples of such multiple baptisms are frequent.[17]

In their work on Terling in Essex, Wrightson and Levine note that as late as 1679 approximately 15 per cent of the householders of Terling were practising only a very severely limited conformity to the restored Church of England, while in addition something over 20 per cent of householders were failing to attend church at all. They go on to note, 'A number of former Baptists or Quakers were also won back in the course of the 1670s, bringing in droves of children to be baptized all at once and to have their dates of birth and baptism entered in the parish register.'[18]

Only one comment in the registers of the Cranbrook parishes contributes directly to the picture of non-registration, and that is the heartfelt cry of the vicar of Cranbrook, John Cooper, in August 1664, '*Multi in Parochia nostra nati, pauci Sacramento renati*'. This indication that many were born but few were baptised can be linked to the returns made for the Compton Census of 1676 in which the percentage of non-conformists in Cranbrook area parishes is high or very high (Figure 2.7). There is clear evidence in these registers throughout the period 1660 to 1700 of nonconformist families using the church for marriages and funerals but not for baptisms; they were not lost altogether to the registers, and therefore to the reconstitution. Quakers alone had the resources to eschew the intervention of the Anglican incumbent when it came to burial, and therefore escape registration altogether (page 187).

What makes the registers of Cranbrook and Benenden so significant is that, unusually, they provide both birth and baptism dates for a proportion of their entries at this time. For 28 per cent of baptisms in the Cranbrook registers between 1650 and 1700 the dates of birth are given as well as the dates of baptism. Of these, 75 per cent delayed the process of baptism by more than a month, a proportion which represents 21 per cent of all known baptisms; delays could be for as long as 30 years (Figure 1.2). Benenden, where the registers increasingly recorded both birth date and baptismal date during the period 1663-1699, shows a similar pattern (Figure 1.3). Between 1663 and 1679 the birth date is given as well as the baptismal date in 61 per cent of entries; this proportion rises to nearly 98 per cent between 1680 and 1699. Again lengthy delays occur, with cases of 28 and 29 years being recorded in the 1680s, but the concentration of delays of more than a year is in the 1660s and 1670s. Between 1663 and 1679, of the population of Benenden for whom the dates of birth and of baptism are known, only 48 per cent had their children baptised within a month of birth. By 1680-99 (when virtually all entries have birth and baptism dates) this figure had risen to 74 per cent. (See Table 1.1)

Figure 1.2   *Analysis of baptismal delay, Cranbrook, 1650-99*

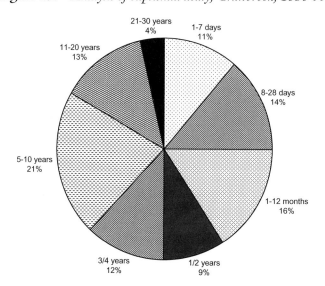

Figure 1.3   *Analysis of baptismal delay, Benenden, 1663-99*

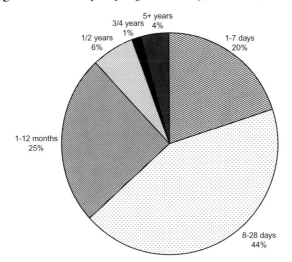

Table 1.1   *Birth-baptism delay, Cranbrook and Benenden, 1661-99*

	Cranbrook 1661-99	Benenden 1663-79	Benenden 1680-99
Percentage with both dates known	28%	60.7%	97.5%
Percentage of those baptised			
within 1 week	11% (75%)	8% (44%)	28% (30%)
4 weeks	25% (79%)	48% (68%)	74% (72%)
1 year	41% (83%)	76% (85%)	92% (92%)

Note: Percentages in brackets represent <u>maxima</u> for those baptised within a week, a month and a year; thus at Benenden, 1663-1679, no more than 68% could have been baptised within 4 weeks.

It might be argued that the reason why the registrars at Cranbrook and Benenden provided dates of birth and baptism for some but not all their entries is that they only recorded exceptional delays in this way. Such a suggestion, however, is disproved by the many instances when the interval given between dates of birth and baptism was but a few days. On the other hand, when only the baptism date is given, one must assume for statistical purposes that baptism occurred within a week or two of birth as statute required.[19] The resultant percentages of those delaying are therefore *minima*, with the unknown 'true' percentages almost certainly higher than those calculated. At the very least, therefore, 21 per cent of people in Cranbrook at this period delayed their baptism by a month or more, and 17 per cent by a year or more. In Benenden during the first half of the period the equivalent figures are 32 per cent and 15 per cent, while during the second half of the period those figures had reduced to at least 28 per cent and eight per cent. It follows that one cannot treat baptisms from these two parishes as if they were births. Because the Restoration of the established church in 1660 affected every parish in the country, baptism dates may bear little relationship to birth dates in many parishes where the nonconformist element was strong.

Three strands of evidence help to quantify omissions from baptismal registers. The first, quite simply, is statements in burial registers which indicate that the deceased had not been baptised. Burial registers regularly record infants buried without baptism, who are therefore known only from their deaths. They are normally identified as 'unbaptized infant' or 'unbaptized child' or 'chrisomer'; those recorded as 'stillborn' have not been included on the grounds that they never lived in the parish. Table 1.2 quantifies those stated in burial records to have missed baptism, and shows that, on average, six per cent of children born to families in the Cranbrook region were omitted from the baptismal registers in this way.

Table 1.2 *Live births recorded in burial, but not baptismal, registers*

	Benenden	Biddenden	Cranbrook	Hawkhurst	Staplehurst	Total
children recorded	1474	1562	3129 *	1601	922	8688
buried unbaptised	103	177	213	20	24	537
as a percentage	7	11.3	6.8	1.3	2.6	6.2

Note: * The Cranbrook burial register often refers to deaths of children simply as 'child of ...', without specifying a name. As a result, in 284 out of 3,271 entries it has been impossible to tell whether the deceased was an established child or new-born. The figure of 3,129 represents the mean between the maximum of 3,271 and minimum of 2,987 children born alive. Correspondingly, the percentage given for Cranbrook represents the mean figure between maximum and minimum.

The second strand of evidence for the non-registration of children concerns those revealed by probate accounts. These list under-age children who were due to benefit from the estate of a deceased parent who died intestate; comparison of such lists with the names of those recorded in the baptismal registers reveals the children who were omitted from the registers. Before they can be used statistically, there has to be sound evidence that the parents were living in the area for the whole period of the formation of their family, and that their children could, and should, have been registered. As a result of these necessary restrictions, only 113 of the children mentioned in probate accounts match the criteria, and the unregistered children (32, or 27 per cent) seem to represent occasional omissions. The main exception is Cranbrook, where some families appear to have been resident in the parish throughout their formation without their children being registered. The implication is that these were Baptist or Quaker families; Drake found much the same in Yorkshire especially after 1660.[20]

A minimum, therefore, of six per cent of those born in the Cranbrook region died unbaptised, and maybe another 27 per cent of nonconformist children were missed from the record for one reason or another at this time. The probability is that as many as a tenth of the births in our parishes went unrecorded, and that other heavily nonconformist parishes would show the same pattern in the aftermath of the Restoration in 1660.[21] General statements about the fall of local or national populations at this time, so often based on crude comparisons of baptismal and burial figures, are therefore at least untrustworthy.

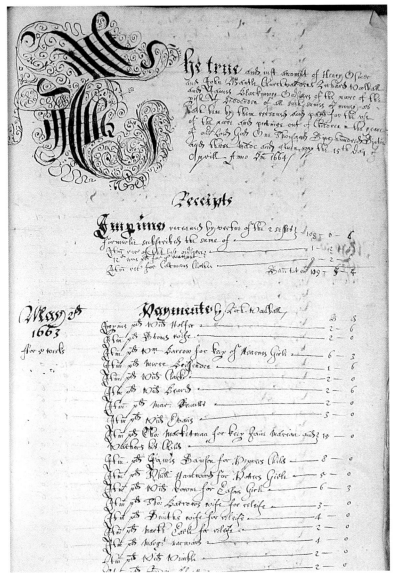

2. John Beale had been writing much of the material in the Biddenden parish chest for some years; this extract from the Biddenden Overseers' Accounts gives an indication of the pride he took, and illustrates the sequence of standard payments to the poor in May 1663. (CKS P26/12/1)

A third, unquantifiable, group of children escaped registration in their parish of birth because of the contemporary practice of some families to baptise their children in another parish, often that of the wife's parents. Stephen and Mary Smith, for instance, had all their children baptised in Staplehurst but buried in Cranbrook. Henry, son of Thomas and Mary Baseden, on the other hand, was born at Milkhouse in Cranbrook in June 1666 but baptised at Benenden in April 1667 'being at nurse here'. These and many similar examples highlight the benefit of covering more than one parish and incorporating information from sources other than the registers.

Other Primary Sources

Marriage Licences

Many couples avoided the standard practice of having their banns read in their own parishes and applied to the Archdiocese of Canterbury for a special licence to marry. These licences have been published.[22] In numerous cases they have confirmed the details of the family reconstitution where families have been built up from baptisms alone, and have provided an approximate date for the marriage (that of the licence). They are also invaluable, especially those before the mid-1670s, because they frequently add details such as the bridegroom's occupation, the pre-marital state and sometimes the approximate age of the bride and groom, and the names, home parishes and occupations of their fathers and of those acting as bondsmen.

There is little cause to question the accuracy of the information contained in the licences, except that the ages ascribed to bride or groom can be misleading. In 41 cases the reconstitution provides a definitive birth date, or a baptismal date, against which the ages provided by the licences can be checked. In 30 of those cases (73 per cent), the ages given by the licences are inaccurate, usually only by one or two years; sometimes the discrepancy is as many as four years, in one case nine years. Such discrepancies are not surprising in a period when approximations normally sufficed. There is no evidence that licences inflated the socio-economic status of their subjects.

Funerary Inscriptions

Another useful check on the accuracy and comprehensiveness of the reconstitution is provided by inscriptions from tombstones or monumental slabs in churches and churchyards. The most useful additional piece of information provided by inscriptions is usually the age of the deceased, precisely expressed. The inscription to Samuel Hunt of Benenden, 'in the 84th year of his age', is exceptional in giving his wife, her age, her parents and their children, and specifying those who survived and those who had died, providing an ideal check on the accuracy of the reconstitution. In general, because of the comparative strength of the marriage and baptismal registers in the parishes under consideration, it has proved possible to reconstitute families with some confidence. That confidence was reinforced by the coincidence of information provided by marriage licences and inscriptions. Other sources, in particular wills and probate accounts, have continued to reinforce the reliability of that reconstitution.

The Compton Census

The Compton Census provides us with the replies from Anglican incumbents to the request, issued in 1676 by Henry Compton, Bishop of London, for details of the numbers of Anglicans and nonconformists living in each parish.[23] This information should be invaluable in assessing the strength of nonconformity in our parishes. There are, however, problems in using the Census.[24] In the first place the wording of the request does not make it clear whether the return was to be of the whole population (men, women and children), or men only, or those over 16 only, or the heads of families and therefore families only. Secondly, the request presumes a consistent definition of nonconformity and that each incumbent knew who did and did not attend his church.

In practice the returns from Cranbrook, Benenden, Hawkhurst and Staplehurst leave no doubt that the incumbents interpreted the request for information as being for those aged 16 and above, and the others, in common with all the Kentish returns, appear to have done likewise.[25] Moreover, the incumbents of many parishes, including the Cranbrook ones, sent additional information, and this helps us to evaluate the accuracy of their returns; the vicars of Benenden and Cranbrook actually specified numbers of communicants. One might expect incumbents to be conservative in their estimation of nonconformists in their parishes, but Anne Whiteman comments that they 'seem, in fact, to have done their best to make a truthful answer in accordance with their understanding of the question'. Indeed she picks out the Rector of Frittenden for giving a detailed break-down of known nonconformists, while branding the reply of the Rector of Biddenden as an example of one given in a 'slipshod or feckless way' (page 42).[26]

Hearth Tax Returns

Use of the Hearth Tax returns as an aid to understanding the social and economic context of any area has been transformed in recent years. The Kent returns[27] list the names of householders and the number of hearths in each individual's occupation; on larger estates the number might include those in lodges or mills as well as in the main house.[28]

The tax, which was instituted by Act of Parliament in 1662, was to be levied on each hearth or fireplace in all non-exempt property in England and Wales, at a rate of one shilling every six months, collectable at Lady Day (25 March) and Michaelmas (29 September). The returns for Lady Day 1664 are frequently the best available, and were the first to list both those who were to pay and those who were exempt from payment. A householder was exempt from paying the Hearth Tax who, 'by reason of his poverty, or the smallness of his estate is exempted from the usual taxes, payments and contributions toward the church and poor', or who lived in a house 'not of greater value than of twenty shillings per annum upon the full improved rent', or who neither 'useth or occupieth any lands or tenements of their own or others, of the yearly value of twenty shillings per annum, nor hath any lands, tenements, goods or chattels, of the value of ten pounds in their own possession, or in the possession of any other in trust for them.' Exemption was decided by the Anglican incumbent together with one of the churchwardens or overseers of the poor, and subsequently certified by two Justices of the Peace.[29]

In the Cranbrook region, as with most of Kent, the administration of the Hearth Tax was based not on parishes but on divisions called hundreds and sub-divisions of the hundreds called boroughs.[30] As a result, none of the divisions or sub-divisions which list the people who lived there equates with the parishes which form the basis of the reconstitution. For example, the hundred of Cranbrook includes parts of the parishes of Benenden, Biddenden, Cranbrook, Frittenden, Goudhurst and Headcorn. Conversely, the parish of Benenden includes parts of the hundreds of Rolvenden, Selbrittenden, Cranbrook and Barkley. A few householders listed in the Hearth Tax returns do not appear in the reconstitution, and some heads of household in the reconstitution do not figure in the tax lists. Nevertheless, it has been possible to ascribe the appropriate parish to the vast majority of householders, and, conversely, to ascribe to most of the householders the number of hearths on which they were taxed. The extent to which this can be taken as an indication of wealth and economic prosperity is explored later (page 37ff).

Heralds' Visitations
Returns from the Heralds' Visitations of Kent made between 1663 and 1668 are available.[31] The purpose of these visits was to correct the abuse of arms by persons not entitled to bear them, and to find those who were entitled to bear them but had not been granted them, and supply the deficiency. To this purpose, the High Sheriff would prepare a list of the gentry of the area and call them to meet the herald, usually at the chief inn of the district, on a certain day. They were to bring with them any documents which might support their claim to gentlemanly status.[32]

Nineteen families relevant to the seven parishes are included in the Visitation returns; two generations, sometimes three, were listed as at 1663, and latest births within the family were included. For the wealthiest families they form a useful check on the information contained in the registers, and fill in gaps which result from marriages taking place in far distant counties or from avoidance of the local Anglican church.

Probate Wills
It has been the generally accepted view, as typified by the findings of Wrightson and Levine in their work on Terling, that those who left wills in early modern England came from the wealthier social groups in society.[33] Takahashi, on the other hand, has shown that from 1560 to 1640 'at least a quarter, and possibly well over a half, of the wills passing through the Consistory Court of Ely were made by labourers and husbandmen', and suggests that this Cambridgeshire pattern was the

more common one, because it takes its evidence from a larger stage than a single village.[34] The pattern from the Cranbrook region falls between these two extremes. Of the 304 wills which have survived from the Archdeaconry Court for the seven Cranbrook area parishes, 1660-1700, the status of 289 (95 per cent) of testators is known.[35] Of these, 149 (52 per cent) figure as gentlemen, yeomen or clothiers, representing the wealthier groups in the parishes, 30 (10 per cent) represent the poorer elements of husbandmen, weavers, labourers and servants; another 53 (18 per cent) were women.[36]

The basic information provided by wills is likely to be accurate. Testators are unlikely to falsify names; when they refer to 'kinsman' it is likely that there was a kin relationship, and when specified messuages or tenements and parcels of land of approximate size are bequeathed, the likelihood is that they did exist and that they were the testators' to bequeath. Testators tended to write their wills at or near the time of death rather than years in advance, and, by dating them, specified the time at which the information was correct. The usefulness of wills is many-layered; most mention the testator's occupation, and the Cranbrook area experience is that these identifications are reliable; if there were conflict between the testator's own claim (yeoman, for instance) and an inventory reference (husbandman, for instance) it might be as well to prefer the independent view.[37] At their most basic they provide an insight into a testator's wealth and land-holdings, although one must remember that he or she may have distributed property or cash before making the will.[38]

Most usefully in the context of this book, however, wills clarify the family circle which the testator felt was important, and thereby lead to an understanding of inter-kin and inter-neighbour relationships both within the parishes and across the parish borders and further afield. They can also tell us much about the circle in which the testator moved. The wording of preambles, or the lack of such preambles, can provide a glimpse of the religious leanings of their authors, or maybe of the scribe who set down the testator's wishes, whether they favoured the established church or some form of nonconformity. Because the Cranbrook area wills tend to be office copies of the originals, it is not possible to draw conclusions about the literacy of testators, but identification of the witnesses to wills does further our understanding of their friends and acquaintances (page 149).[39]

Probate Inventories

Inventories itemised and gave a value to a deceased person's goods, chattels, moveable assets and debts owing to them, often in detail; they included livestock and stored grain, as well as grain awaiting harvest, but excluded real estate, which was the preserve of the secular courts. For some 50 years scholars have used inventories extensively as a guide to several areas: farming practices; prices, trades, crafts and local industry; the problem of debt; house size, wealth and social status; and to provide a comparison between different regions of the country.[40]

For Cranbrook and its neighbouring parishes, 757 inventories have survived dating to 1660-1700.[41] They are of particular use to us here because they are sometimes the sole indicator of an individual's occupation, and their contents frequently show the importance of husbandry to those variously categorised as clothiers, cordwainers and the like. They certainly add to the overall impression of the deceased's comparative wealth and standing, and, by naming those who conducted the appraisal, they provide a further clue to relationships (page 158). They provide valuable insights into the sums owed to the deceased, but they need to be used with very considerable care because they rarely take account of what he or she owed. The Cranbrook region provides many examples of individuals who appear to be quite wealthy on the basis of their inventory value, but who died with such large debts that their personal estate could not meet them; they were, in fact, insolvent unless they could offset those debts by selling their real estate. Several made provision in their wills to do precisely that (page 178).

Probate Accounts
Far fewer probate accounts have survived nationally than wills and inventories, but Kent, with more than 13,000, outstrips all other counties.[42] From the Cranbrook region 234 probate accounts have survived from the period 1660-1700; while this is hardly a large number, they exceed the totals for most counties.[43] They list every person to whom the deceased owed money at the time of his or her death, and therefore clarify our understanding of the real value of an individual's personal estate (page 172). Not infrequently they give some indication of what those debts were for, thereby providing literally thousands of clues to the interplay between people at this time. Further insights into relationships are furnished by the choice of administrator of the account, whether a personal friend, or relative, or a major creditor, and the provisions made for the guardianship of any children.

The administration of probate accounts was carefully regulated, and the account was complete when all debts had been paid and the process had been duly written up and lodged with the court.[44] If there was no will (as was the case with most probate accounts in the Cranbrook region), and if there was still some surplus, it was the role of the court to decide how to divide among the heirs what was left of the value of the inventory. These decisions of the court were appended to the account, and provide the most accurate possible listing of the relict (if any) and surviving children. In the Cranbrook region, following the Kentish principle of partible inheritance, the divisions among children were uniformly fair and equal. Where there were no children, and especially when the deceased was unmarried, the account provides a list of siblings.

Churchwardens' Accounts
Churchwardens' accounts[45] have survived from five of the seven parishes under review and provide two kinds of valuable evidence. In all cases they incorporate an annual summary of expenditure, and in the process provide the names of the churchwardens and of individuals who worked for the parish or witnessed accounts. They thus provide a picture of the clique which ran the parish under the vicar or

3. The first page of the assessment made by the churchwardens of Benenden in July 1667 for the repair of the Church and other necessaries, showing the rate to be charged (two pence in the pound), the fact that the rate was on yearly rents (or value of goods), and listing the parishioners in Westend Quarter. (P20/5/1)

rector, and make it possible to explore the oligarchy of village life (page 123). In many cases the accounts also provide a list of all the householders of the parish who were assessed for tax for the upkeep of the church. Those from Benenden give the rental value of each person's holding, indicating which payers were occupying their own land and which were renting land from others. As these lists tend to be repeated each year for church assessment purposes it is possible to trace changes in occupation and/or ownership, and changes in the value of land.

The Benenden accounts are exceptionally full, and assessment lists are frequent especially in the early years. The Biddenden churchwardens' accounts are confined to the annual record of income and expenditure for the parish, providing a total received from the assessment, rather than a breakdown of each parishioner's land holdings. While they provide the names of those active in prosecuting the affairs of the parish, they do not contain the wealth of evidence which one finds at Benenden. The Frittenden churchwardens' accounts provide a brief summary of annual income, as a global sum, and expenditure. They also provide some references by name to individuals working for the parish, and the signatories beneath the accounts are the main evidence for vestry members and the offices some held. The Cranbrook accounts provide details of income and expenditure, and several lists of parishioners who contributed to charitable demands. Their most significant contribution to the picture of relationships in the parish concerns the provision of names of those appointed surveyors of the highways, and, occasionally, of the parishioner chosen to be schoolmaster of Dence's free school where the poorer children of the parish might receive some education.

Overseers' Accounts

The accounts of the overseers of the poor have survived from four of the parishes, with those from Biddenden the most complete; they consist of assessment lists and monthly disbursement lists.[46] In Biddenden and Goudhurst, the assessment lists were written up in alphabetical order by Christian name, rather than by districts. The disbursement lists indicate monthly payments to the poor within the parish, with extra details in April and October of rents paid, and in April of annual clothing payments. They give us a remarkable insight into the poorest in the parishes, and their relationship with those whose resources supported them (page 133).

The Biddenden overseers' accounts provide full coverage of the period from 1652, whereas the Cranbrook ones are either missing or fragmentary before the mid-1670s. The information they provide usefully parallels that provided by Biddenden, listing every householder who held or worked land in the parish, and supplying the names of the poor to whom the payments were made.

Quarter Sessions Records

Records of the quarterly meetings of the justices of the peace, held at Canterbury and at Maidstone, survive in unbroken sequence throughout the period.[47] They reflect the business of the justices, both administrative and criminal, indicate which of the parishioners of the Cranbrook area were appointed to serve on the grand jury, list some who were fined for attendance at nonconformist meetings, and name the individuals who were held in gaol but omit their parishes of origin. They are useful in providing valuable insight into the relationship between officialdom and parishioners, and especially between the vestry and the individual.

Other Unpublished Sources

Several settlement and removal notices of the 1690s have survived from Frittenden, all following the standard format for such documents.[48] The settlement certificates were written by the churchwardens and overseers of Frittenden to local parishes, assuring their officers that Frittenden would honour the individual's settlement.[49] The removals represent the reverse situation, with the Frittenden officers informing those of other parishes that individuals had given no evidence of settlement in Frittenden.[50] The parishes mentioned were all local.

Of more immediate relevance to the question of inter-relationships in village societies are the 15 indentures, dating across the period, which apprenticed poor children of Frittenden to masters and mistresses locally and in neighbouring parishes. They show how the overseers of the poor fulfilled that part of the poor law legislation which required them to find placements for poor children (page 141).[51]

From Staplehurst there has survived a handful of notices of inclusion of sons of paupers in the local parish school. They open with 'We, the Feoffees of the School's Lands in the Parish of Staplehurst given for the teaching of several poor boys, do appoint these boys under named to be entered into the same school paying unto the Master 12d. for their entrance ... ,' and proceed to name the four boys concerned. They are signed by the rector and four leading parishioners.[52]

Finally the Kent Quarterly Meetings Sufferings Book 1655-1759 is available in manuscript, and in some 400 pages gives details under six headings of ways in which individual Quakers suffered persecution at this time (page 190).[53]

Conclusion

Macfarlane has argued that, given records of a suitable quality, it is possible to undertake complex sociological and historical work on a parish, or preferably on a region, from at least the mid-16th century.[54] The records of the Cranbrook region match up to those demands; it is to be hoped that the following pages will justify his confidence.

Chapter 2

The Cranbrook Region

Environmental Effects of Geology and Topography

Two long fingers of chalk, the North and South Downs, stretch eastwards from the hub of Salisbury Plain to meet the English Channel at Dover and Beachy Head respectively. These Downs flank the geologically older clay and sandstone Weald of East Sussex and Kent, which with its far heavier soils and thick afforestation proved difficult for people to penetrate and settle (Figure 2.1).[1] In general the Low Weald is based on a heavy clay sub-soil, while the High Weald exhibits a lighter soil resting on sandstone.

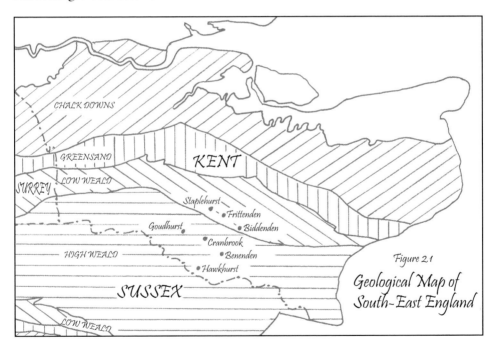

Figure 2.1

Geological Map of South-East England

Cranbrook, Goudhurst, Benenden and Hawkhurst lie firmly on the High Weald; Staplehurst, Frittenden and Biddenden largely sit beyond the geological transition from High to Low Weald but share much the same environment. Hawkhurst, the most southerly parish, is defined by the Kent Ditch (formerly Dyke) on its southern border; beyond lies Sussex. To the west the River Teise borders Goudhurst, to the north the Beult (formerly Lower Medway) borders Staplehurst and both rivers feed the Medway to the north. Into these rivers flow the numerous streams which rise in the Weald and cut their way through the land, and which were a major factor in enabling the development of the local industries of cloth and iron.

The subsoil of the Cranbrook region meant that the area had been dominated by thick woodlands.[2] Over time, however, the region had been exploited by many upland towns, villages and manors which secured the right to pasture their swine there. Three of the chosen parishes share the suffix -den, indicating their origins as woodland pastures especially for pigs; they provided summer pastures at the southern end of drovers' tracks. Three parishes have the suffix -hurst, the characteristic word for a wood in those parts of Kent which were settled late, especially the Weald.[3] By the latter half of the 17th century, much of the ancient woodland, especially the great oak standards used for ship-building, had been destroyed; the woodland which survived, all the more valuable, was farmed by coppicing.[4]

Movement about the Weald itself, especially in winter, could be very difficult because of the clay subsoil. Farms and hamlets were isolated for weeks on end in a wet season, with by-roads 'so very deep and miry as to be but barely passable till they are hardened by the drouth of summer'.[5] Such conditions necessarily bred an isolated and inward-looking countryside, a Wealden characteristic on which many contemporaries commented.

While penetration of the parishes was difficult for several months each year, access to the area from outside was less problematic, with a road branching south to Maidstone and beyond from the London-Dover highway, and an alternative route from London, via Tonbridge to Hawkhurst and on to Rye with specified side-roads to Goudhurst, Cranbrook, Benenden and Biddenden.[6] Indeed, a complex network of scheduled public carrying services was run on major routes, using wagons especially over shorter distances.[7] Carriers from the Cranbrook region habitually journeyed to London by travelling north via Maidstone and crossing the Darenth at Farningham (Figure 2.2).[8]

While the really wealthy built for themselves brick houses of considerable magnificence, the plentiful timber of the Weald enabled local carpenters to build timber-framed houses of quality in the 15th and 16th centuries so that the 'Wealden' has become synonymous with a particular style of farmhouse.[9] The Cranbrook area boasts some of the finest. They were mostly constructed before 1500, and heated by central hearths. By the 16th and 17th centuries, however, many owners followed fashion and enclosed their fires, usually by the construction of a brick stack. Together with the building of a first floor to the hall, this allowed the number of hearths in the house to be quadrupled by opening them either side of the stack and on both floors, and, incidentally, encouraged the government to institute the Hearth Tax.[10] Timber-framed houses which were upgraded in this way nevertheless had fewer hearths than those which were purpose-built in the 17th century. Especially after 1660 these tended to be built in brick or stone, with most living rooms having hearths of their own. As a result, new houses tended to have more hearths in the Hearth Tax returns than older houses of the same or greater size.

4. Section of the road map from London to Rye in Sussex, taken from the 1939 facsimile of John Ogilby's 'Britannia', 1675, showing the main road along the Kent and Sussex border with side roads to the Cranbrook area parishes.

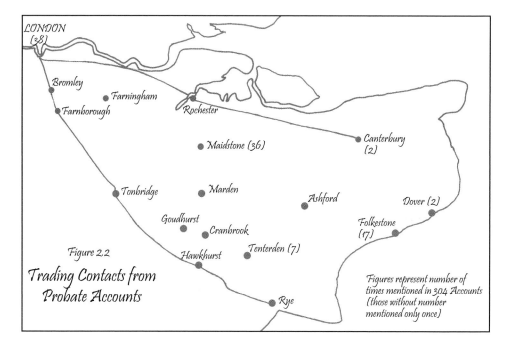

Figure 2.2

Trading Contacts from
Probate Accounts

Figures represent number of
times mentioned in 304 Accounts
(those without number
mentioned only once)

The 'Wealden' may well have predominated among men of yeoman and clothier status, but far less impressive dwellings were the norm, with maybe 20 per cent of the population, the landless labourers, in fairly squalid two roomed cottages, one downstairs, one upstairs. The majority lived in dwellings with one or two hearths, maybe with four acres of land associated with the cottage as required by the Act of 1589.[11] They were not necessarily poor, and their houses were often well-built; the Biddenden husbandman, James Willard, exempt on his one-hearth house in 1664, had a kitchen, wash-house, tub-house, milk-house and buttery, inner chamber, middle chamber, outer chamber and shop in his 1671 inventory![12]

Two environmental factors which greatly affected the lives of local people at this time were disease and climate. One took life, the other threatened it. Despite the severity of the plague of 1665 in London, however, the effects on the Cranbrook region were muted, striking down some individuals in Cranbrook and Frittenden in 1666, and arriving in Biddenden in the summer of 1667 (page 139). Smallpox appears to have been a more consistent killer than plague, with mentions of death from smallpox in registers and probate accounts. In general, however, specific diseases are very rarely identified as killers of the local population; accidents of one kind or another, like that which robbed Thomas Beale of both his legs, feature rather more often but still infrequently.

Climate was life-threatening both because of its effects on crops, cattle and therefore food, and because of its link back to disease. A mini ice-age combined with other exceptional weather features to harass local farmers at this time. John Evelyn records periods of intense cold interspersed with torrential rain and destructive winds in the late 1650s, 1660s and early 1670s. In December 1672 the Benenden church bell-tower was destroyed by storm, and the Staplehurst spire, and other buildings locally, were blown down the following year. The 1680s saw exceptionally cold winters, severe drought (it rained only once between December and May 1681), and very hot summers. In 1682 and 1683 intense winter cold caused the Thames to freeze from December until February; trees split, men and cattle perished, and in Tenterden one-third of all the sheep perished. The 1680s closed with what Evelyn refers to as 'no other than an Hurocan' which uprooted trees and ruined houses, and was followed by a similar storm in January 1690.[13]

Table 2.1   Pattern, nationally of harvests and prices, locally of weather, 1645-99

	wheat harvests	effect on prices	weather
1645-51	poor	grain prices relatively high	severe winter 1648/9
1652-55	no comment	grain prices relatively high	fairly calm (hail 1652)
1656-63	poor	grain prices relatively high	some severe winters
1664-72	good	agricultural prices low	storms latterly
1673-84	no comment	agricultural prices low	terrible cold/drought latterly
1685-91	good	agricultural prices low	terrible winds latterly
1692-94	no comment	grain prices relatively high	fairly calm
1695-99	poor	grain prices relatively high	heavy snow 1697/8

Note: Harvests and prices from Bowden (1985) 56; weather from Tenterden Municipal records, see Taylor (1917), and from John Evelyn's diary.

It is easy to reconcile the pattern of wheat harvests and prices given in Table 2.1: poor harvests led to relatively high prices, and good harvests reduced those prices. It is not possible to relate that pattern to the micro-climate of the Weald and the atrocious weather suffered in the south east of the country during these 40 years.

The Population of Cranbrook and Adjacent Parishes

We have no population figures for the parishes of the Cranbrook area prior to the Census figures of 1801, but we do have the Compton census of 1676, the reconstitution 1660-1700, and the Hearth Tax returns of 1664. Each of these has major defects as a source for population if taken on its own, but by combining the results it is possible to suggest approximate totals.[14] In each case the use of appropriate multipliers is required: the Compton figures relate to adults over 16 years of age, and the Hearth Tax returns relate to householders. Multipliers have long been used in population calculations: Gregory King, the archetypal statistician, himself used them in the 1690s.[15] Too often, however, an arbitrary single figure has been employed, with questionable results. Michael Zell has produced mid-16th century population figures for our parishes which, he admits, are crude, but which probably approximate to the truth.[16]

Tom Arkell has recently looked at contemporary evidence taken from work on various parishes where there was a known percentage for those aged below 16 in the period 1676-1701, and found a range from 29 per cent to 41 per cent.[17] Application of Arkell's range to the figures provided by the Compton Census produces a putative total population for each of the seven Cranbrook area parishes in 1676. Those totals can then be compared with ones derived from the second major source, the reconstitution and the Hearth Tax returns.

It is possible to extract from the reconstitution the fathers of families who, it can reasonably be inferred, were living in the parishes in 1664. To these can be added those individuals, single men and widows, who are named as householders by the Hearth Tax returns. The combined figures provide a total for heads of household in 1664 which must still be regarded as a minimum. In his discussion of mean household, Arkell again prefers a range of multipliers between 3.7 and 5.2.[18]

Table 2.2 presents the figures suggested by Zell for the 1560s, together with those derived from the reconstitution and Hearth Tax and the Compton Census, and the fixed totals of the 1801 census. It may be argued that Arkell's multipliers cover too wide a span for them to be of great use, but that span gives a far more convincing impression of population than a total produced by a single multiplier, and the mean figures in each case, when compared, provide useful approximations. One must not, however, attempt to draw hard and fast conclusions from these figures.

Table 2.2 *Estimated populations for seven Wealden parishes, 1660s & '70s*

	Zell 1560s	from Hearth Tax & reconstitution, 1664				from Compton Census, 1676			Census 1801	Acreage 1801
		low	high	mean		mean	high	low		
Benenden	950	725	1019	872	↔	869	949	789	1300	6693
Biddenden	1050	710	998	854	↔	1086	1186	986	1151	7191
Cranbrook	2000	1820	2558	2189	↔	2017	2203	1831	2561	10372
Frittenden	400	296	416	356	↔	334	364	303	551	3509
Goudhurst	1500	1465	2059	1762	↔	1551	1695	1408	1782	9797
Hawkhurst	1170	780	1097	938	↔	1551	1695	1408	1742	6493
Staplehurst	650	529	744	636	↔	706	771	641	1220	5897

Note: The source for the 1560s figures is Zell (1984); for the Compton Census figures, Whiteman (1986)

The mean figures for Benenden, Cranbrook, Frittenden and Staplehurst are remarkably similar. Those for Biddenden and Goudhurst equate less well, while nevertheless suggesting approximate populations; one suspects that the reconstitution figure for Biddenden, very much a minimum figure, is less secure than the Compton Census figure, whereas the reconstitution/Hearth Tax figure for Goudhurst is probably close to the truth because of the coterminous nature of the parish and district. The greatest discrepancy applies to Hawkhurst. The Compton Census figure of '1000 men and women over 16' is clearly a rounded approximation;

on the other hand, there are problems with the Hawkhurst figures based on the Hearth Tax and the registers, which seem considerably too low (page 82). There is sufficient general agreement, however, to suggest total populations for the parishes in the 1660s and 1670s of 900+ in Benenden, 1,000+ in Biddenden, 2,200+ in Cranbrook, 350+ in Frittenden, 1,700+ in Goudhurst, 1,200+(?) in Hawkhurst and 700+ in Staplehurst.

Socio-economic Factors

There were several tiers of land-ownership in Kent.[19] At the top of the pyramid were three great ecclesiastical landlords, of whom the Dean and Chapter of Christ Church, Canterbury, figure on several occasions among major landlords to whom inhabitants of the Cranbrook region paid rents; the other two were the Archbishop of Canterbury, and the Dean and Chapter of Rochester. Almost comparable in size, but more compact in location, were the estates of perhaps a dozen wealthy noblemen and gentry. Among these were the Baker family of Sissinghurst in Cranbrook parish, whose lands centred on the middle Weald with some outlying properties near Maidstone (page 111).

Smaller in scale were the properties of several hundred gentry and scores of wealthy yeomen with lands in up to a dozen parishes. In the Cranbrook region at this time few will-makers claimed such a spread of estates, although Stephen Ginder's reference to lands in Braborn in Kent, marshland in Newchurch parish, and 'all other my lands and tenements in the Realm of England' has a certain ring about it.[20] Finally there were many thousands of freeholders, mostly with land in just one parish, often comprising no more than a small farm, but with fields in different areas. It was this feature of land tenure in Kent which led Boys to remark, at the end of the eighteenth century, that 'the property in land in this county is very much divided, there being few extensive possessions but what are intersected by other persons' property'.[21]

It would be wrong to equate possession of land with farming. Individuals, from gentry to quite modest husbandmen, and even labourers, owned land. Normally the gentry did not farm all their land, often retaining their home farm for their own use, and renting out farms or fields to others. Yeomen farmers usually owned some land, but frequently worked land belonging to others, either the gentry or fellow yeomen farmers. Other landowners might be neither yeomen nor gentry. It was rare, for instance, for a clothier to have no land to pass on; indeed, more often than not the local probate inventories of the period show clothiers, and tradesmen generally, possessed of a far greater value of livestock or grain than of goods, chattels or stock in trade.[22] Virtually everyone at this time was a husband-man or -woman whatever their stated occupation.

Craftsmen and traders such as tanners, blacksmiths, butchers, grocers, millers and victuallers supplemented the income from their activities by working their own land, and passed it on to their children. Most husbandmen and some labourers can

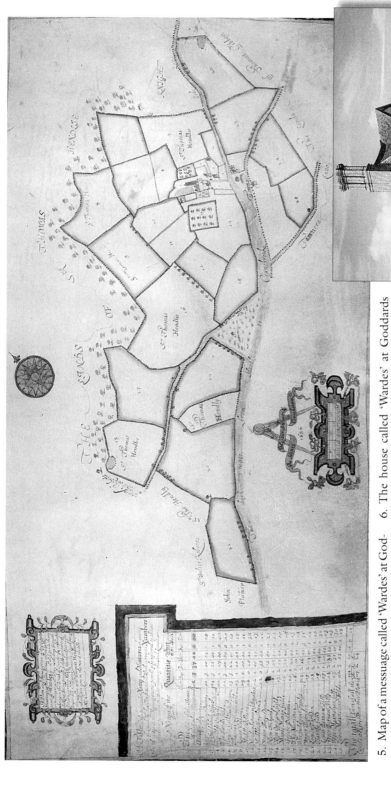

5. Map of a messuage called 'Wardes' at Goddards Green in Cranbrook, the inheritance of Peter Courthop Esq., drawn for Sir Thomas Hendley by Henry Couchman, 1636. (CKS U814 P8)

6. The house called 'Wardes' at Goddards Green in Cranbrook, showing little change since its depiction on the estate map above. It was the home of the Courthope family for several generations before it passed by marriage to the Campion family.

be shown to have owned small holdings. William Waller, labourer of Benenden, for instance, held land valued at £2 from 1663 to 1672; in the assessment lists his name is frequently followed by '*or ye occ*', implying that even at this level of economic activity he was leasing out his plot, taking rent from others.

Local Industry

Farming

Farming of one form or another occupied the energies of most people living in the Cranbrook region, but precise figures for the size of Kentish farms in the 17th century have proved elusive,[23] and the same is true for acreages owned or rented in the Cranbrook region. Churchwardens' and overseers' assessments provide precise rental figures, and some wills provide acreages, but identification of one with the other is fraught with uncertainty. Some testators had already passed on fields and farms, some had retired from active farming, so that property bequeathed does not necessarily equate with property farmed. It is also unrealistic to ascribe rental values to acreages because the quality of the land in question varied enormously; some was valued at more than £1 per acre, other at considerably less.[24]

The Weald was 'parcelled out generally into small farms' in contrast to 'the best cultivated parts of East Kent'.[25] Chalklin has suggested a notional average of 40 acres, which implies that holdings of between five and 30 acres were common; in the manor of Southborough in Tonbridge parish, for instance, half the 46 freeholdings in 1621 were under ten acres in size, and only a tenth were 50 acres or more.[26] The countryside therefore consisted of thousands of little properties varying in size between a cottage with one or two acres of land, and a farmhouse with perhaps 50 acres or more. Holdings of less than five acres would have been too small to enable people to maintain themselves and their families; they were therefore worked as a sideline by those involved in other occupations or by farm labourers when they were not hiring themselves out.[27]

The Kentish practice of partible inheritance had a marked effect on land-holding in the Weald by fragmenting holdings into units which were too small to be economic.[28] It found its origins in gavelkind, the right of tenure peculiar to Kent by which sons of a tenant who died intestate should divide their inheritance equally; if there were no male heirs, division should be made among the females.[29] Most local wills involving land left it to one son or, if the testator possessed several parcels of land, then he might well apportion them between sons (page 107). The principle of partible inheritance most effectively manifests itself in probate accounts, the great majority of which concerned those who died intestate. They invariably partitioned goods and chattels equally among sons and daughters irrespective of their age and gender. As a consequence, partible inheritance caused more tenants, smaller tenements and the need for tenants to turn as well to cottage industry to survive.[30]

Farmhouses in the Weald tended to be isolated down lanes or tracks several hundred yards from the main roads on sites chosen for their supply of fresh water, often with an adjacent pond. Most of the fields associated with the farmhouses were contiguous, with perhaps two or three scattered parcels, often water meadows or woodlands, lying at a little distance from the rest. On large farms the labourers' cottages were scattered over the estate; otherwise such labourers occupied cottages in the vicinity of the town or parish centre. There was little common land for the labourers to work, and what there was tended to be in the form of small heaths of little use for pasture. On the other hand the bracken and heather of these common areas provided essential material for the bedding of poorer inhabitants, and the underwood provided faggots for fires for cooking and keeping warm. Associated with the typical yeoman's farmhouse were barns, stables, a vegetable garden, an orchard of maybe a quarter or half an acre in size, and a hop garden; in the later 17th century the hop garden came to take up a greater acreage than the orchard, with inventories talking of 4,000 and 7,000 hop poles.[31]

Most land tenure in the Kentish Weald in our period was freehold or leasehold. Those who held their land freehold were required to pay nominal quit-rents and heriots to the lord of the manor.[32] Quit-rents, often fixed for centuries, had become trifling amounts (5s. or 2s. 6d.) which represented a mere fraction of the annual value of the property.[33] The heriot was a payment to the lord of the manor, in kind or commuted to cash, at the death of the freeholder or tenant, or at the time of purchase or inheritance of the land. It had to be the 'best good', usually an animal.[34] Most Wealden small farmers, however, were tenants who owned some of the land they worked and leased the rest. They normally paid rack rents, representing the full economic value of the land which they were leasing.[35] These leases tended to be for comparatively short periods, with the seven-year term popular in post-Restoration Kent,[36] but Wealden farmers preferred to hire their lands from year to year.

The nature of the Wealden subsoils meant that the land was more suited to pasturing livestock than for arable farming, leading to what has been described as a 'mixed farming wood-pasture economy, generally very reliant on animal hus-bandry'.[37] This led to a high degree of self-sufficiency among the farms of adequate size, which suited the Wealden temperament. The late development of the hamlets and scattered farms of the area meant that fields tended to be enclosed from the beginning, and the history of their development meant that they were frequently bordered by 'shaws', thin copses of wood or underwood, usually of oak, beech or ash. Where such strips of woodland did not survive, the fields were bounded by hedges. Shaws and copses might make up ten per cent of the available acreage; they were frequently coppiced, and provided work in wood crafts such as carpentry, turning and charcoal-burning.[38]

Plans of contemporary farms bear out all these features. The large estate of Captain George Pix of Hawkhurst, for instance, shows 222 acres of 'plain land' and 23 acres of 'wood land', the woodland representing ten per cent of the whole.[39] Some of the woods were in the form of shaws, usually less than an acre in area; elsewhere they matched the largest fields in acreage. Some 40 fields are noted altogether, ranging from just over an acre to eight acres and three-quarters. The mean and median size of the fields was approximately four and a half acres (Figure 2.3).

The main arable crop of the region was oats, possibly occupying rather more than half the cultivated land, with wheat occupying another third of that land. Approximately one eighth of the cultivated land was therefore left for barley, peas and tares, and maybe buckwheat or flax.[40] To make the fields productive, continual applications of dung, marl or lime were essential; the normal practice was to add between 300 and 500 cart-loads of marl per acre dug from the pit or pits which served each field. Leases customarily contained covenants stipulating just how tenants should care for the rented land.[41]

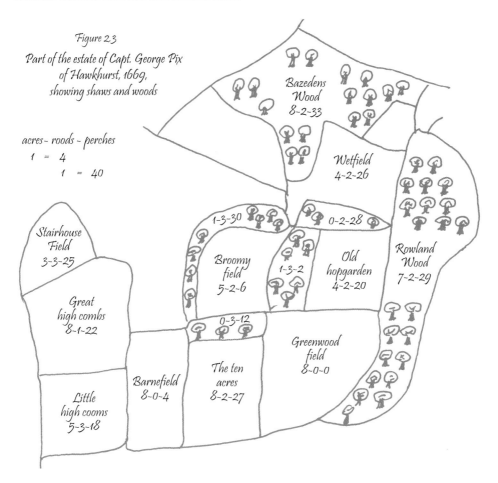

Figure 2.3

Part of the estate of Capt. George Pix
of Hawkhurst, 1669,
showing shaws and woods

acres ~ roods ~ perches
1 = 4
1 = 40

Bazedens
Wood
8-2-33

Wetfield
4-2-26

Stairhouse
Field
3-3-25

1-3-30

0-2-28

Rowland
Wood
7-2-29

Broomy
field
5-2-6

1-3-2

Old
hopgarden
4-2-20

Great
high combs
8-1-22

0-3-12

Greenwood
field
8-0-0

Barnefield
8-0-4

The ten
acres
8-2-27

Little
high cooms
5-3-18

Inventories bear out the concentration on oats in the Cranbrook region, but make it clear that the breeding and fattening of animals was the most important enterprise in the Weald, with livestock the main investment. Because of the size of the farms, however, the number of animals involved was not large. Most farms had two or three cows, some had six or seven, which would be sufficient to provide for the domestic requirements of the average household in terms of milk, butter and cheese, and supply a surplus. A husbandman of 1640 in the Low Weald maybe had a herd of 14 animals, some being fattened before being sold to local butchers.[42]

Oxen, the most valuable animals in most Cranbrook inventories, pulled the ploughs, working in teams of four and six, unshod so that they could better cope in the heavy soils. At the age of seven they were sent to market for beef. There were also sheep on the pastures, with a yeoman having maybe 100 or 200 animals in his flock. Larger flocks, under flockmasters and sheep fatteners, were pastured on Romney Marsh, rich in perennial rye grass, where some flocks ran into thousands; at nearby Tenterden George Wightwick had nearly 6,000 sheep in 1666.[43] While the standard yield from these animals was their wool, there was an increasing emphasis on meat production as the Wealden cloth industry declined. Of the two main breeds, the Southdown, ideally suited to the heathlands because of its short coat, was bred more for meat, while the Romney, also known as 'Kent' sheep, was bred for its long fleece as much as for meat.[44] Pigs, goats, poultry and horses also feature among the animals of the 17th-century farm, with the horses used more for riding than for draught purposes.

Cloth

The coincidence of partible inheritance, parcels of land of uneconomic size, and the comparative freedom which pastoral farming brought to people, provided the classic environment for the development of local industry.[45] As early as 1336 Edward III had encouraged weavers, dyers and fullers from Flanders to settle and teach the English the art of making woollen cloth, and the Weald of Kent had been specified as a major area for the production of broadcloth. The Cranbrook area was rich in the necessary raw materials: wool from the fat sheep of the Romney marshes or from the sheep on the Downs; fast-flowing streams to drive the fulling mills; fuller's earth and marl, the former especially from Boxley parish; and timber for the mills, the hammers and the machinery required to drive them. As a result the Cranbrook region, which in 1334 shared one of the lowest assessments of wealth in England, had been transformed into one of the highest yielding parts of the country by 1524.[46]

The Wealden cloth industry was at its height in the middle and later years of the 16th century; in 1573 Cranbrook famously welcomed the queen herself. The clothiers who ran the Wealden cloth industry in its heyday made fortunes. They built magnificent houses, funded extensions to the churches, occupied the main pews in those churches, filled almost all the places on the governing body of Cranbrook school and acted as captains for the local muster; as late as 1667 Philpot could claim 'for making durable broadcloth with very good mixtures and perfect colours, Cranebroke doth with most that way excell.'[47]

By our period, however, the cloth trade was in decline. It had suffered in the 1610s, reached crisis point in the 1620s, and suffered again during the civil war of the 1640s and its aftermath.[48] In the 1650s prices fell sharply, and even more so in the 1680s, but clothiers continued to be active at least to the end of the century, although on a far less profitable basis than earlier. Cloth remained an important occupation for a large proportion of men and women in Cranbrook and its environs because much of the work of producing the broadcloth was carried out in their own cottages, and clothiers still provided that work.

One does not find 'carders' or 'spinners' in the registers because it was the women and children who spun the wool; they worked in their own homes, on raw wool supplied by the clothiers.[49] The men wove the broadcloth; 'broadweavers' figure frequently in the registers of 1660-1700. Although broadweavers and spinners were paid by the clothiers for their work, they were not their employees; in essence they were self-employed. They often kept looms in the attics and wove the cloth there from the wool prepared by their wives and children in what was genuinely a family business.[50]

In 1683 the rector of Biddenden neatly summed up the situation with: 'The parish of Biddenden ... not soe populous now as formerly when the clothing trade there flourished.' By 1724-6 Daniel Defoe could write 'that Trade is now quite decay'd, and scarce Ten Clothiers left in all the County'.[51] The last clothier to be so designated in the parish registers of Cranbrook was John Stunt, who was buried on 24 November 1740.

Iron

The coincidence of a plentiful supply of iron-ore in the Weald together with an even more plentiful supply of timber, latterly through coppicing, meant that iron-working was an industry likely to flourish. It developed earlier and more comprehensively on the Sussex side of the county boundary; in Kent the industry was slow to take off, possibly because of the primacy of the clothiers who, in 1635, complained that the setting up of John Browne's ironworks at Brenchley was threatening their industry because of the vast quantities of timber it consumed. Not only did it consume timber on a vast scale; it also employed considerable manpower in the early part of the 17th century.[52]

By the 1660s, however, the industry was very much on the wane in this part of Kent, with John Ray (1674) saying that it was dying, if not dead, by the end of Charles II's reign. Its demise, no doubt hastened by the importation of iron from Europe, was not complete in 1740, at which time four furnaces were still at work in the county, but in the registers of our parishes any mention of occupations connected with iron-working (as opposed to blacksmithing) is exceptionally rare after 1660. The iron industry figured little in the everyday lives of people in the Cranbrook area at this time.[53]

The Occupational Balance

The balance between those engaged in the broad areas of farming and cloth-making, as well as those occupied outside these industries or wealthy enough not to need an occupation, can be gauged by reference to the exceptionally detailed banns of marriage 1653-62 and the reconstitution itself. Certain caveats, however, need to be aired at the outset. Areas of occupation do not reveal wealth or social status. Broadweavers and clothworkers earned their pittance by hard grind, while clothiers, some of whom had been among the wealthiest in the community, sourced work for them. Similarly, those who worked the land ranged from labourers, who relied for their subsistence on hiring themselves out, to affluent yeomen, many of whom owned more land than they needed, let it out to others, and benefited from the rents which accrued. Among traders and craftsmen there was a similar differentiation between those who barely maintained themselves and their families by their work, and those who, like mercers and tanners, had to be wealthy enough to carry a considerable stock of goods or raw materials. Nor is one able always to distinguish the difference in nuance between 'yeoman' and 'husbandman', 'clothworker' and 'clothier', 'weaver' and 'broadweaver'. Those who used these terms at the time did not necessarily set out to use them with precision.

Frequently individuals were given more than one occupational label. Indeed, multiple occupations like those noted by Wrightson & Levine at Terling,[54] and highlighted by Arkell,[55] are frequently reflected in the Cranbrook region. Richard Haffenden of Biddenden, for instance, was variously described as clothier and yeoman,[56] and Richard Caffinch of Cranbrook was actually referred to as 'ripyer or husbandman' at the burial of his daughter Mary in 1656. Individuals also progressed and regressed in the course of their working lives. Nathaniel Fosten of Cranbrook, once a clothier, became a victualler; Richard Amit, earlier a 'husbandman', became a 'labourer, poor'; others retired from active work, sometimes living in the house of another, and omitted their occupation in their wills. Alexander Luckhurst of Plushinghurst in Cranbrook was a 'miller' at marriage in 1658, a 'husbandman' in 1659, and a 'broadweaver' in 1660; was this progress, or did he have a hand in all three areas of work at the same time? Categorising the main occupation of some people involves a considerable element of judgement.

The banns of marriage for Cranbrook from October 1653 to June 1662 provide a detailed breakdown of the occupations of the bridegrooms (355 of them) and, in most cases, of fathers of bridegrooms (280) and fathers of brides (278). Licences were not available. The banns of marriage for the same period at Benenden and Hawkhurst, while not as informative about parental occupations, are nevertheless comprehensive on those of the bridegrooms, making it possible to draw a general picture of the occupational balance of these three parishes.

Figure 2.4 shows that some 45 per cent of the marrying population of Cranbrook at this time were involved in the cloth industry, and Hawkhurst, with 41 per cent, was similarly biased. At Benenden, however, the figure is only 25 per cent. These figures contrast with the equivalent figures for all bridegrooms irrespective of parish of origin, which for Cranbrook and Hawkhurst show some ten per cent fewer involved in cloth and proportionally more involved in the land and trade or manufacture. Even among local parishes, therefore, Cranbrook and Hawkhurst parishioners were more heavily involved in cloth production than most. When the proportion working the land is considered, however, roles are reversed: Benenden, with 40 per cent, was more involved in farming than Cranbrook with 29 per cent or Hawkhurst with 30 per cent. It is not possible to treat parishes as if they were alike even in this small cluster; Benenden, however, appears more typical of Wealden parishes in general than the other two.

Figure 2.4   Balance of landworking and clothworking from banns, 1653-62

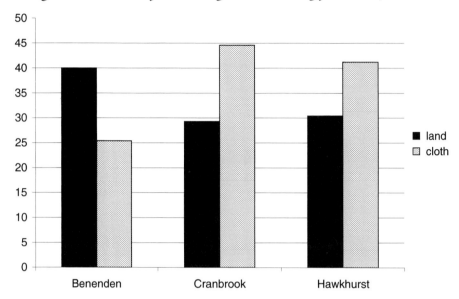

The most consistent occupational group across the three parishes was the 23 to 29 per cent of the population involved in servicing others by their skills as blacksmiths, thatchers, mercers and the like. The group who did not need to work with their hands to earn their living is so small (two to five per cent) as to suggest that the wealthiest members of society, whom they represent, shunned the whole process of civil banns and ratified their marriages at this time in some other way.

The database provided by the reconstitution draws from a wide variety of sources, but the same *caveats* about trying to be too specific apply as above. The analysis has been limited to the year of the available Hearth Tax returns, Lady Day 1664, and, as for the population calculations above, inclusion has been confined to heads of household mentioned in those returns or who are known to have been living in the parish as householders in that year (Table 2.3).

Gentry figure more prominently in the reconstitution than in the banns of marriage, which supports the suggestion that the wealthiest members of village society did not have their banns read. The proportion of villagers involved in crafts or retailing shows a fairly consistent pattern across all the parishes, with Cranbrook, as the central market town, having the greatest share. Similarly, the proportion of widows across the parishes is fairly uniform at between nine and 15 per cent. In both these areas the Wealden parishes parallel the figures from Ely. The balance between cloth and land exactly parallels the pattern shown by the banns of marriage, with Benenden more oriented towards farming, Cranbrook more towards cloth. Of the other parishes, Hawkhurst and Staplehurst have a slight leaning towards cloth; Biddenden looks more agricultural.

Table 2.3 *Householders by occupation: from reconstitution and Hearth tax, 1664*

Occupational Description	Benenden		Biddenden		Cranbrook		Frittenden Staplehurst		Hawkhurst		Ely 1651-1700
		%		%		%		%		%	%
Gentry	14	10.4	18	16.1	16	4.0	9	7.5	11	10.0	5.2
Farming											
husbandmen	11		13		53		9		13		
yeomen	24		17		11		25		11		
gardeners etc	1		1								
labourers	22		3		5		2		6		
total on land	58	43.3	34	30.4	69	17.2	36	30.0	30	27.3	53.3
Cloth											
broadweavers	8		7		65		16		10		
linen-weavers			1		4				2		
clothiers	13		13		67		15		18		
clothworkers	1		1		4		1		2		
cardmakers etc.	1		2		9				1		
total in cloth	23	17.2	24	21.4	149	37.2	32	26.7	33	30.0	3.7
Other craftsmen and retailers	25	18.7	21	18.8	99	24.7	28	23.3	20	18.2	18.8
Widows	12	9	14	12.5	60	15.0	14	11.7	15	13.6	17.0
Others	2	1.5	1	0.9	8	2.0	1	0.8	1	0.9	1.3
total occupations known	134	68.4	112	58.3	401	81.7	120	53.8	110	52.1	

Notes: Frittenden and Staplehurst have been taken together because of the small size of Frittenden and because some contemporaries even assigned themselves ambivalently.
Ely figures have been adjusted to accommodate widows (17%).
Source: Diocese of Ely   Evans (2000) 180, Table 9.2

Figures 2.4 and 2.5 confirm the similarity of these two patterns, and show that in these Wealden parishes in the 1650s and 1660s the cloth industry was still active.

Some continuity of occupation across generations is discernible, with sons following fathers in rather more than half the known instances, as in Table 2.4. Farming shows the highest incidence of continuity at a time when a stake in the land was a major factor in the stability of life. Only half of those working in the cloth industry followed in their fathers' footsteps despite the network of contacts which clothiers and broadweavers must have set up, and the value of their equipment. Among craftsmen and retailers it is noteworthy that bricklayers, ripyers, thatchers and to a less extent blacksmiths, carpenters, tailors and tanners did tend to follow their fathers into those occupations; the cordwainer John Scott, for instance, left his 'lasts and all other my instruments belonging to my trade' to his son.[57]

Figure 2.5   *Balance of landworking and clothworking from reconstitution, 1664*

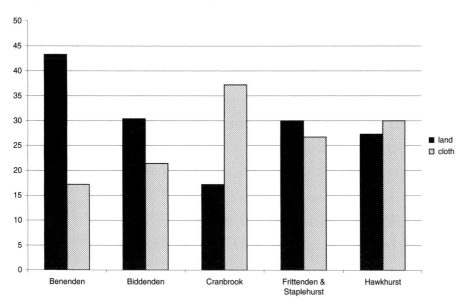

Table 2.4   *Continuity of occupation between father and son, 1653-62*

	correlation		no correlation	
cloth	75	51%	72	49%
land	83	65%	44	35%
craft	42	49%	43	51%
retail	6	32%	11	68%
overall	206	55%	170	45%
(Cranbrook only	113	54%	96	46%)

Skills and interests imbibed in the home did not necessarily direct youngsters into their fathers' occupations; the practice of apprenticing youngsters at the age of thirteen or fourteen did not at all presume that the apprenticeship should be in the father's area of expertise. Those fathers who could not afford to apprentice their sons for seven years, or who for some reason did not wish to do so, would customarily send them and their daughters as servants to the homes of others, either locally or in neighbouring villages. Their offspring helped in the home or on the land of the host, became part of that household for a year at a time, and learnt new skills while there. Such putting out of sons and daughters might be repeated for several years from the middle teens onwards, and introduced the young people to a variety of skills.[58] It is not therefore surprising that continuity of occupation was as tenuous as the Cranbrook evidence suggests.

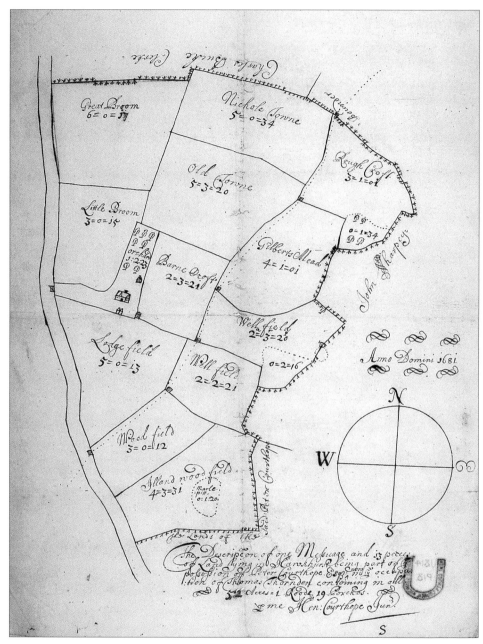

7. Map of a messuage and thirteen pieces of land in Hawkhurst, part of the possessions of Peter Courthope Esq., 1681, prepared by Henry Courthope. The farm was occupied at the time by Thomas Thornden (=Thornton), whose will and probate account have survived. He is referred to as a husbandman, but he left £223 after payment of his debts. Note the marl-pit in the southernmost field, and that the vicar of Cranbrook, Charles Bucke, held lands to the north. (U814 P13)

The Balance between Rich and Poor

Margaret Spufford has shown that the Hearth Tax can provide an indication of the balance between the wealthy, the middling and the poor of any parish in the late 17th century. In her work on Cambridgeshire parishes she successfully established a rough correlation between the number of rooms indicated by probate inventories and the corresponding number of hearths; between social status and the number of rooms; and between inventory value and the number of hearths on which individuals were assessed.[59] The Cambridgeshire pattern provides a close parallel to that of the Cranbrook region (Table 2.5); remarkably, however, the detail suggests that the poor in the Weald were better off than those in Cambridgeshire, whereas the middling group in Cambridgeshire were better off than those in Kent.

Table 2.5 Comparative wealth groupings by hearths, 1660s

No. of hearths	Cambridgeshire, 1661-70		Cranbrook region, 1665-79	
	range of appraisal	median appraisal	range of appraisal	median appraisal
one	80%+ had under £50	£ 25	77% under £100	£ 52
two	75% between £10 & £100	£ 60	all but one below £200	£ 78
three	£30 to £500, mainly £30-£200	£141	£60 to £400	£144
four	£34 to £1132, 60%+ over £300	£360	£13 to £862	£211

Cambridgeshire: Hearth Tax returns Michaelmas 1662, revised Michaelmas 1664 / Lady Day 1666; appraisal from inventories 1661-70 of householders who can be directly linked to Hearth Tax lists; Source: Spufford M. (1974), 39-41.
Cranbrook region: extracts from Kent Hearth Tax returns Lady Day 1664; appraisal from inventory totals ('the charge') in probate accounts 1665-79 of householders who can be directly linked to Hearth Tax lists.

Spufford also explored the link between the value of a man's inventory and his occupation, thereby drawing economic and social links together more closely. Again the pattern of the Cranbrook region is similar to that in Cambridgeshire and that found by Bower in Lincolnshire (Table 2.6).

When inventories or the Hearth Tax are used to establish comparative wealth patterns, certain *caveats* must be noted. Tables 2.5 and 2.6 show that no category is exclusive: someone with one hearth may be wealthier than someone with three; yeomen, especially retired ones, may appear poorer than some labourers. One cannot argue from the particular to the general, whether from individuals to whole parishes, or from one parish to other parishes, or from one county to another. Inventories themselves are especially crude indicators of wealth both because they do not take into consideration the value of the deceased's land and because debts owed by the deceased might, and frequently did, outweigh the value of his goods and chattels.[60] Kent, being so rich in probate accounts, clarifies this point (Table 2.7). Nor is the Hearth Tax a definitive indicator; Ralph Josselin, for instance, the Essex minister and diarist, moved from an 11-hearth house to a six-hearth house at a time of increasing prosperity in a search for greater comfort, and newer but smaller houses in Kent tended to have more chimneys than large ancestral timber-framed mansions.[61]

Table 2.6   *Comparative wealth groupings by occupation, from inventory appraisals, 1600s*

| category | Cambridgeshire 1661-70 | | Lincolnshire 1630-83 | | Cranbrook region 1660-99 | | |
	range	median	range	median	data base	range	median
	£	£	£	£		£	£
labourer	up to 80	15	12-89	29	40	7-476	69
husbandman	10-250	30	9-388	62	33	14-417	62
craftsman		40			62	3-1597	66
yeoman	12-1131	180	18-2583	149	120	20-2173	169
clothier					77	6-1146	120
retailer					42	7-882	106
widow					87	6-730	88
gentleman					37	10-2475	210

Sources: Cambridgeshire: Spufford, M. (1974) 36-9; Lincolnshire: Bower (1999), lxxxvi. In the Cranbrook section, 36 weavers (median £81) have been combined with the four labourers (median £48).

Despite the considerable reduction in the value of a person's effects as a result of payment of debts as shown in Table 2.7, the median value of a labourer or weaver's residue (£19) was lower than that of a husbandman (£46), and the value of the husbandman's residue was on balance lower than that of a yeoman (£50), just as was the case with the Hearth Tax. Provided that one bears in mind the reservations already expressed, the Hearth Tax remains a useful arbiter of prosperity. Table 2.10 at the end of this chapter provides a profile of the Cranbrook region in a format which makes it comparable to the analysis for Kent and other counties.

Table 2.7   *Wealth groupings, before and after payment of debts, Cranbrook region 1660-99*

category	median appraisal before payments (£)	median appraisal after payments (£)	percentage reduction
labourer/weaver	42	19	55
husbandman	64	46	28
yeoman	167	50	70
clothier	163	37	77
craftsman	73	23	68
retailer	144	34	76

Source: probate accounts

The percentages, parish by parish, of those households exempt from paying Hearth tax (Table 2.10, column 8) have been superimposed on the map, Figure 2.6a. These percentages, derived from the reconstitution, indicate clearly the proportion of poor in the parishes, and are fully consistent with Sarah Pearson's figures for the hundreds taken directly from the Hearth tax returns (Figure 2.6b).[62] At 46.2 per cent 'no charge', Cranbrook has a very high proportion of poor, exceeded only by Goudhurst with 50.7 per cent. As Cranbrook was the only 'town' of the area, and, with Goudhurst, the main cloth-producing centre, it is not surprising that the poorest gravitated there in search of work or alms.[63] Indeed, with 57.1 per cent, the borough of 'Cranbrook town' itself, as distinct from the whole parish, had the highest proportion of poor of any borough in the county.[64] The parishes to the north, east and south-east had a proportion of poor which was also considerably higher than the average for the whole county (32.1 per cent). If one includes among 'the poor' those living in one-hearth houses who did pay tax, the proportion of poor rises from 41 to 53 per cent.

The exception to this picture of poverty is the remarkably low percentage of exempt in Hawkhurst and in the equivalent hundreds. It is unlikely to be a genuine reflection of their comparative prosperity; more likely, it reflects a failure to list all the householders who should have been included as exempt. Certainly the population total generated by the Hearth Tax and reconstitution (Table 2.2) seems to lack some householders.

The converse of this picture of large numbers of poor is that the region was also comparatively bereft of really wealthy people at this time (1664). It featured no peers of the realm, and only two baronets and one knight; only four of the 85 houses of Kent with 20 or more hearths are found in the region. Whereas most of the more prominent members of old county families in Kent occupied houses with between six and 18 hearths, branches of such families in the Cranbrook region tended to pay on between six and 12 hearths. On the other hand the region figures strongly in the distribution map of comparatively wealthy people paying on between five and nine hearths (six to 12 per cent); these are the houses of the prosperous gentleman, yeoman and clothiers of the area.[65] As for those with three to four hearths and two hearths respectively, most of the Cranbrook area sits in the middle of the scale; the exceptions are Little Barnfield, with its high proportion of very poor and super-wealthy, and Great Barnfield, with its very low proportion of very poor.

Labourers (84 per cent of them), weavers (72 per cent) and widows (77 per cent) figure prominently among the 53 per cent of the population of the Cranbrook region who can be labelled poor or very poor. Also among the poor (but not paupers) were most of those occupations which fall at the lower end of the skills market: the millman, not the miller; the leather-dresser, not the tanner; the alehouse-keeper, not the inn-keeper.[66] Some carpenters lived humbly, while others, especially joiners, were much more affluent. Some men were more successful than others in the pursuit of their trade, like the bricklayers paying on two or three hearths, and the cordwainer on four (page 175). Retailers prospered, but had to support considerable stock

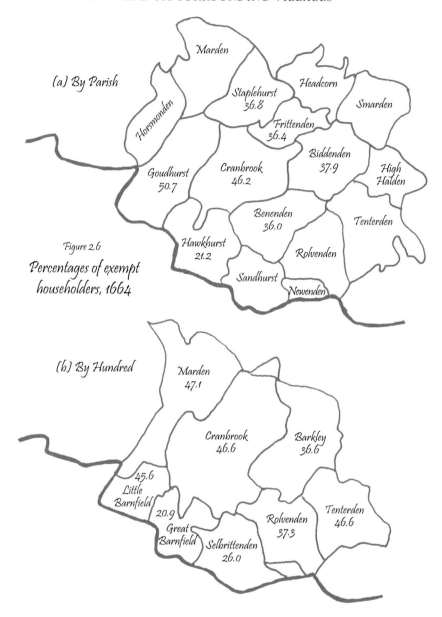

(a) By Parish

Marden

Horsmonden

Staplehurst
36.8

Headcorn

Smarden

Frittenden
36.4

Biddenden
37.9

Goudhurst
50.7

Cranbrook
46.2

High
Halden

Benenden
36.0

Tenterden

Figure 2.6

*Percentages of exempt
householders, 1664*

Hawkhurst
21.2

Rolvenden

Sandhurst

Newenden

(b) By Hundred

Marden
47.1

Cranbrook
46.6

Barkley
36.6

45.6
Little
Barnfield

20.9
Great
Barnfield

Selbrittenden
26.0

Rolvenden
37.3

Tenterden
46.6

and withstand delay in receiving payment (page 166). Butchers tended to pay on two or three hearths, and haberdashers, mercers and victuallers had even larger premises, often with a separate shop; mercers figure quite prominently as 'principal creditors' in the probate accounts of deceased parishioners. Some tailors did well for themselves, as did carriers and millers, while among the more affluent craftsmen were blacksmiths, dyers, saddlers and tanners, each of whom would have been apprenticed in their craft, and needed considerable material resources in metal or leather.

The position of 'clothier' is compromised by an increasingly generous use of the term to describe someone involved in the cloth industry;[67] of 126 'clothiers', 20 (16 per cent) were in houses with no charge or only one hearth. Similarly, 14 of the 84 'yeomen' (17 per cent) were exempt; at least some of these men were no doubt elderly, and had passed on their property while retaining some independence in a cottage of their own. In at least 50 cases owners paid tax on more than one house; Thomas Bayly 'of the Dane House' in Cranbrook, for instance, moved to Staplehurst in 1664; he was taxed on six hearths in Cranbrook and exempt on a one hearth house in Staplehurst. Edmund Luckhurst of Cranbrook, clothier and sometime miller, was charged on a two-hearth house and on an empty five-hearth house in his home parish. Such examples do not compromise the general principle that the Hearth Tax is a good arbiter of wealth; they do reinforce the dangers inherent in making judgements on individual examples.

Table 2.8 places the Cranbrook region Hearth Tax figures in a wider context, and shows that the proportion of 'exempt' was comparatively high, possibly reflecting the presence of the cloth industry. On the basis of those living in one- or two- hearth houses, however, percentages approximate to those found in rural Essex and Terling, where most worked on the land.

Table 2.8 *Comparative percentages of Hearth-tax payers, 1660s & '70s*

category (a) No. of hearths (cohort)	IV 1 (b) %	III 2 (b) %	II 3-5 %	I 6+ %	(exempt) %
Whickham 1666	(367)	79	11	7	3	79
Eccleshall, Staffs, 1673	(317)	83	9	7	1	53
Colyton 1674	(187)	33	23	40	4	53
Cranbrook region '64	(1656)	42	26	25	7	41
Herefordshire 1674	(11034)	74	13	10	3	39
Warwickshire 1669-70	(14509)	69	16	12	3	36
Rural Essex 1669/70	(20897)	48	19	25	8	34
Terling 1671	(122)	51	17	24	8	33
Kent 1664	(27077)	35	29	27	9	32
Bedfordshire 1669-70	(7730)	62	18	16	4	30
Chippenham 1674	(72)	49	18	26	7	23
Cambridgeshire 1674	(5377)	50	30	16	4	19
Willingham 1666	(149)	40	46	14	1	---
Willingham 1674	(150)	39	41	19	1	15
Holland Fen 1665	(940)	56	25	17	3	9

Sources: Wrightson and Levine (1979) 35; Spufford M. & Takahashi (1996) 400; Levine and Wrightson (1991) 157; Hindle (1998) 75; Sharpe (2002) 69.
Notes: (a) categories as given by Wrightson & Levine; (b) includes exempt.

Nonconformity and the Established Church

The administrative units which most affected the lives of people living in the Cranbrook region were the parishes. They provided the constables and the surveyors of the highways, the churchwardens and the overseers of the poor (page 123). Parishes were also, by definition, ecclesiastical units, and religion and religious persuasion were of profound importance in the life of virtually everyone living in the region at this time. The Restoration of 1660 may have brought an end to many of the more esoteric sects, but it did not end dissent in the form of nonconformist congregations; in fact, officially, it defined nonconformity, because now all parishioners had to attend the Anglican church on Sundays under pain of fine (page 179).[68]

In Kent generally most incumbents were willing to side with the restored church in 1660/62. The extent of nonconformist feeling in the Cranbrook region, however, is highlighted by the fact that in six of the seven parishes the ministers refused to conform, whereas 62 were ejected out of a total of approximately 400 in the whole of Kent. Calamy portrays the Wealden parishes as a hotbed of potential nonconformity, stimulating the comment of a contemporary in 1661 that 'The Wild of Kent is a receptacle for distressed running parsons who vent abundance of sedition'.[69]

By the time of the Compton Census (1676) little had changed (Table 2.9). Nonconformity was rife. Robert Newton, for instance, made a typically precise return for Frittenden; he recorded about 215 'persons of yeares of discretion men and women', and near '100 under age boyes and girles; in all 300 and over'. He also reported 'Professed Presbiterians wholly refusing society with the Church of England ... we have not above 2 or 3 obstinate dissenters' as well as 31 Anabaptists or so suspected, two Quakers, two Brown, between 30 and 40 'Newtralists between Presbiterians and Conformists', and 11 or 12 'Licentious or such as profess no kind of Religion', adding up to a total of 84; he closed with 'Other infrequent

Table 2.9   *Conformists and nonconformists in the Cranbrook region, Compton Census, 1676*

	conformists		nonconformists		total	communicants	
	No.	%	No.	%		No.	%
Benenden	491	88	69	12	560	82	15
Biddenden	610	87	90	13	700		
Cranbrook	898	69	402	31	1300	100	8
Frittenden	131	61	84	39	215	(practising=45)	
Goudhurst	900	90	100	10	1000		
Hawkhurst	850	85	150	15	1000		
Staplehurst	295	65	160	35	455		
totals	**4175**	**80**	**1055**	**20**	**5230**		

Source: Whiteman (1986)

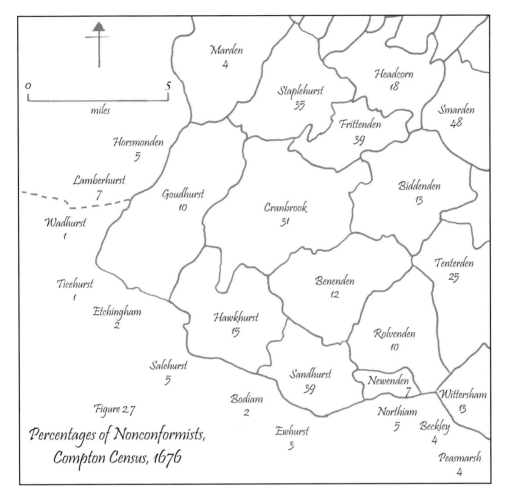

Figure 2.7

Percentages of Nonconformists,
Compton Census, 1676

Resorters to their Parish Church we have between 30 and 40 living and residing in Frittenden'.[70] This reply is by far the most detailed, treats of a parish in which the incumbent could easily have known each parishioner because of its comparatively small size, and by recognising that some were 'obstinate', some were 'neutralists', some professed no religion and some were 'infrequent resorters to their parish church', carries conviction.

The extraordinary intensity of dissent in the Cranbrook region is indicated on the map of the Kentish parishes and those which lie just across the border in Sussex (Figure 2.7). Among the Sussex parishes the median figure is three per cent nonconformity in a range which runs from one to five. Across the border in the parishes of the Cranbrook region, the median figure is 15 per cent in a range which runs from 10 to 39 per cent. When the Compton Census provides an average for nonconformity of four per cent across the whole country, and eight per cent for Kent, then Cranbrook, Frittenden and Staplehurst really do stand out as hot-beds of dissent.[71]

Table 2.10 Hearths in the seven parishes of the Cranbrook region, 1664

(to parallel the format used in Kent Hearth Tax, page xxx & lviii-lxii, for comparison)

Parish (a)	1 Total entries(b)	2 Total hearths(c)	3 1 hearth households No.	%	4 2 hearth households No.	%	5 3-4 hearth households No.	%	6 5-9 hearth households No.	%	7 10+ hearth households No.	%	8 Exempt households(d) No.	%	9 Exempt hearths (e) No.	%
Benenden	186	482	66	35.5	54	29.0	45	24.2	17	9.1	4	2.2	67	36.0	109	22.6
Biddenden	182	474	83	45.6	39	21.4	32	17.6	26	14.3	2	1.1	69	37.9	84	17.7
Cranbrook	484	1170	201	41.5	138	28.5	100	20.7	39	8.1	6	1.2	223	46.2	311	26.6
Frittenden	77	199	25	32.5	20	26.0	24	31.2	7	9.1	1	1.3	28	36.4	43	21.6
Goudhurst	400	866	200	50.0	101	25.2	67	16.8	27	6.8	5	1.3	203	50.7	255	29.4
Hawkhurst	203	524	81	39.9	49	24.1	45	22.2	24	11.8	4	2.0	44	21.7	51	9.7
Staplehurst	125	351	35	28.0	34	27.2	41	32.8	14	11.2	1	0.8	46	36.8	65	18.5
Total for Cranbrook area	1657	4073	690	41.6	435	26.3	354	21.4	154	9.3	23	1.4	680	41.1	924	22.7
Total for all Kent county	27077	72644	9636	35.6	7813	28.9	6080	22.4	2975	11.0	588	2.2	8695	32.1		

Notes: (a) Parish is the parish as reconstituted; the Hearth Tax returns are not by parish but by lathe, hundred and district.

(b) Total entries refers to householders in the reconstitution for whom the hearth tax supplies a listing, charge or exempt, but figures are not identical to those in Table 2.2 (population figures) because some householders paid on more than one house.

(c) Total hearths refers to the hearths listed by the assessors, whether charge or exempt; the four cases of householders whose entry is blank have been counted with the one-hearth people following the precedent of the Kent volume.

(d) In most instances, exempt households had one or two hearths, but there were exceptions, as follows: Benenden: 4 x 3 hearths, 3 x 4 hearths, 2 x 6 hearths; Biddenden: 1 x 3 hearths; Cranbrook: 6 x 3 hearths, 4 x 4 hearths, 1 x 5 hearths; Frittenden: 1 x 3 hearths; Staplehurst: 2 x 4 hearths.

(e) With the exception of 'exempt hearths' all percentages are of the total of householders, whether charge or exempt. The 'exempt hearths' percentage is of the total of hearths.

Chapter 3

Making the Family

Kinship: Nuclear and Extended Families

Each village or parish consisted mainly of the families living in it, and the relationship of those families to each other determined village society. Each family had its origin in marriage: the creation of a new economic unit and the lifelong association of two previously separate persons from existing families. Marriage and the making of the family is therefore an appropriate starting-point in this exploration of village societies. At the outset, however, we need to distinguish between family, household and kin; *family*—those related by blood or marriage who live together under one roof; *household*—those living under one roof including the family, apprentices, resident servants, boarders and lodgers; and *kin*—those related by blood or marriage who are currently alive.[1]

The standard view of the *family* in the latter half of the 17th century is that it consisted of parents and their children (the 'nuclear family'), to whom might be added youngsters in service, apprentices where appropriate, and, in wealthier households, more permanent servants, thereby making up the *household*. It also recognises that there were exceptions to the simple family household: elderly widows or widowers did live with their married children, and sometimes newly-weds stayed on for a while in the parental home until their new home was available.[2] The Cranbrook region bears this out; most families were of the nuclear type, but there are examples of more diffuse situations. For instance the will of Richard Webbe, gentleman of Frittenden, specifically required his brother George to take on the care of their uncle, then living with Richard, and to provide him with meat, drink and lodging, washing and apparel, for the term of his natural life, and 'see that he want nothing fitting for such a man of his degree to have as well in sickness as in health'. George seems to have taken over Richard's household, including his servants.[3]

There is less agreement on the importance of wider *kin* (brothers and sisters, uncles and aunts, nephews and nieces, cousins). While some commentators accept that they frequently appeared 'at critical junctures in the life course', like starting work or raising capital, there is an underlying view that at this time relationships with cousins were 'very remote and casual'.[4] In fact such contacts varied from one set of personal circumstances to another, and between one status group and another. Ralph Josselin's diary is frequently quoted as evidence that, apart from uncles, wider kin were of little importance; but he was a clergyman, geographically isolated from his kinsmen, and he had lost both his parents before he reached the age of 21.[5] The diary of Nicholas Assheton, on the other hand, shows him as a bachelor frequently meeting his kin, especially in social gatherings, and his life 'heavily oriented by ties of kinship'.[6] In his analysis of mean household size in England from the 16th to the early 19th centuries Laslett showed that status affected the proportion of wider kin who lived together in the family group; 27.6 per cent of gentry households

Table 3.1 *Kin relationships of 304 testators with their legatees, Cranbrook region 1660-99*

nuclear family	wives	141				
	sons	353				
	daughters	396	890	42%	890	42%
grandchildren	grandsons	119				
	granddaughters	92				
	unspecified	84	295	14%		
at one remove	brothers	88				
	sisters	102				
	fathers	7				
	mothers	13	210	10%		
at two removes	aunts	1				
	uncles	7				
	nephews	89				
	nieces	84	181	9%	686	33%
in-laws	brothers in law	43				
	sisters-in-law	9				
	sons-in law	49				
	daughters-in-law	15				
	fathers-in-law	3				
	mothers-in-law	4	123	6%		
kin	cousins	202				
	kindred	182				
	step-relations	16	400	19%	523	25%
Total: 2099						

Table 3.2 *Comparative kin relationships by number of wills*

		Cranbrook region 1660-1700 (304 wills)		Terling 1550-1699 (192 wills)	
nuclear family	wives, husbands, sons, daughters	221	73%	140	73%
grandchildren		82	27%		
at one remove	brothers, sisters, fathers, mothers	95	31%	20-35	10-18%
at two removes	aunts, uncles, nieces, nephews	59	19%		
-in-laws	brothers-, sisters-, sons-, daughters-	87	29%	less than 18%	
kin	cousins, kindred, step-relations	90	30%	far less than 18%	

For Terling see Wrightson & Levine (1979) 92.

contained resident kin beyond the nuclear family, as compared with only 17 per cent of yeoman households and 7.9 per cent of the households of the poor.[7]

The weight of opinion is that kinship ties beyond those of the nuclear family were of limited significance in the social structure of village communities.[8] Even the Tudor Poor Laws laid it down that 'those relations for whose welfare individuals might be held responsible at law went no further than parents and children, grandparents and grandchildren'.[9] The terms used for the inner core of father, mother, grandfather, grandmother, brother, sister, uncle and aunt are specific; those for peripheral relationships, like kinsman, cousin and even 'friend', are very unspecific. Such vagueness in the usage of terms like 'kinsman' and 'cousin' can be exemplified from the Cranbrook region, where nephews and nieces were sometimes referred to as cousins (in the wills, for instance, of Robert Newton, gentleman of Cranbrook, and William Austen, brickstriker of Staplehurst).[10] William Austen left legacies to three female cousins, the wife of a male cousin and eight children of two other male cousins, while Thomasine Rucke included in her legatees 'three kinswomen' and Anna Parton, 'daughter of my cousin James Parton'.[11]

Table 3.1 provides an analysis of individual legatees in the 304 wills from the Cranbrook region towards the close of the 17th century which closely parallels a similar analysis of Powick, Worcestershire, 1676-1775.[12] The highest percentage of legatees belonged to the nuclear family itself, but it is significant that, at 42 per cent, they represent less than half the total being recognised in wills. The proportion of family members outside the nuclear family, but with specific relationships including in-laws, figured almost as highly at 39 per cent. Most telling of all, however, is that as many as 19 per cent of those who were remembered in wills had a so-called 'remote' and unspecific kin relationship as cousins, kindred and step-relations. One cannot, therefore, accept that these groups were of little significance when brothers, sisters, mothers or fathers comprised 'only' ten per cent of legatees, and grandchildren comprised 'only' 14 per cent. It would be ridiculous to conclude that brothers, sisters, mothers, fathers, and grandchildren had little significance.

Relationships in the Cranbrook area of Kent were far from the 'genealogically narrow and shallow' range found at Terling, or indeed experienced by Josselin. Table 3.2 contrasts Cranbrook with Terling by providing a break-down of kin-relationships by will rather than by legatee, and shows that in the Cranbrook area, just as at woodland-pastoral Myddle, wider kin relationships remained very much alive.[13]

Choice of Marital Partner

It was a feature of marriages in England at this period that brides and bridegrooms commonly found their spouses locally. Studies of several villages, six in Lancashire and one near York for instance, show that, at the level of agricultural labourers, husbandmen and artisans, two-thirds of all grooms who married where they were born chose brides from the village itself; about 90 per cent came from within ten miles and all but a negligible proportion from within twenty miles. At Myddle 'nearly everyone found a husband or wife within a radius of ten miles of his or her dwelling'. This comparatively close proximity has been linked to the distance a suitor was prepared to travel, as well as to the restricted range within which most boys and girls took up employment as living-in servants (see below). Gentlemen might look much further afield; only 60 per cent of the squirearchy of Lancashire, and 50 per cent of that of Dorset, married within the county in the early 17th century.[14]

A close look at the Cranbrook evidence suggests that the region was no different from Myddle when it came to choosing a marital partner locally, but there are some factors which are worth highlighting. The compilers of the Cranbrook and Benenden banns 1653-62, which relate almost exclusively to those below the social level of gentry, had a genuine interest in the people whom they were recording, their genealogy and their origins, and they provide the main evidence.

Table 3.3   Parental parish, brides and grooms, compared with that of settlement

	total number	those living in parental parish		those living in different parish	
		number	percentage	number	percentage
Banns of marriage					
Cranbrook brides	224	149	66%	75	34%
Cranbrook grooms	239	146	61%	93	39%
Benenden brides	52	29	56%	23	44%
Benenden grooms	61	32	52%	28	48%

Note: More bridegrooms' fathers have a parish assigned to them than brides' fathers, hence the discrepancy in numbers. Only first marriages of brides have been used.

Table 3.3 summarises the data, and shows that during these years a third of Cranbrook brides, and a slightly higher percentage of bridegrooms, were no longer living in the same parish as their parents when they came to plan their marriages. The percentages for Benenden are even higher, but this may be because the database is much smaller. This does not, however, mean that these brides and grooms were comparative strangers to each. Contemporary custom was for youngsters to leave their family homes to be apprentices or servants in the houses of others. Gregory King, in his 1688 analysis, has one in ten of the population at any one time acting as a servant in the household of another family, though not necessarily in a different parish. Such service normally lasted a year, and therefore earned the 'servant' settlement in the parish where he or she was working; on average such placements were approximately four miles from their place of birth.[15]

All but one of the brides in the marriage banns came originally from within the borders of Kent and Sussex, the exception coming from Leicestershire. Four bridegrooms had fathers living well beyond the county boundary, in Somerset (feltmaker), Suffolk (clothworker), Cornwall (miller) and Bedfordshire (gentleman). No obvious reasons for their moves to Kent present themselves.

Table 3.3 shows that most of those about to be married were living at or near home, and this is reflected in Figures 3.1 and 3.2 for Cranbrook itself. Of the 224 cases in which the banns specify a parish for both brides and their fathers, 86 per cent of brides were living within a radius of six miles of their home. The picture for grooms is very similar. To the 146 living in the same parish as their parents can be added a further 30 from adjacent parishes and 16 from those parishes just beyond; some 80 per cent of bridegrooms, therefore, were living within a radius of six miles from home.

In more than a quarter of the 171 marriages in the Cranbrook banns which provide the necessary information, the bride, the groom and their respective fathers are shown as being of the same parish; the couple were therefore probably living with their parents and in close proximity to their future in-laws. The most overwhelming evidence from the Cranbrook banns of marriage, however, is that all but five of the 204 men who were registered as living in one of the home parishes, and who were marrying spinsters, married girls from those parishes or those in the immediate vicinity. In other words, 98 per cent of these marriages were between young people who were living in the same or the neighbouring parishes.

The fact that so many of these young people were living and working near each other but apart from their parents might suggest that they were able to make their own decisions about whom to marry, albeit often with parental consent. Macfarlane, discussing Adam Martindale's problems with his daughter who wished to marry a boy whom she met while out at service, concludes that, ultimately, the choice was the child's.[16] Ralph Josselin tried to guide his four daughters, but ultimately they chose their own husbands because they were out of the parental home for so long. Others would agree that, with the exception of gentry marriages, when the preservation of property was crucial, the initiative in courtship usually came from the young people themselves.[17]

In only two instances in the Cranbrook region is there evidence of parental pressure. John Dunke, clothier of Benenden, left his 15-year-old only daughter, Susanna, £200 provided she did not marry the vicar's son, then aged 22, nor marry without 'the consent or approbation of her mother'; if she married contrary to her mother's wishes she was to forfeit the £200. Allen Foster, yeoman of Hawkhurst, when his only daughter was but two years old, left her £500 to be hers at marriage or at age 21, provided she married with her grandfather's consent; if not, the sum would be reduced to £200.[18]

The main consideration especially for bridegrooms was to have completed their apprenticeship or period of service, and to have accumulated the resources to be able to maintain an independent household. Young people in service in the households of others were free to meet at dances, alehouses, in church and elsewhere without being chaperoned. Kissing, fondling, and spending a good deal of time alone together were tacitly sanctioned. When courtship became serious it was considered right and proper to inform parents, who would formally give or withhold their approval to continue. If approval was obtained, courtship could continue and intensify. Although

Figure 3.1   Origin of brides from Cranbrook banns, 1653-62

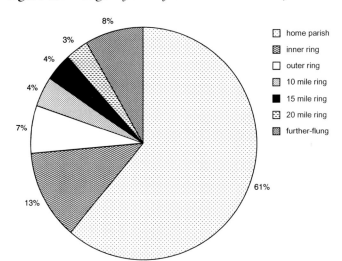

Figure 3.2   Origin of bridegrooms from Cranbrook banns, 1653-62

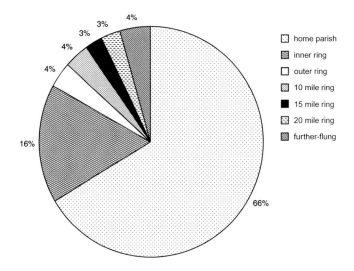

parental consent to marriage was not required by law, in practice it no doubt took an uncommonly determined couple to proceed in the face of open opposition.[19]

Proximity may have been a most important factor for those below gentry status in their choice of a partner for life, but one might expect occupational link and social grouping to have played some part in that choice. In fact occupation proves not to have been a major factor. The reconstitution of the parishes of the Cranbrook region yielded 427 marriages or remarriages in which the occupation of the groom and of the bride's father or, in the case of a widow, her former husband, could be identified with some confidence. Of these, 53 involved 'gentlemen' who, by virtue of that ascription, had no occupation, and have therefore been left out of consideration for the moment. Consistency of occupation featured in only 86 of the remaining 374 marriages (23 per cent), with the lowest correlation found in the central market town of Cranbrook (18 per cent) which, with its far greater variety of ways of making a living, provided a far larger marriage market.

Occupational descriptors are very imprecise, but even broad categories yield fairly low correlation levels between grooms and their brides' families, as shown in Table 3.4. Among the retailers and craftsmen, a very disparate group ranging from humble thatchers and bricklayers to affluent victuallers and mercers, where one might expect the tools and skills of the trade to influence matters, only 12.5 per cent actually married within the same occupation, as cardmaker to cardmaker's daughter, tanner to tanner's daughter. Specific examples of such occupational links can be cited: Richard Curd, a Benenden blacksmith, married Judith Neeve whose younger brother Simon Neeve was also a blacksmith; Simon's eldest son set up as a blacksmith in Frittenden. Mary Curd married Oliver Harris, a carpenter, while Isalte Curd married the labourer Edward Drilee, and John Curd plied his trade as a thatcher. Typically Elizabeth, the widow of William Playford, went on to marry another labourer, Henry Roots.

Table 3.4   *Consistency of occupation between bride and groom by occupational groups, Cranbrook region, 1660-99*

	broad correlation	percentage	no correlation	percentage
cloth	40	28%	104	72%
land	39	32%	83	68%
retailer/craftsman	47	43.5%	61	56.5%
gentleman/professional	45	85%	8	15%

Note: for this analysis, the 53 'gentlemen' have been included together with the 374 unions of those below gentry status.

Among the gentlemen and professional group, however, there was a very close correlation between the status of groom and bride in almost every case. The two baronets married the daughter of a baronet and of a knight respectively; the knight married the daughter of a knight. Of seven esquires, two married daughters of knights and two the daughters of esquires, the other three marrying gentlemen's daughters. Among the gentlemen (including a lawyer and a physician), rectors, vicars and schoolmasters, all the clerics married the daughters of gentlemen as did the vast majority of the others. There was clearly a status barrier, erected by the local gentry to preserve their exclusivity. The only breaches in this barrier were made by the daughters or relics of four clothiers, two yeomen, a tanner and a victualler,

8 Hancocks, a 15th-century farm house, and little changed over the years; in the 16th century it was the property of Thomas Sheafe before passing to the Courthope family. It probably remained a small tenanted farm in the 17th century. The chimney-stacks have clearly been added.

each of whom was anyway on the verge of gentry status, as revealed in the records by the occasional use of the epithet 'Mr'.

This high correlation in status between gentry bridegrooms and their brides prompts one to ask whether social background was a more important factor than general occupational groupings in determining marriage links. Such an analysis can only be approximate. On the other hand, most of those involved in the basic skills of cloth manufacture, like broadweavers, clothworkers, weavers, woolcombers and cardmakers, together with beer-brewers, bricklayers, masons, labourers, sawyers and thatchers, were generally defined as poor by their exemption from paying Hearth Tax. At the upper end of the scale were the yeomen and clothiers, although some clothiers in particular tended to have an inflated ascription. Skilled and semi-skilled craftsmen, the blacksmiths, tanners, saddlers, coopers, dyers and the like, together with grocers, butchers, millers and, most numerous of all, husbandmen, make up the very broad band of workers of 'middling' wealth and status.

Even as an approximation, the evidence tabulated in Table 3.5 is remarkably persuasive. Eight out of every ten among the gentry found an alliance in his own social grouping. Lower down the wealth and social scale the exclusivity of each social division diminished. Nearly seven in every ten of the yeomen and clothiers found a match in their own social sphere, while for the middling sort it was rather more than five in every ten, and for the poor it was four in ten.[20] Intermarriage

Table 3.5 *Consistency of occupation between bride and groom by wealth and status groups, Cranbrook region, 1660-99*

	broad correlation	percentage	no correlation	percentage
gentleman/professional	45	85%	8	17%
those comfortably off	57(a)	67%	28(a)	33%
the middling sort	100	55%	81(b)	45%
the poor	44	40%	64	60%

Notes: (a) 29 'yeomen' and 56 'clothiers' of whom 72% of yeomen and 64% of clothiers married their like or into the gentry.
(b) 59 of the 81 (73%) enjoyed a possibly advantageous match, with a yeoman, clothier or even the gentry; 22 of the 81 (27%) had a possibly disadvantageous match with someone in the 'poor' category.

across social boundaries was therefore more frequent the further down the social scale you were. The poor had a more than evens chance of marrying above their natural status group, which may suggest a healthy society; they were more likely to achieve advancement than any other of the groupings. Those in the middling or comfortably-off groupings might move up or down the social scale. The evidence suggests that the middling sort were more likely to marry up the scale than down, while for clothiers and yeomen marriage into the gentry was a more difficult step.

Age at Marriage

Marital age, especially the age at which brides were married, has a major effect on family size, as will become clear. It is now an accepted fact that brides in the 17th century were more likely to be nearer 25 than 20 years of age, and their husbands some three years older. These figures originate from Hollingsworth's analysis of 1,007 Canterbury Marriage Licences (1619-43) and were used by Peter Laslett to correct the mistaken belief that girls at this period married in their teens; they yielded mean ages of 23.58 for brides and 26.65 for bridegrooms.[21]

Biddenden provides a useful check on these findings in that the mean age for its 50 brides from the same source for the same period was 23.7 years and for bridegrooms 26.4 years. The correlation between Biddenden brides and grooms and the generality of Canterbury applicants is so exact as to suggest that in this regard Biddenden can be taken as an absolutely average parish at this time. This picture of precise ages is, however, very misleading. A more careful look at the Biddenden marriages shows that in 11 cases the bride was actually older than the groom, in one case by nine years, in three other cases by six or seven years; this gives the lie to the cosy 'average' which has become the accepted version. In another eight cases the bride and groom were the same age—meaning that in nearly 40 per cent of the Biddenden sample the groom was either the same age or younger than his bride. On the other hand in seven cases the groom was ten or more years older;

and although of our 50 brides eight were in their teens, in only two of these cases was the husband much older than she was. One couple married for the first time at 43 and 40 respectively, another at 20 and 18. Not one bridegroom of 26½ married a bride of 23½; indeed Edmund Crutwell and Edmund Randolph were the only bridegrooms aged 26, and they married respectively Rebecca Peat, aged 27, and Deborah Master, aged 22.

The *average* view of human activity may well bear little relationship to the reality on the ground, and statistical analyses which produce mean or even median figures may well give completely false impressions. This is not an argument for eschewing statistics; they do have a place. It is, however, an argument for treating them with the care appropriate to their ability to mislead. No statistics should be taken at face value, and all should be seen in context. Outhwaite sums up the situation judiciously by referring to the arithmetic mean as 'not always the most appropriate measure of central tendency', while yet 'the one encountered most frequently in literature'.[22]

The Canterbury Licences provide similar material, albeit less detailed, for each of the seven parishes in the Cranbrook area for the period 1660-99, as summarised in Table 3.6. These figures suggest virtually no difference between the average marital age of those from the Wealden parishes who sought licences after the Civil War and those from the whole of the Canterbury district before that War. On average, people did not rush into marriage.

Table 3.6   *Mean (and median) age at first marriage by licence, 1660-99*

	cohort	mean age, bridegrooms	mean age, brides	difference
		(median in brackets)		
Benenden	13	26.1 (26)	23.3 (22)	2.8
Biddenden	44	27.0 (25)	22.3 (21)	4.7
Cranbrook	39	27.7 (26)	23.6 (22)	4.1
Frittenden	13	25.7 (26)	23.2 (23)	2.5
Goudhurst	8	24.8 (24)	22.4 (23.5)	2.4
Hawkhurst	11	25.6 (25)	24.2 (23)	1.4
Staplehurst	27	26.4 (26)	23.9 (23)	2.5
Total	155	26.7 (26)	23.2 (22)	3.5
(1619-1643)				
Canterbury licences	1007	26.65	23.58	3.07
(1600-1649)				
Aldenham, Herts		29.1	25.3	3.8
Bottesford, Leics		29.2	25.9	3.3
Colyton, Devon		27.4	27.3	0.1
Hawkshead, Lancs		27.8	24.8	3.0
Willingham, Cambs		26.7	24.8	1.9

Source: Volumes 3 and 4 of Cowper's Canterbury Marriage Licences; Laslett (1983) 82; and Wrightson (1982) 68 for the last five parishes.
Note: Cranbrook parishes limited to marriages where ages are given for bride and groom.

Again, however, the picture provided by the averages for the seven parishes is misleading. One bridegroom under 20 years of age figures in the lists, while at the other end of the scale five married for the first time when past their 40th birthdays, one of them aged 45. These older bridegrooms married girls of 21, 24, 25, 30 and 30. On the distaff side, 23 girls were under 20 years of age at first marriage, whereas only two were over 30; the age of another 13 was given as 30 (clearly an approximation). Within these extremes, couples of widely differing ages joined together in matrimony. Sarah Sceeles at 18 married William Lanes of Biddenden, clothier, who was twice her age at 36. Bridget Fowle at 18 was 20 years younger than her husband, John Relfe of Cranbrook, gent., although the fact that she gave birth on the day following the marriage may account for this exceptional match. Ann Barr was only 21 when she married Samuel Furner of Biddenden, husbandman, aged 40.

Less frequently one finds younger men marrying older women, as the 20-year-old Thomas Stroud of Staplehurst, husbandman, and Obedience Glover, aged 26; John Bridge of Staplehurst, 'grosier', aged 24, and Susan Longley aged 30; and Stephen Chittenden of Biddenden, yeoman and William Lowes of Benenden, tanner, both 24 years old, marrying respectively Margaret Bayden and Susan Tamms who were both 30. Finally it was not uncommon for the bride and groom to be the same age; what is uncommon is any example of a 26-year-old bridegroom marrying a 23-year-old bride; indeed of 12 bridegrooms aged 26 not one married a girl of 23!

One further *caveat*, about the inaccuracy of the ages given on licences, has already been expressed (page 10), but this is not on such a scale as to nullify the general point which Laslett was making. It does, however, call into question any slavish reliance on statistics based on approximations, and the provision of mean ages for brides and grooms correct to the nearest two decimal places.

More to the point here, possibly, is that those who applied for marriage licences were not typical of the population in general. The normal practice before marriage was for the couple to have the banns of marriage promulgated during a service and in front of the congregation on the three Sundays prior to the date of their proposed wedding.[23] Banns were called to allow anyone who wished to state an impediment to the proposed match the opportunity to make their objections. Purchase of an ecclesiastical licence provided an alternative route to marriage which avoided what for some might be a too-public process. All one had to do was 'to apply to the episcopal authorities, present one's *bona fides*, and pay the requisite fee of 5s or 7s'.[24] The presiding official needed to satisfy himself that each of the couple was free to marry, and that in the case of a minor there was appropriate consent, by requiring the deposit of bonds and allegations (page 145ff).

Wealthier groups were always better represented than poorer ones in surviving marriage licences.[25] The advantages brought by the acquisition of licences included being able to marry in haste; to marry during seasons when matrimony was prohibited by the church; to marry away from home; and to plan marriage away from the glare of publicity. Hence marriage by licence rather than by banns became

9. Coursehorn is a medieval hall house which was occupied for four centuries by the Hen[d]ley family, clothiers.

an increasingly common practice in the later 17th century, especially among the gentle and commercial élites; 'To proclaim banns is a thing nobody now cares to have done; very few are willing to have their affairs declared to all the world in a public place, when for a guinea they may do it snug and without noise.'[26]

The profile of those who married by licence, therefore, is not typical of villagers as a whole; they tend to be more affluent and more independent. Certainly the gentry tended to marry young, sometimes very young, and their marriages tended to be arranged, precisely because of the need to preserve, or improve, the family's social and/or economic standing. Sir Ralph Verney, for instance, was 16 when, in 1629, he married his 13-year-old bride.[27] John Evelyn was 26 when in 1647 he married Mary, daughter of Sir Richard Browne, who was then aged 12; as in the case of Ralph Verney, this was an arranged marriage.[28]

The Cranbrook evidence goes some way towards supporting this picture of earlier marriage among the affluent and social *élite*, but we do not meet the same extremes. Sir Thomas Roberts was 24 when in 1683 he married Jane Beale, daughter and coheiress of Sir John Beale, Bt., of Farningham, Kent, who was 18 at the time. His sister Bridget was also 18 when she married. Sir John Henden's daughter Elizabeth was 19 when she married James Turner, gent., but the daughters of Samuel Boys Esq. of Hawkhurst were 20, 24 and 28 when they were married. He himself had been 29; his son was 25. None of the Roberts family of Glassenbury seems to have married young, with the exception of Bridget. Robert, son of Edward Guldeford Esq. of Benenden, who was created Baronet in 1685, was 29 when he married.

The tendency of the more affluent to marry younger and by licence may well account for the discrepancy between the figures for mean age at first marriage given by Laslett, and those given by Wrigley and Schofield which are based on the reconstitution of 12 parishes (Table 3.7). While Laslett's figures may be a fair reflection of the average age of those who married by licence in east Kent, the greater mean ages given by Wrigley and Schofield may be a more accurate reflection of the average ages of villagers as a whole. The importance of this conclusion is that the Wrigley and Schofield average age of 26 or 26½ years for females more accurately reflects the physical development of brides from the Cranbrook area at the time of their marriages than the figure of 23 provided by the Cranbrook area licences (Table 3.6). Even given the fact that these averages do not reflect the actual age of any one bride, nevertheless the two and a half or three years difference between them does represent a loss to the community of one or two children per family because of the 'birth-control' effect of the greater age of the brides at marriage. Because no woman could expect to remain fertile much beyond the age of 40, any delay in marriage reduced the number of children she was likely to bear.

Table 3.7   Mean age at first marriage from 12 reconstitution studies, 1600-1849

	1600-49	1650-99	1700-49	1750-99	1800-49
Male	28.0	27.8	27.5	26.4	25.3
Female	26.0	26.5	26.2	24.9	23.4

Source: Wrigley and Schofield (1989) 255, Table 7.26; 423, Figure 10.8.

The First-born

Marriage marked the point at which men settled down, as householders and/or as tenants, and therefore came into the orbit of tax-assessment; it also normally marked the beginning of the process of family formation. The reconstitution of the families who were living in the Cranbrook region immediately comes into its own, because it can readily supply the basic data from which we can calculate, for instance, the length of time between marriage and first birth, and therefore the frequency of pre-marital conception. Before the pattern of the first-born in the Cranbrook area is explored, however, some major *caveats* need to be highlighted.

The first is that for the dates with which we are dealing, and in the geographical area of our parishes, baptismal dates do not necessarily equate with birth dates (page 5). Precision in pinpointing dates of birth is therefore unattainable, and approximations must suffice. This does not in any way invalidate the conclusions which are to follow provided due weight is given to the problem. The second *caveat* links with the first; that human behaviour cannot be reduced to numbers. Not only did some families delay baptism for much longer than a week, but some wives did not deliver their babies exactly 38 weeks (the average gestation period is 39 weeks) after conception, as some have postulated.[29] A wife who delivered a live baby eight-and-a-half calendar months after marriage may well have conceived after the marriage ceremony. It follows that, even if the problem of delay between birth and baptism at this time did not exist, any apparent precision in analysing the delay between marriage and the birth of the first child in our period must be illusory.[30]

The third problem is the fact that some children were not baptised in the parish of parental residence. They therefore do not appear in the parish registers which record any given family's development, and therefore sabotage the accuracy of any analyses which do not include neighbouring parishes. There is evidence that in some areas it was customary for the first-born child to be baptised in the parish of his or her mother.[31] If this were so, then any attempt to arrive at a meaningful statistical analysis of average intervals between marriage and the birth of the first child by looking at one parish only must be doomed to failure; even where clusters of parishes are examined baptisms will have taken place beyond the boundaries of the area studied.

The evidence for the parishes of the Cranbrook area between 1660 and 1700 tends to support the view that baptism, especially of first-born, sometimes took place in the parish of the mother's family. It does not, however, suggest that the practice of having the first-born baptised away from home was so common as to be the norm. It may well be that the custom would have been more frequently observed had it been common for the mother's parents to be living in a different parish in the first place, or more frequently alive at the time of the birth of their grandchild; expectation of life being what it was at this period wives had frequently already lost their parents at the time of marriage.

The example of Gothard Harper clarifies the problem. He appears as a 'Cranbrook husbandman' in the marriage register, but he was the son of a Biddenden husbandman; on 2 December 1654 he married Ann Shephard of Cranbrook, spinster, whose father was a Cranbrook husbandman. Bride and groom were living in Cranbrook at the time of their marriage, but presumably Gothard had been in service in Cranbrook because his parental home was in Biddenden. The couple made their home in Biddenden where the registers record four children, of whom the eldest, Elizabeth, was baptised in June 1656, 18 months after the marriage itself. The picture of Elizabeth as the first-born, however, is inaccurate; the Cranbrook registers reveal that their first-born, a chrisomer, was buried at Cranbrook on 28 April 1655, just under five months after their marriage, and 14 months before the baptism of their *second* child Elizabeth. The fact that Ann came to term within five months of marriage might suggest a preference for staying away from the public gaze of their new home.

Two other examples must suffice. John Chittenden, a Cranbrook clothier, married Susannah Hawkins of Hawkhurst at Hawkhurst in July 1662. The Cranbrook registers imply a delay of 34 months between marriage and the birth of James, the eldest recorded son, baptised May 1665. The Hawkhurst registers show that in fact *John* was the first-born, baptised there in June 1663 after 11 months of marriage. Richard Banks, gentleman of Thakeham near Storrington in Sussex, married

Margaret, daughter of Samuel Boys Esq. of Hawkhurst, on 19 December 1682. They lived in Storrington, but their son, Henry, was actually born in Hawkhurst and baptised there in September 1684 as 'son of Richard of Storrington, co. Sussex, gent., and Margaret his wife'.

Such cross-parish registrations were not confined to the first born. There are plenty of instances of parents arranging the baptism of one or more of their children at any time in another parish. Sometimes the reason for this is stated, as for instance the temporary absence of their local incumbent, or the special request of relatives in another parish. More frequently the reason is not known. Such cases do not affect the examination of intervals between marriage and first birth, but do have a bearing on discussion of birth intervals in general.

To these problems, for which there is local evidence, one might also add that John Evelyn's wife Mary miscarried with her first pregnancy, thus delaying the first birth, but of course there is no record of that in the registers. In the case of Anne, wife of the East Anglian clergyman, Isaac Archer, she did not give birth to their first child until a period of 18 months had elapsed because she was ill with an ague for the first six months of their married life. Illness and miscarriage were all too common occurrences in the latter half of the 17th century, and all too readily distort calculations of mean and median intervals between births.

If precision in analysing delays between marriage and first birth, or between subsequent births, is unattainable, then the question arises of how best to achieve a useful and honest picture of the relationships between couples, and the pattern of family development at this time, while avoiding distortion due to the problems mentioned above. The answer lies in the use of histograms.[32] When the 'x' axis represents the number of months from marriage to birth or baptism, and the 'y' axis represents the number of examples taken from the reconstitution, then a visual pattern can be presented which does have meaning. Unusually long intervals, created by intervening children unrecorded or recorded in other parishes, or by abnormally long intervals between birth and baptism, disappear beyond the right-hand margin. Because the histogram is calculated in months, and because it avoids means and medians which are distorted every time a child is missed or a baptism delayed, the pretence of precision is avoided but the pattern of human activity is portrayed. Moreover, by using the same principle for each of the parishes, or for all of them together, it is possible to see at a glance whether the pattern of human behaviour in one parish is different from that in another, and to determine whether a norm emerges (Figures 3.3 to 3.9).

Figure 3.3 shows that the most common delay between marriage and first birth at Benenden was 10 or 11 months, with a rapid rise to that peak starting at nine months and the peak falling off through 12 and 13 months. A total of 89 out of 147 first births noted, or 61 per cent, fell within the ninth to the 13th month; within 14 months of marriage 76 per cent of Benenden newly-wed wives had given birth.

It is difficult to create meaningful parallels with published work on other parishes because it is not always clear to what extent consideration has been paid to the

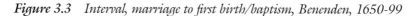

Figure 3.3 *Interval, marriage to first birth/baptism, Benenden, 1650-99*

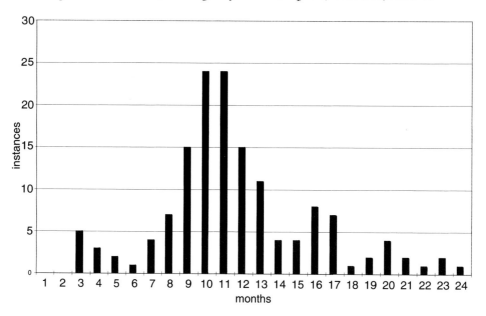

Figure 3.4 *Interval, marriage to first birth/baptism, Biddenden, 1650-99*

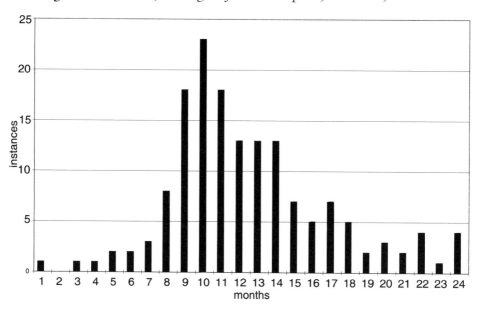

caveats expressed above. Apparently only 11.6 per cent of the inhabitants of the market town of Ludlow in Shropshire, for instance, had their first child baptised within 14 months of marriage, with most taking between 18 and 26 months to produce their first child.[33] There is no difficulty, however, in comparing Benenden

Figure 3.5   *Interval, marriage to first birth/baptism, Cranbrook, 1650-99*

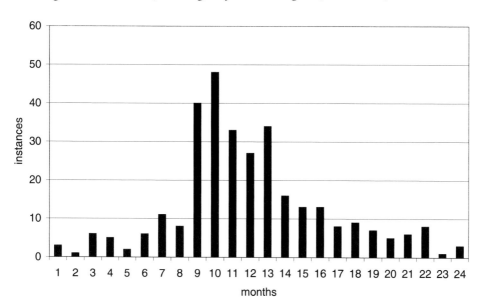

Figure 3.6   *Interval, marriage to first birth/baptism, Goudhurst, 1650-99*

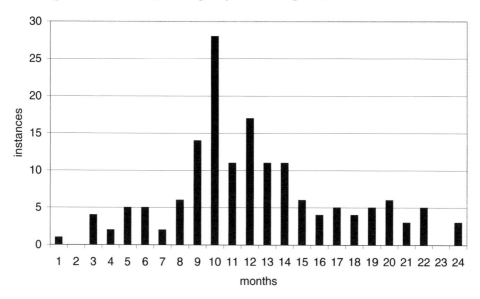

with its neighbouring parishes. Figure 3.4 shows that a delay of ten months was the most common at Biddenden, but that again the graph rises from nine months to that peak and falls back via 11 months to 14 months. Putting it another way, within 14 months of marriage 74 per cent of Biddenden newly-wed wives had given

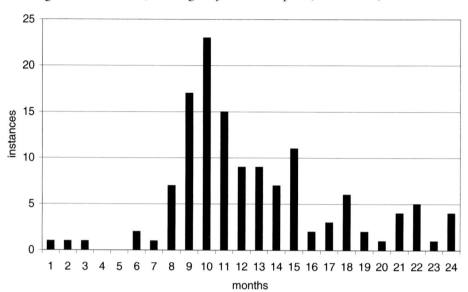

Figure 3.7   Interval, marriage to first birth/baptism, Hawkhurst, 1650-99

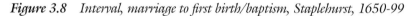

Figure 3.8   Interval, marriage to first birth/baptism, Staplehurst, 1650-99

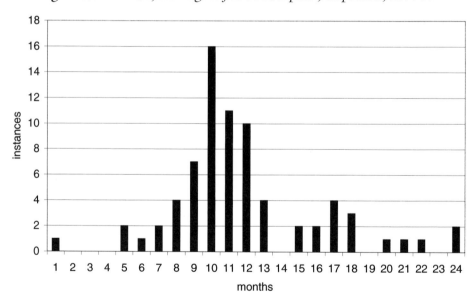

birth. The Figures for Cranbrook, Goudhurst, Hawkhurst and Staplehurst (Figures 3.5-3.8) show the same general pattern, with a concentration in the ninth to 13th months, by which time more than 70 per cent of mothers had given birth. Figure 3.9 combines all the parishes, and accentuates the importance of the peak months,

Table 3.8   *Optimum delay, marriage to birth/baptism of first child, 1660-99*

	cohort	peak month(s)		main concentration		by end of 14th month	
				Nos.	%	Nos.	%
Benenden	147	10/11th	(9th-13th)	89	61	111	76
Biddenden	156	10th	(9th-14th)	98	63	116	74
Cranbrook	313	10th	(9th-13th)	182	58	224	72
Goudhurst	184	10th	(9th-14th)	92	50	117	64
Hawkhurst	132	10th	(9th-15th)	91	69	93	70
Staplehurst	74	10th	(9th-12th)	44	59	54	73
Totals	1006			596	59	715	71

Source: Reconstitution of Cranbrook region parishes

Figure 3.9   *Interval, marriage to first birth/baptism, Cranbrook region, 1650-99*

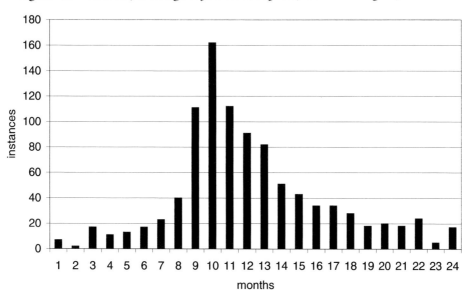

which can be tabulated as in Table 3.8. One can see little sign here of a reluctance to conceive; if anything the reverse was true.

Pre-marital Pregnancy

The pattern of first births highlights the fact that some brides had been indulging in pre-marital sex and were already pregnant at the time of their marriage. One needs to stress here that there was a real difference in perception between the birth of a child outside wedlock altogether, and the birth of a child inside wedlock even though it was conceived before marriage.[34] The former was regarded as a deviant form of behaviour in the way that the latter was not. When Hair drew a sample of marriages from many parishes over the period 1550-1820, he found that 32 per cent of all first births or baptisms occurred within eight and a half months of the marriage, and 21 per cent within six months of marriage.[35] In Terling in Essex Wrightson and Levine found that 'one third of all brides traceable to the baptism of their first child in Terling between 1550 and 1599 were pregnant when they married'.[36] In one parish, Lamplugh in Cumberland in the early 17th century, 60 per cent of brides were pregnant at the time of their marriage.[37]

Across the country the general pattern shows bastardy and bridal pregnancy rising and falling in concert, rather than one supplanting the other. The illegitimacy rate for England as a whole fell dramatically from a high point in 1600-1610 to a low point in 1651-1660, whence there was a gradual rise to 1700 and beyond.[38] Adair's main contribution to the debate has been to show that there were marked differences in pattern between the regions, and that illegitimacy rates in the highland zone were very much higher than those in the lowland zone (Table 3.9). That being said, all districts showed a trough which coincided with the so-called Godly revolution and the period just after the Civil War. The pattern of pre-marital pregnancy in the parishes of the Cranbrook region shows an average rate of 13 per cent, which matches very well with the pattern which Adair postulates for the Lowlands in general for the last half of the 17th century (Table 3.9).

Table 3.9   *Comparative Bridal Pregnancy*

Regional variations in bridal pregnancy, 1538-1754 (%)			Bridal pregnancy in the Cranbrook area parishes, 1660-99 (%)		
Cohort	Highlands	Lowlands	Benenden	15	[22 of 147]
1538-1580	25.1	19.5	Biddenden	12	[18 of 156]
1581-1620	24.7	18.6	Cranbrook	13	[42 of 313]
1621-1660	21.1	12.3	Goudhurst	10	[19 of 184]
1661-1700	16.7	15.3	Hawkhurst	10	[13 of 132]
1701-1754	24.0	20.6	Staplehurst	14	[10 of 74]
			Average	**13**	**[105 of 822]**

Source: Adair (1996) 101, Table 3.2.   Source: Reconstitution
Note: bridal pregnancy is number of first baptisms in parish within eight months as a proportion of the total number of baptisms in the parish, as Adair (1996) 98.

Adair also set out to test a question raised by Wrigley as to whether analysis of the balance of early and late pregnancies before marriage might provide a clue as to the motivation for the marriage itself.[39] In the late 17th century most bridal pregnancies would not have been detectable at the time of marriage; as the 18th century wore on, however, pre-nuptial pregnancy not only became more common, but the pregnancy tended to be in a more advanced state by the time of the marriage ceremony. Might it not be, Wrigley wondered, that in the late 17th century it was the decision to marry which led to intercourse, whereas in the 18th century it was increasingly the pregnancy which led to the marriage? Adair selected 28 parishes for analysis on the basis of the completeness of their registers. He then divided the parishes into highlands and lowlands, and arrived at the data in Table 3.10, into which the equivalent information for the Cranbrook parishes has been incorporated.

Table 3.10   *'Degree of pregnancy' data (% of births within months of marriage)*

cohort	Region	0-3 months	4-6 months	6-8½ months
1581-1650	Highlands	36.1	40.0	23.9
	Lowlands	17.0	29.8	53.2
1651-1700	Highlands	23.2	33.8	43.0
	Lowlands	16.1	30.3	53.6
1660-1700	*Cranbrook*	*20.0*	*27.7*	*52.3*
1700-1754	Highlands	25.3	37.6	37.1
	Lowlands	19.7	45.9	34.4

Source: Reconstitution and Adair (1996) 107, Table 3.6.

Again it can be seen that the Cranbrook parishes follow very closely the pattern suggested for the lowland area of England at this time. The implication remains that, for the most part, the couples of the region indulged in intercourse only when preparations for the marriage were far advanced.

Chapter 4

Growth of the Family

This chapter examines the pattern by which the family, formed by the birth of the first child, was continued and completed. In the process the opportunity arises to explore such topics as fertility, family limitation, infant and child mortality, and attitudes to children in general. The chapter closes with five short case-studies of families taken from the reconstitution which provide useful points of reference for many of the experiences which are the topics of discussion in the earlier part of the chapter.

Family Formation

Histograms again provide the most useful picture of the growth of families in the Cranbrook region. The early ones illustrate in most general terms the intervals in months between successive births after the arrival of the first-born child. Later ones distinguish more precisely the intervals between the first and second child from those between further children, and address the question of the effect of social grouping on such patterns. For ease of representation, intervals have been paired, so that 13 and 14 months have a single vertical indicator, as do 29 and 30, 41 and 42 and so on. No attempt at precision has been made, because to suggest precision would be to create false expectations. There can be no precision, especially at this period, when sometimes the interval known is between a date for birth and a date for baptism, sometimes between baptism and baptism, and sometimes (more especially in Benenden), between birth and birth.

The intervals allowed in the histograms run from nine to 60 months. Intervals greater than 60 months do occur in the reconstitution, but they are comparatively rare; there were two less than nine months, and they no doubt stem from the late baptism of the previous child. Intervals greater than 60, even towards the end of a particular mother's reproductive life, can of course happen naturally, but the implication of such a long interval is that a birth or baptism is missing from the sequence; it may be that there had been a miscarriage, or a stillborn child had gone unrecorded, or a child was unbaptised, or baptised in another parish. If one applies the same principles to a known family, for instance, there is a gap of 79 months between the births of John Evelyn's fourth and fifth children, 1657 and 1664, which his diary shows was occasioned by his wife Mary's miscarriage in October 1660 following a fall.[1] In the case of William Springett of Goudhurst, on the other hand, we know that the 62-month interval between second and third child was occasioned by his imprisonment for debt![2] The advantage of portraying the birth interval pattern as a histogram, therefore, is that the eye is drawn, quite rightly, towards the norm where bars are tallest while recognising that there was a tail which ran to and beyond 60 months. In each of Figures 4.1 to 4.6, the darker columns indicate the number of

Figure 4.1   *Intervals between births/baptisms, Benenden, 1650-99*

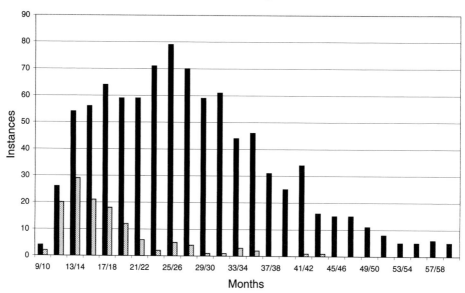

Figure 4.2   *Intervals between births/baptisms, Biddenden, 1650-99*

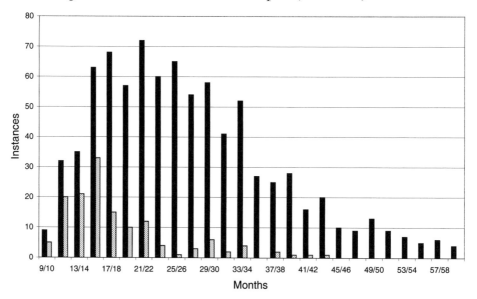

birth intervals in general, and the lighter columns those birth intervals immediately following an infant death (page 82).

The histograms of the individual parishes display a marked consistency, indicating that there was virtually no difference between the patterns of family formation from

Figure 4.3   *Intervals between baptisms [some births], Cranbrook, 1650-99*

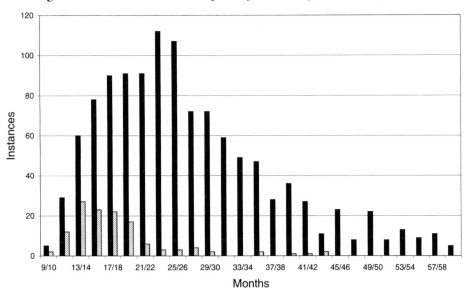

Figure 4.4   *Intervals between baptisms [some births], Goudhurst, 1650-99*

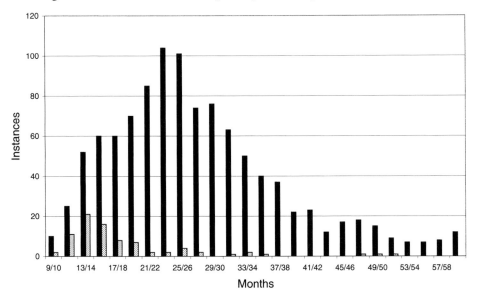

one to another. We are therefore perfectly justified in seeing the Cranbrook region as a whole and concluding that, across the span of the reproductive life of women in the region at this time, the interval between births tended to be between 15 and 30 months, with a modal point of just over two years.[3]

Figure 4.5   *Intervals between births/baptisms, Hawkhurst, 1650-99*

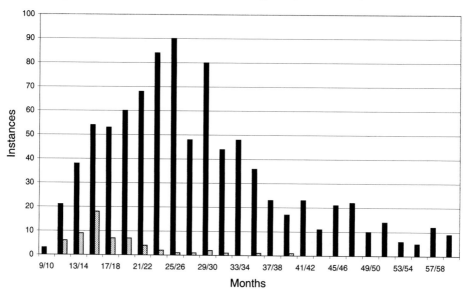

Figure 4.6   *Intervals between births/baptisms, Staplehurst, 1650-99*

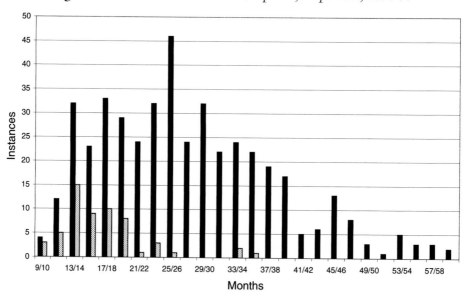

Figure 4.7   Intervals between births/baptisms, all Cranbrook region parishes, 1650-99

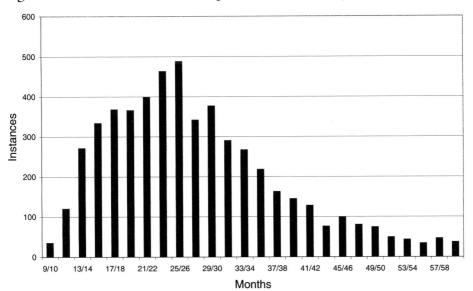

The Evidence for Family Planning

It has been suggested that couples in the latter half of the 17th century set out to limit the size of their families. The suggestion derives from Wrigley's work on Colyton in Devon which seemed to indicate that, in the period 1647-1719, unlike the periods 1560-1646 and 1720 onwards, the population was falling because the number of burials usually exceeded the number of baptisms. In his view, for some 70 years 'after the terrible mortality of 1646-7', women had a marked tendency to delay marriage until they were in their 30s, and to practise some form of birth control once they had a few children.

As far as the first point is concerned, there can be no doubt that if, on average, women were marrying three or four years later than usual, they could expect to produce families with at least two less children. The argument that this was a major factor at Colyton, however, is weakened by the fact that Wrigley's figures show a marked drop in the number of known marriages in precisely the middle period as compared with the other two.[4] Lots of marriages, therefore, were missing from the registers of Colyton, as elsewhere, in the decades following 1646, and it might well be that those marrying clandestinely were young![5]

The evidence for active birth control in Colyton is possibly more persuasive. For the middle period Wrigley noted a marked rise in the interval between the penultimate and final birth in completed families, and argued that a disinclination to have more children would extend intervals, especially the last interval; the last child would, in effect, be a mistake, or the result of a reversal of an earlier decision not to increase family size, maybe from a desire to replace a child who had died.

He interpreted a marked rise in the mean interval between the penultimate and last births as typical of a community beginning to practise family limitation'.[6] In her recent reappraisal, Sharpe is not convinced.[7]

The material from the parishes of the Cranbrook region allows one to tabulate it for comparison with Colyton, as in Table 4.1. This shows that the Cranbrook region reproduction intervals are considerably shorter than those at Colyton for the equivalent period; indeed they equate much more closely with the Colyton figures for the earlier and later periods, thereby reinforcing the impression that what is exceptional is the experience of Colyton from 1647 to 1719, not the period 1647 to 1719 in general. The reason for this Colyton experience would need to be sought in that parish, maybe with its exceptional death toll in 1646-7 following a last, virulent outbreak of plague, which would have led to barrenness among women who survived, or maybe as a result of female commitment to the lace industry and male emigration.[8] One cannot argue from Colyton to the wider view, any more than one can from Cranbrook.

Table 4.1 *Mean birth intervals (in months) for Colyton and the parishes of the Cranbrook Region, 1650-99*

		1-2	No.	2-3	No.	3-4	No	Last	No.
Colyton	1560-1646	25.2	87	27.4	84	30.1	77	37.5	76
	1647-1719	**29.1**	**23**	**32.6**	**26**	**32.1**	**18**	**50.7**	**34**
	1720-1769	25.1	24	29.8	24	32.9	22	40.6	24
Benenden	1650-99	21.6	60	26.4	60	28.4	60	35.9	60
Biddenden	1650-99	23.6	61	26.9	61	27.4	61	37.3	61
Cranbrook	1650-99	25.3	65	27.8	65	29.9	65	36.9	65
Goudhurst	1650-99	21.6	43	28.5	43	33.7	43	39.6	43
Hawkhurst	1650-99	23.5	92	26.6	92	29.7	92	39.5	92
Staplehurst	1650-99	22.3	35	29.6	35	34.1	35	35.3	35
Cranbrook region	**1650-99**	**23.2**	**356**	**27.4**	**356**	**30.0**	**356**	**37.6**	**356**

Source: Wrigley (1966b) 93, and reconstitution of Cranbrook area parishes.
Note: Wrigley used some families with only four children; Cranbrook data are based on families with five or more children: numbers are therefore consistent throughout.
   The mean intervals for Benenden are largely based on birth dates, those for Colyton and the other Wealden parishes on baptismal dates. Because they are mean intervals, and because they reflect different types of interval, one should not treat figures such as these as if they were precise. They are merely a guide.

The table also shows that in the Cranbrook parishes birth intervals increased as the process of family formation continued. A woman's fertility normally declines as she approaches the end of her active child-bearing period; Table 4.1 reflects that fact.[9] Figures 4.8 to 4.11 combine the parishes and show that the concentration between 1st and 2nd birth/baptisms lies between 13 and 30 months; that for 2nd to 3rd birth/baptisms the interval has spread to between 15 and 34 months, for 3rd to 4th birth/baptisms it is much the same, and for the interval between the penultimate and last birth/baptisms it has moved to between 25 and 42 months. The Cranbrook area figures therefore show no great rise in the interval between the births of the penultimate and last children, and no evidence of deliberate family limitation.

Figure 4.8   Intervals, 1st to 2nd birth/baptisms, Cranbrook region 1650-99

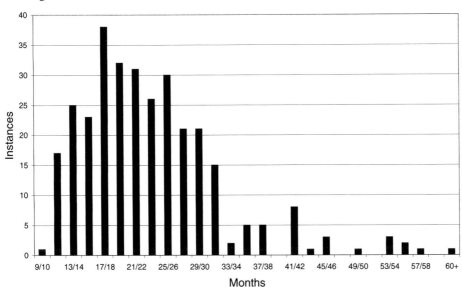

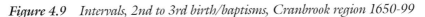

Figure 4.9   Intervals, 2nd to 3rd birth/baptisms, Cranbrook region 1650-99

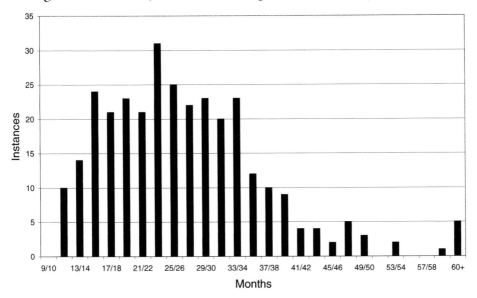

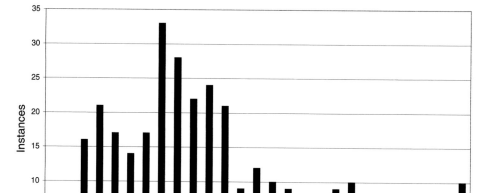

Figure 4.10 *Intervals, 3rd to 4th birth/baptisms, Cranbrook region 1650-99*

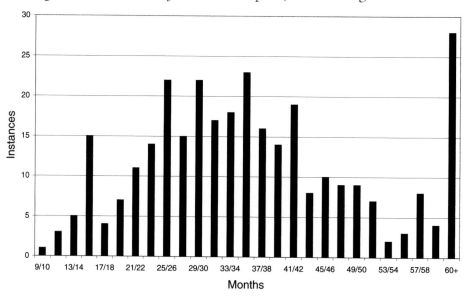

Figure 4.11 *Intervals before last birth/baptism, Cranbrook region 1650-99*

The highest concentration in Figure 4.11 lies in the column marked 60+, or more than five years between births/baptisms; the 28 intervals thus portrayed consist of 14 between five and six years, seven between six and seven years, five between seven and eight years, and two where the gap was longer than eight and nine years respectively. It might well be suggested that the 'tail' thus revealed did indicate some attempt at family limitation in these parishes, like that perceived at Colyton. On the other hand there had been one case of an interval over five years between the first and second child, five over five years between the second and third child and 10 over five years between the third and fourth child. In the circumstances, therefore, the extended delays between the penultimate and final birth, which are found in less than one in ten of the families examined, look more the result of natural loss of fertility, or other unknown causes like miscarriages or illness, rather than of family limitation. Just so did Ralph Josselin's wife, Jane, suffer five miscarriages late in her child-bearing career; Isaac Archer's wife, Ann, also miscarried five times, and John Evelyn's wife, Mary, twice.[10]

Social Groupings and Family Formation

The reconstitution also provides the necessary evidence to determine whether different social groupings had recognisably different patterns of child-bearing. There has to be a *caveat* here too. A rapid rate of child-bearing might well be the preserve of those sufficiently affluent to be able to take advantage of a wet nurse, and thus fulfil what John Evelyn suggests was the cultural requirement of the day 'for persons of quality';[11] or it might stem from the need to provide a male heir which marked the outlook of such gentry families as the Verney's which had a title to pass on.[12] It might also be the result of a desperate determination on the part of parents to establish any sort of family when faced with the loss of previous children soon after birth.

Figures 4.12 to 4.16 show birth/baptism intervals for the first four children of families in the Cranbrook parishes by social groupings: gentlemen (34 families,

Figure 4.12   Birth/baptism intervals, gentlemen, Cranbrook region 1650-99

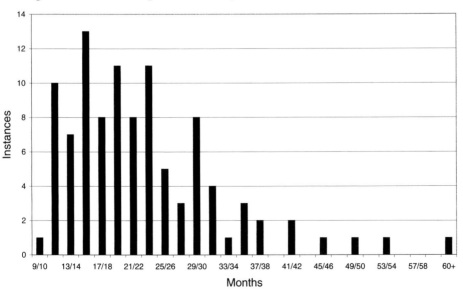

Figure 4.13 Birth/baptism intervals, labourers, Cranbrook region, 1650-99

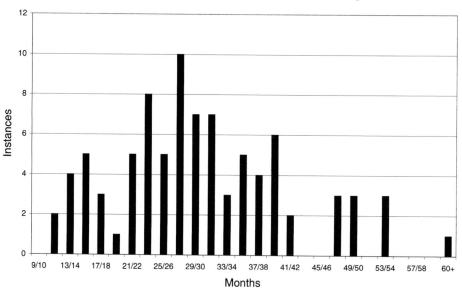

Figure 4.14 Birth/baptism intervals, yeomen and clothiers, Cranbrook region, 1650-99

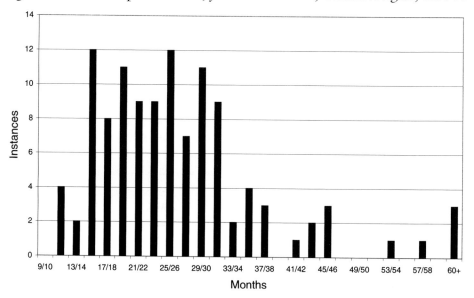

including clergy and esquires); the poor (29, including weavers, bricklayers and a thatcher); yeomen and clothiers (38, those comfortably off in society below the level of gentlemen); husbandmen (15, the smallest sample); and craftsmen/retailers (a disparate group of 36 including blacksmiths, carpenters, joiners, mercers, millers, butchers, tailors and a tallow-chandler).

Figure 4.15 *Birth/baptism intervals, husbandmen, Cranbrook region 1650-99*

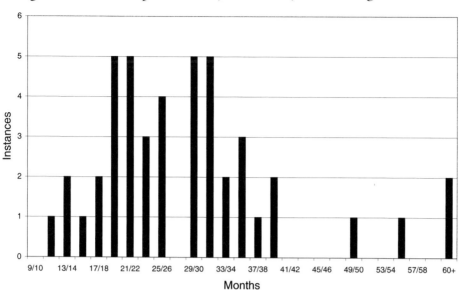

Figure 4.16 *Birth/baptism intervals, craftsmen and retailers, Cranbrook region, 1650-99*

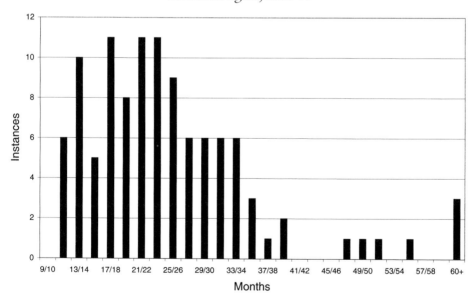

Despite the *caveats* mentioned above there is sufficient contrast between birth/ baptism intervals in the families of gentlemen and those of the poor to suggest that there was a genuine difference between the rate of reproduction of the two groups. The most common interval for the gentlemen is 15/16 months, for the poor it is

27/28 months; the concentration for gentlemen is between 11 and 30 months, with few births taking place after longer intervals, whereas the concentration for the poor is between 23 and 40 months.[13] The wealthiest in society, those with a status to be maintained, therefore reproduced more rapidly than the least wealthy who had no status to maintain. The probability is that the concentration of birth-intervals around the one-year mark among the gentlemen represents the use of wet-nurses as well as, occasionally, infant deaths, while the dozen or so short birth intervals discernible among the poor simply represents a rapid second pregnancy after the endogenous loss of a child.

The histogram for yeomen and clothiers indicates a pattern which falls neatly between the gentlemen and the labourers, and the same is true of the husbandmen. Neither group seems, in general, to have been in a hurry to procreate, with the clothiers and yeomen concentrating the pattern of intervals between 15 and 32 months, the husbandmen between 19 and 36 months. It is true that the pattern of the clothiers and yeomen approximates more closely to that of the gentlemen, the pattern of the husbandmen more to that of the labourers, and in so doing these two social and economic groupings reinforce the evidence that there was an economic factor in play in family formation.

Finally the pattern of birth intervals of the craftsmen and retailers really covers the whole spectrum as portrayed by the other four groups. There is no clear modal point, and the concentration of birth intervals covers from 11 months at one extreme to 34 months at the other, as one would expect from such a mixed group which ranges from carpenter and miller to mercer and victualler. Overall, there is also clear support for the view that wealthier couples were likely to have children more rapidly than those lower down the social scale. Whatever the main reason for this contrast, whether it was some Malthusian desire on the part of the poor to limit the number of their offspring according to the availability of food and accommodation, or whether relieving the wealthiest mothers of the duty of feeding their own children led to more frequent pregnancies among their status group, the most powerful factor determining the size of families at this time was not so much rate of birth as rate of death.[14]

Infant and Child Mortality

The seriousness of the problem of infant and child mortality is all too starkly brought home by the process of reconstitution. Time and again, as one builds up the families from the baptismal register, no sooner has a child been entered on the sheet than the burial register confirms how brief was his or her life. If the revelations become depressing for the researcher, how much more depressing might they have been for those who suffered the loss in their own family.

In this connection, one school of thought, pioneered by Philippe Ariès in the early 1960s, and typified by Laurence Stone's work, maintains that parents could not allow themselves too deep an attachment to their children; the ever-present reality

10. In the 17th century a massive chimney stack was inserted centrally into an earlier dilapidated medieval house; the hearth, part of which is shown to the right, warmed the living area. The south doorway to the house can just be seen to the extreme left; the contemporary stairs rise in the space to the left of the stack; between them are contemporary cupboard doors which retain their original butterfly hinges.

11. The original treads of the 17th-century stairs provide access to the first floor; the chimney forms the 'wall' at the back of the picture.

12. The space on the north side of the chimney-stack was used to form a closet above the north door entrance lobby.

of death is seen as the psychological key to the mentality of family relationships.[15] Supporters of this view see family life in terms of a distant relationship between parents and their children, and, at least before 1640, with little evidence of real love, or of time and energy, given to their children. They argue that babies were little regarded; they were swaddled, inadequately fed and washed, and put out to wet-nurse; their arrival occasioned little joy, their death little grief. Such ideas tend to be based on attitudes exhibited by some upper gentry families; there are hints of them in the correspondence of the Verneys of Claydon House,[16] but they would be recognised by very few inhabitants of the Cranbrook area.

A second school, championed by Alan Macfarlane and neatly expressed by Linda Pollock, has challenged such ideas, providing a more positive picture by use of diaries and biographies.[17] She has argued that Ariès and others have limited their perspectives by looking at too selective a range of sources. David Cressy affirms that 'far from there being a paucity of emotional warmth in these families, I find their emotional lives to have been complex and intense, especially affected by grieving and loving.' This may well be because, as he says earlier, he is dealing with a large number of individuals, many below the level of the gentry and clergy, men and women, who are 'temporarily dislodged from obscurity'.[18] Most commentators would now accept that families in the 17th century could be happy, and that parents did love their children.[19]

The nature of the reconstitution process readily allows one to calculate the incidence of infant and child mortality in the parishes of the Cranbrook region at this time. For comparative purposes the figures have been calculated according to principles established by Roger Schofield in the 1970s;[20] the infant mortality rate is therefore presented as the number of deaths under age one per thousand live births. Some idea of the incidence of infant mortality in the Cranbrook area at this time can be seen in Table 4.2. In looking at those figures, however, it is important to realise that, because they depend on data from parish registers, they are *minima*. Many children were born dead, and some were born alive but too weak to be taken

Table 4.2   Infant and child mortality statistics from the reconstitution of the parishes of the Cranbrook region, c.1650-99

Number of	Benenden	Biddenden	Cranbrook	Hawkhurst	Staplehurst	Total
... children recorded	1474	1562	3129*	1601	922	8688
... dying aged under 10	444	580	1399	326	286	3035
... of whom infants†	275	375	548	110	111	1419
Percentage of children						
... dying aged under 10	30.1	37.1	44.7*	20.4	31.0	34.9
... dying as infants†	18.7	24.0	17.5*	6.9	12.0	16.3

Notes: * The Cranbrook burial register often refers to deaths of children simply as 'child of ...', without specifying a name. As a result, in 284 out of 3,271 entries it has been impossible to tell whether the deceased was an established child or new-born. The figure of 3,129 represents the mean between the maximum of 3,271 and minimum of 2,987 children born alive. Correspondingly, the percentages given for Cranbrook represent mean figures between maxima and minima. Frittenden (very small numbers) and Goudhurst (unhelpful burial register) have not been included.
      † 'infant' means before reaching first birthday.
Known still-born children (Benenden 22, Biddenden 15, Cranbrook 25, Hawkhurst 11 and Staplehurst seven) have not been included in the above figures.

to church for baptism, and died soon after birth. It has been calculated that an interval of a month between birth and baptism could have the effect of reducing the infant mortality rate by half, as a percentage of the births would not have been recorded as baptisms.[21] We know that such an interval was commonplace at this period in the Cranbrook region (page 5ff).

In addition, some burials went unrecorded. Comparison of the Biddenden overseers' accounts with the burial registers between January 1660 and December 1662 shows that of 11 pauper burials noted in the accounts, several of which were of infants, only two were recorded in the registers. While the Biddenden discrepancy can be shown to have been short-lived, the Hawkhurst and Staplehurst registers rarely mention the burial of unbaptised children at all; this helps to explain the very low figures for those two parishes in Tables 4.2 and 4.3. Maybe the incumbents there followed the instruction from the church authorities that those dying unbaptised should not receive a Christian burial. For all these reasons, therefore, these infant mortality figures considerably under-represent the true death rate.

Table 4.3   *Comparative infant mortality figures, c.1650-1700*
(rates per thousand live births)

		males	females	male/female
Hawkhurst, Kent	**1650-1699**			69
Hawkshead, Cumbria				74
Gedling, Nottinghamshire	1650-1699	101	103	
Colyton, Devon	1650-1699	104	100	
Aldenham, Hertfordshire	1650-1699	112	97	
Staplehurst, Kent	**1650-1699**			120
Terling, Essex	1650-1699	135	145	
12 parishes (1981)	1650-1699	154	133	
12 parishes (1983)	1650-1699	170	133	
Cranbrook, Kent	**1650-1699**			175
Willingham, Cambs.	1650-1699	186	224	
Benenden, Kent	**1650-1699**			187
Biddenden, Kent	**1650-1699**			240
Wrangle, East Fens	1654-1703			246
Gainsborough, Lincs	1650-1699	255	221	
Leake, East Fens	1654-1703			263

Sources: West (1974) 41-44 for Leake and Wrangle; Reynolds (1979) 32 for Willingham, Aldenham, Colyton, Gainsborough, Gedling and Terling; these six were included in the 12 parishes (1981) used by Wrigley and Schofield (1989) 249, and updated by Laslett (1983) 112.
Note: Within the 12 parishes there were very marked variations in apparent death rate, from Gainsborough (284 and 245 per thousand) to Hartland (85 and 75 per thousand).

With all these *caveats* in mind, Figure 4.2 shows that between 1650 and 1700 *at least* 35 per cent of children in this area of Kent died before they attained the age of ten years, and that *at least* 16 per cent, probably nearer 20 per cent, died as infants below the age of one year.[22]

Comparison of the infant mortality figures of the Cranbrook area with those from some other parishes throughout the country for this period suggests that the Kentish parishes appear towards the higher end of the spectrum of child mortality (Table 4.3). Hawkhurst stands out as possessing a remarkably low rate of infant mortality, for which there can really only be two main reasons: either the parish represented an area three times as healthy as Benenden for rearing babies, or there was inadequate recording of infant burial in Hawkhurst. The latter would appear the likelier cause.

Causes of Infant and Child Mortality

The lighter columns in Figures 4.1 to 4.6 represent babies known to have been born following the death of a child at or within days of birth; they have already been counted within the darker columns. The concentration of such births towards the left-hand side of the histograms, where birth intervals are shortest, confirms that the interval between births tended to be considerably shorter when the previous child had died in early infancy than when a child survived. The natural implication is that mothers commonly suckled their babies; the death of a baby in infancy naturally removed this barrier to conception and so subsequent births occurred after much shorter periods, often deliberately in order to replace the dead child.[23]

The causes of the comparatively high rate of mortality among infants at this time merit comment. There was certainly a plethora of diseases of many kinds; after 1666 there was an enormous increase in smallpox, as well as various fevers including typhus, influenza, diphtheria, malarial ague, spotted fever, relapsing fevers and dysentery which came down 'like rain through a leaky roof'.[24] Plague had been a cause of widespread death in the generations before 1660, but 1665-6 saw the last major outbreak in England, and its effect on the Cranbrook region was marginal (page 139). Smallpox had been a relatively mild disease of childhood in the earlier 16th century but, by the later 17th century, it had changed to be not only much more frequently fatal but also generally epidemic rather than endemic, killing adults and children.[25]

While attacks of smallpox and other diseases may well have been devastating, the likelihood is that poor living conditions, rudimentary and frequently counter-productive medical intervention, and a profound lack of personal hygiene were far more frequently the insidious causes of premature death. 'Men and women rarely if ever washed their bodies, and they lived in the constant sight and smell of human faeces and human urine'.[26] Even in the later 17th century the ground floor of most houses was simply beaten earth, dusty and strewn with straw, rushes or grasses, and with dog and cat excrement seeping into the floor.[27] Indeed, the penetration of earth floors by human urine and the like, even in quite substantial dwellings, produced a material rich in nitre, the saltpetre used in the production of gunpowder. The Crown, in need of such a rich source of war material, empowered 'saltpetre men' to enter people's homes and dig up and take away their earthen floors.

The 'powers of seisin' of the saltpetre men may have been revoked in 1656, but earthen floors continued to be used as a source of saltpetre until the end of the century, and therefore to remain highly unhygienic.[28] Not until the early 18th century, with the rebuilding of houses in brick and tile, did the revolution in domestic hygiene take place which led to a decline in premature mortality. Such poor levels of hygiene in contemporary domestic dwellings would therefore have contributed to the high mortality rate of infants in the latter half of the 17th century. These conditions, however, and the incidence of fever, were universal; they cannot account for the comparatively high rate of child mortality in the Cranbrook region.

Poverty was not the sole, nor indeed the main, cause of the high incidence of infant mortality. James Bunce, among the wealthiest and most influential in the parishes, lost nine of his ten children in infancy, while the Amit family of Benenden, labourers and registered as poor of the parish, lost 'only' six of their children as infants out of a total of 15 (Case Studies 1 & 5).

Birth at this time was a hazardous experience for the child as well as the mother, and the process of birth and nurture was governed by a mixture of contemporary medical knowledge and old wives' tales. Most 17th-century physicians advocated breast-milk for feeding the baby, but some advised that it should not suck any milk at all on the first day of its life, and 'ideally should be put to the breast of another woman until the eighth day or so'.[29] Isaac Archer gives a dramatic account of his wife's problem with their daughter, then nearly two weeks old, which highlights the desire of the parents that the child should be breast-fed: 'We had tried all meanes to make my child ... suck of my wife. She would suck greedily of others ... we had a child older, and that would not fasten; we gott a puppy, and could not make it lay hold, in so much that we despaired of what I had so desired of God, the blessing of the breast as well as that of the wombe ...'.[30]

Breast-feeding was an extended process; Culpepper and John Ward, in the mid-century, advocated weaning at one year if a child was strong; Sharp and others said that it should not be weaned until it had its main teeth: 'the stronger the child is, the sooner he is ready to be weaned; some at twelve months, and some not till fifteen or eighteen months old; you may say two years if you please'.[31] John Evelyn records that, after his birth in October 1620, he was sent away to nurse for 14 months, and Ralf Josselin's wife weaned each of their children between 12 and 19 months.[32] Despite the 'obvious' dangers of employing wet-nurses, and contemporaries pointing out that nurses were not as careful of another's child, even infecting their charges with venereal disease, it is quite clear that families which could afford to employ them continued to do so.[33] Archer relates the classic case of the death of his last child. By now (1682), after nearly 15 years of marriage, nine children and three miscarriages, his wife was no longer well enough to nurse her own children, so he hired a wet nurse. Tragically, this child who 'was well the night before, and never sick in its life' was overlain by the nurse 'when she turned to quiet her owne child, there being 4 in the bed: and this she might not know, and yet stopp the breath as soon as overlaying'.[34] John Evelyn's fifth child died in the same way.[35] It still happens.[36]

While the practice of wet-nursing is unlikely to find many mentions in register-based evidence, Cranbrook does have the case of Henry, son of Thomas Basden, clothier of Cranbrook, who was sent away to Benenden to be wet-nursed. Wills and probate accounts also refer to the use of wet-nurses. Evidence for their comparatively widespread use by those who could afford them, however, is best provided by the rapidity with which some wives were able to conceive after the birth of their previous child (Case Studies 4 & 5). The frequency of endogenous deaths would ensure a ready supply of those able to provide the necessary service.

The majority of the population, however, had little choice because they could not afford a wet-nurse.[37] On the other hand, children who survived the traumas of infancy then had to face a barrage of diseases irrespective of their social backgrounds. Rickets, convulsions, constipation, consumption, scabs, scales, thrush, ringworm, snuffles, warts and worms are a sample of such disorders for which the commonplace books of the time were full of popular beliefs and magical cures.[38] Several of the ailments listed above, which must have assailed the infants and children of the Cranbrook region, can be illustrated from the diaries of Archer and Evelyn among others; they include ague, with its attendant convulsions;[39] worms;[40] and teeth.[41]

Accidents also abounded. Archer gives examples of his children falling into the fire, and recounts how, as a very young child, he was nearly drowned on several occasions, and how he was nearly killed in a fall from his horse when he was six or seven years of age.[42] His East Anglian contemporary, William Coe, gent., from Cambridgeshire, is another whose diary is full of mishaps suffered by his son and six daughters. They ranged from drowning, choking on pins in their food and setting their clothes alight to being hit by missiles, bitten by dogs and trodden on by horses.[43] The Cranbrook area registers are not without their mishaps, which remind us how thin was the line between life and death. Thomas Beale, yeoman of Frittenden, died within a month of 'a sad accident [which] happened to me by breaking of both my legs'.[44] In addition to two girls who were drowned, in 1666 and 1694, the Biddenden burial register includes several epitaphs: 'who came to her end by a gate falling on her' (1658); 'who was killed by a waggon' (1665); 'bruised by a cart and died two days afterwards' (1697); 'died from a fall from his horse coming from Tenterden fair at Casselden's oak' (1657); and 'was killed by a pistol' (1666). As Stone said, 'Death was at the centre of life, as the cemetery was at the centre of the village'.[45]

Case Studies: a sample of families from the Cranbrook region

The following families, chosen to illustrate some of the factors of family formation which have already been discussed, have not been selected at random; they cover five strata of society from labourer to baronet; they represent five of the parishes under scrutiny; they each show a substantial number of children; and they are typical in that many alternative examples could have been chosen which would display just the same features.

Case Study 1: A labourer's family from Benenden

Richard Amit, husbandman of Rolvenden, married Margaret Dereson of Benenden there in March 1655. Richard's father was a Benenden man, so they had probably known each other for years; they set up their home in Benenden. The baptismal registers of Benenden duly record the births of Richard after 13 months and Mary 50 months later, and the baptism of John after a further 45 months. At first sight Richard and Margaret had produced a small family of three children with remarkable prudence.

Father	marriage	burial	occupation	Mother		burial
AMIT, Richard	Be'55 banns	80.03.16	'labourer, poor'	DERESON, Margaret		87.07.02
husbandman, of Rolvenden, son of Lawrence, late of Ben				d. of late John of Ben		

	name	born	baptised	interval	buried	age at death
	Richard	56.04.27		(13)		
	unbapt infant			21	58.01.14	infant
	unbapt infant			16	59.05.15	infant
	Mary	60.06.22		13		
	John		64.03.20	45		
	stillborn			35	67.02.03	infant

As a husbandman Richard might have rented a small farm, but by 1664 we find him labouring for the churchwardens (6s. 8d.) and exempt from tax on his two-hearth house. The burial register confirms the slide in his fortunes. An unbaptised infant of Richard and Margaret was buried in January 1658, a second in May 1659 and a third, stillborn, in February 1667. In other words in 12 years of married life Margaret had borne Richard six children not three, and the intervals between births in months had been 21, 16, 13 (the last two each following infant deaths), 45 and 35. Richard was buried in March 1680, after 25 years of marriage and 16 years after the baptism of his youngest child. He had lived to see his family grow to independence, but was buried on the parish as 'labourer, poor'; his widow outlived him by seven years. The reality as it now presents itself is typical of the period and the area.

Without the burial register, three of the family's six children would not be known; they do not figure in the baptismal register. Margaret conceived her second child one year after the birth of her first, which may imply that she suckled the first child for about twelve months. Conception of her third and fourth children followed rapidly on the loss of the previous baby, but it might be suggested that Margaret was less anxious to become pregnant with her sixth child, before whose birth there was a gap of 45 months; it is also possible, of course, that she had a miscarriage during this time. Both parents lived to see their surviving children grow to independence, a situation frequently not achieved.

In the following generation the elder son, Richard, married Hannah Hopper in May 1682 at the age of 26; she was a spinster of 27 years. They had their first child after nine months, but 44 months later Hannah died in childbirth; her husband was buried four months later as 'labourer, poor'. What happened to their four-year-old son is not known; his grandmother, Margaret, was still alive, but she died within the year. Presumably little Richard was brought up on the parish (page 140).

Father	marriage	burial	occupation	Mother		burial
AMMITT, Richard	Be82.05.02	87.03.18	'labourer, pore'	HOPPER, Hannah		86.10.30**
name		born	baptised	interval	buried	age at death
Richard		83.02.27	83.03.18	(9)		
stillborn**				44	86.10.30	infant

In 1687, at the age of 23, Richard and Margaret's second son, John, married Mary Clifton; his elder brother had been dead for six months, his mother for two. Their daughter, Elizabeth, was born after 12 months, and their son Richard after another 22 months but he died at the age of only 12 weeks. Mary must have died soon afterwards because John married for a second time in September 1691. This second marriage produced five more children, after gaps of 9, 28, 19, 36 and 58 months. The pattern is again a typical one, of a swift birth after marriage and a short interval after the early death of their second baby.

Father	marriage	burial	occupation	Mother		burial
AMITT, John	Be87.09.29			CLIFTON, Mary		unknown
name		born	baptised	interval	buried	age at death
Elizabeth		88.09.09	88.09.16	(12)	1706	adult of c.18
Richard		90.07.26	90.08.10	22	90.11.02	infant
2nd marriage	Be91.09.10			MERRITT, Elizabeth		
John		92.06.22	92.07.24	(9)		
Nathaniel		94.10.08	94.10.14	28	94.11.25	infant
Mary		96.05.14	96.06.07	19		
Margaret		99.05.05	99.06.10	36		
Lydia			Mar. 1705	58		

Case Study 2: A retailer's family from Staplehurst

The family of Stephen Smith of Staplehurst represents those who enjoyed a higher standard of living than the Amits of Benenden. Stephen was the only surviving son of Stephen Smith of Hesseldens Wood, butcher of Cranbrook; his uncles and cousins were also butchers, and his grandfather, George Smith, had been a packcarrier. In 1682, at the age of 22, he married Mercy Munn by licence. The Munn family had been successful butchers for generations, especially in Benenden, so the couple could have met through Stephen's apprenticeship. On the other hand Mercy, referred to as 'of Cranbrook, spinster, aged 18' in the licence (she was actually 19) was the daughter of the Thomas Munn of Cranbrook who earned his living as a woollen-draper. Stephen and Mercy settled in Staplehurst immediately after their marriage, and their children were baptised there.

The family formation of Stephen and Mercy highlights many of the problems aired above. Their first-born child was baptised just 33 weeks after their marriage, suggesting that conception predated the ceremony, and maybe explaining why they sought to marry under licence rather than by the more lengthy and public process of calling banns. The interval between the first and second baptisms is short at 17 months but not so short as necessarily to suggest that Mercy did not suckle her first child for the first few months, and the same can be said for all subsequent intervals. The baptism of their fourth child followed quite closely on the death within weeks of their third child, whereas other inter-baptismal intervals were more than two years; the interval shortened again after the loss within weeks of Katherine, and the birth of the second Katherine caused the death of both the infant child and her mother.

Father	marriage	burial	occupation	Mother	burial
SMITH, Stephen	CM82.07.31		butcher	MUNN, Mercy**	93.08.04
'of Cranbrook', settled Staplehurst (baptisms)				'of Cranbrook', spinster, 18	

name	born	baptised	interval	buried	age at death
Stephen		83.03.18	(8)	87.01.03	child of 3
Katherine		84.08.31	17	86.05.12	child of 1
Mercy		86.04.13	20	86.05.21	infant
Stephen		87.09.13	17		
Mary		89.12.31	27		
Katherine		92.01.26	25	92.02.16	infant
Katherine			19	93.08.04**	
2nd marriage(?)				Elizabeth	
Elizabeth		95.08.04		'of Stephen & Elizabeth his wife'	
Thomas		97.01.08	17	'of Stephen & Elizabeth his wife'	
Jane		98.12.04	23	'of Stephen & Elizabeth his wife'	

In the course of their short married life of 11 years, Stephen and Mercy had seven children, of whom three died as infants and two as very young children. It is a familiar pattern. None of their children was actually buried in the home parish of Staplehurst, but in Cranbrook where maybe there was a special burial area where the Smith family, or the Munn family, were buried. Stephen appears to have married a second time.

Case Study 3: A clothier's family from Hawkhurst

Robert Barham of Hawkhurst married Ann Gibbon there in 1639. He was comfortably off without being a particularly prosperous man: he paid tax on two hearths, was referred to as a 'clothier' in his inventory, and left goods, chattels and personal estate to the value of £261.

The development of this family shows some familiar features and some which mark a contrast. The delay of 24 months between marriage and first known baptism is longer than usual; it may have been a purely natural one, or it may be that there was a rapid birth for which we have no evidence. The intervals between subsequent baptisms fall either side of two years throughout the family build-up until, towards the end, the intervals became more extended, to 30 and then 37 months. The exception is the interval between the baptisms of John and Sarah, a mere 12 months, which implies the death of John within days of childbirth.

Robert and Ann Barham proved successful in nurturing most of their family. Eight children are known, of whom John probably died an infant and Richard at

Father	marriage	burial	occupation	Mother	burial
BARRAM, Robert	H39.07.11	83.05.25	clothier	GIBBON, Ann	78.05.02

(Barham in Prob. Acc; clothier in inventory)

name	born	baptised	interval	buried	age at death
Anne		41.07.18	(24)		
Mary		43.03.26	20		
John		45.06.--	27	(? infant?)*	
Sarah	46.06.24	46.06.28	12		
Robert	49.04.24	49.05.06	34		
Arthur		51.01.26	20		
Richard		53.07.17	30	64.06.28	child of 10
Francis	56.08.05	65.08.26	37		

* No Hawkhurst burials are registered between March 1643 and August 1654.

the age of 10. Francis, born in the period of secular administration (1653-60), was not baptised until he was nine years old. Ann lived for 22 years after the birth of her last child, dying after nearly 40 years of marriage, and her husband survived her by five years. As a result they saw their children through to maturity and beyond. On Robert's death intestate, his eldest surviving son, Robert, acted as administrator of the estate.[46] He divided the personal estate, at £39 each, between his sister Anne, the husbands of his sisters Mary and Sarah, and his brothers Arthur and Francis; he kept the residue of £31 for himself.

Case Study 4: A yeoman's family from Cranbrook

Stephen and Elizabeth Osborne (née Wood) married by licence in 1670 and went on to have an unusually large family. Stephen was a bachelor in his 30s; his spouse had already been married briefly, as second wife to John Potter, yeoman of Goldford in Cranbrook, who paid tax on three hearths and was a key man among those in Cranbrook society who acted as local parish officials, and whose four sisters each married similarly influential husbands. Her new husband, Stephen Osborne, was too young to figure in the Hearth Tax returns, but his contacts show that he was a man of substance. He was of the same family as Robert (HT6) and Alexander (HT7), and in 1683 he was made joint overseer, with John Freebody and Peter Sharpe jnr. of Tenterden, of the will of Peter Sharpe, gentleman of Benenden.

At the time of her wedding Elizabeth already had a son, William, by her first husband, and then went on to have another 12 children within 20 years. Three of those children died as infants and another two died very young; so short were the intervals between baptisms that one suspects the use of wet-nurses. The repetition of the name Elizabeth for the second, fifth and last child shows how keen the couple were to perpetuate their mother's name as a family name, a not uncommon practice. Stephen himself died just 20 years after the birth of his second son and namesake, but because of the size of their family his youngest daughter was only three years old; indeed, all but one of their seven surviving children were under 21 at the time of his death. Elizabeth survived him, but her later history is not covered by the reconstitution.

Father	marriage	burial	occupation	Mother	burial
OSBORNE, Stephen	CM70.10.18.	94.03.21	yeoman	POTTER, Elizabeth	
allegations by Peter Couchman of Cranbrook, clothier				née Wood, wid. of John	

name	born	baptised	interval	buried	age at death
John		71.10.22	(12)		
Elizabeth		73.07.25	21	76.06.23	nearly 3 yrs
Stephen		74.11.24	16		
Peter		76.08.30	21		
Elizabeth		78.06.29	22	78.07.03	infant
James		79.08.07	14		
Mary		80.10.19	14		
Anne		83.03.13	29	83.09.03	infant
Robert		85.01.18	22	87.01.18	2 years
Thomas		86.04.15	15	86.04.20	infant
Ann		88.02.28	22		
Elizabeth		90.08.03	30		

Case Study 5: A gentleman's family from Biddenden

Family formation among the upper echelons of society could be as disastrous as among the poor. In the course of the 1650s, James Bunce, gentleman of Biddenden, married twice and in each case soon lost his wife in child-birth. He then married Susanna. In August 1659 their daughter, also Susanna, was baptised, and survived infancy and childhood. The burial registers tell the subsequent sad story of six consecutive infant deaths.

The ultimate tragedies for James, who had already lost two wives and nine children, must have been the death of his third wife in November 1675 and of his only surviving daughter in June 1678 at the age of nineteen. The altar tomb which he had erected outside the church shows that his wife Susanna was still only 35 when she died.

Father	marriage	burial	occupation	Mother	burial
BUNCE, James		83.07.02	gentleman	YOUNG, -----	56.09.04**
name	born	baptised	interval	buried	age at death
Elizabeth				56.09.10**	infant
2nd marriage				Martha	57.10.06**
Mary ?twin				57.09.25**	infant
John ?twin				57.11.21**	infant
3rd marriage				Susanna	75.11.13
Susanna		59.08.29		78.06.24	19 years
unbapt. son			46	63.06.04	infant
unbapt. dau			29	65.11.21	infant
unbapt. son			15	67.02.26	infant
unbapt. son			29	69.07.27	infant
unbapt. son			42	73.01.08	infant
unbapt. son			"	73.01.08	infant

James Bunce was a wealthy man; he paid tax on six hearths, and was the principal creditor of Richard Glazier, a young clothier, when the latter died in 1672. He was also principal creditor of Peter Lewkner, a clothworker who died in 1675; when he came to finalise that account, James wrote off most of the debt to himself to reduce Lewkner's commitment to zero, and acted as guardian to his two young daughters. James' brother Thomas left the huge sum of £1,216 as the value of his goods, chattels and personal estate after payment of all necessary expenses and debts when the probate account was presented in 1685. Wealth was no guarantee of family success!

Chapter 5

Preservation of the Family

While it is generally accepted that premature death frequently removed one or both parents before their children had grown to maturity, little analysis has been done to substantiate this assertion, or to quantify the effects on families. This can be achieved by looking at parental death rates and their consequences for family size, and showing how contemporary parents tried to cope with their loss. In the process, we need to provide a realistic picture of how long these marriages lasted, because survival of both parents was the key to the stability of the family. We also need a clear idea of the number of children in families at this time if we are to assess the seriousness of problems posed by premature parental death.

The Scope of the Cranbrook Evidence

Once again the reconstitution provides useful data on which to base conclusions about the duration and size of families, but the parameters which define those data need to be specified. Before any couple and their family can be included in the evidence, we have to be reasonably certain that they were resident in the Cranbrook area, though not necessarily in the same parish, throughout their active life, from the time of their marriage to the death of the husband or wife. The predominance of the husband in the available records, as the one who headed the household and gave his surname to the family, means that we are on much safer ground following families only through the male line to start with: the distaff side will be pursued later.

We need to know the date of the marriage and the date of burial or remarriage of the husband, and to have a sequence of baptisms of children which suggests continuity. Couples sometimes moved out of an area and subsequently returned when, for example, the father of one or other of them died, and inheritance drew them back. Such a situation would almost certainly cause gaps in the sequence of baptisms, and bar those families from inclusion in the evidence.

In the Cranbrook parishes for this period 583 marriages satisfy these requirements. While the concentration of the present enquiry is from 1660 to 1700, it has been possible to look back to earlier decades, especially to the 1650s, for the inception of marriages, and forward for the date of death of some husbands. The earliest of these marriages dates from 1621, when Robert Post of Biddenden married Lydia Price; Lydia died in 1667 and Robert in 1669, so they comfortably exceeded forty years of marriage together. The latest is from May 1699, when Richard Nuttley married for the second time, to the widow, Ann Shoebridge; Richard died in 1717, just a year after Ann. Within the global figure of 583 marriage unions, 76 of them were men marrying for the second and, occasionally, third time. As a result one can speak of a total of 507 heads of household, or 507 families, created by 583 unions; one in seven (or 15 per cent) of the men in our sample married a second time or more.

Of all the families living in the Cranbrook area between 1650 and 1700, therefore, only a small proportion satisfies the parameters mentioned above. The need to know the date of the marriage rules out most of the couples who married outside the area, and all those whose marriage was otherwise unrecorded. The date of death of the husband, and/or the date of the death of first or second wife when second or third wives were taken, must also be known, and they are not always to hand. Because a major purpose of this analysis is to deal with the children born to these marriages, the families must be complete; some registers are defective especially for the 1640s and early 1650s, and others, in particular that of Cranbrook, are defective in their method of describing child burials. Reconstitution is an imperfect medium, and even with the addition of wills and other probate evidence, of inscriptions and other contemporary lists and accounts, we cannot be sure that we have a full picture of the families of these parishes. Nevertheless, nearly 600 families during this period do meet the criteria noted above, and these families do provide a sample which, in social and economic terms, represents a cross-section of the far greater number of families who were living in the parishes.

Duration of Marriage as a Key Factor

The duration of any marriage must be of prime importance in considering the stability of the family, because one of the main purposes of marriage was the procreation and education of children. For the education of children to take place effectively at least one of the parents had to extend their protection of those children until the youngest child had reached the age of 13 or 14 and was therefore of a normal age to go into service.[1] A typical couple, expecting their first child between nine and 11 months, and succeeding children between 15 and 30 months, would expect to have five or six children in 10 years. It would be a source of disruption if one of the partners died prematurely, and potentially disastrous for the children if the marriage were to end early with the deaths of both partners. For the marriage effectively to nurture the first of any children it would need to last until that child was in his or her mid-teens. Any marriage ending within 15 years must therefore have disrupted the upbringing of even the oldest child; in a family in which there were several children, the youngest would be quite incapable of fending for itself, and therefore in urgent need of care and protection.

We live now in an age when divorce, or casual liaisons rather than marriage, tend to be the limiting factors whereas in the 17th century it was death. It has been suggested that, for most families, the median duration of marriage was between 17 and 20 years.[2] Whatever the truth of this assertion, it is a generalisation which, by

Figure 5.1 *Duration of marriages, excluding remarriage by husbands,
Cranbrook region, c.1650-99*

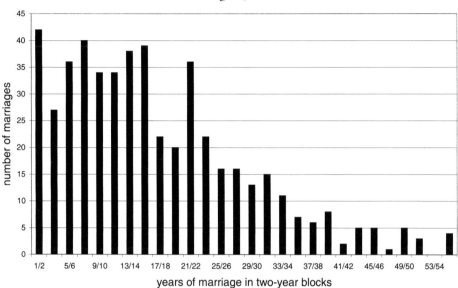

Figure 5.2 *Duration of marriages, including remarriage by husbands,
Cranbrook region, c.1650-99*

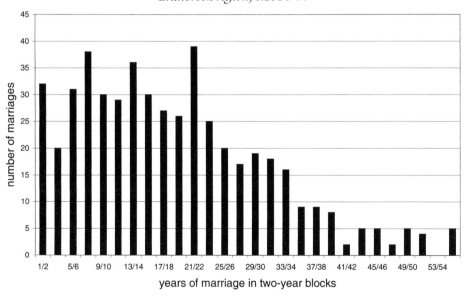

its nature, can be misleading. The median does not necessarily reflect the experience
of any actual family. Statistically, the median life of a marriage may have been between
17 and 20 years, but that allows for the possibility of large numbers of marriages

ending very quickly, with the corollary of lots of marriages lasting well beyond the time when the children of those unions had reached maturity at 21 years of age.

The family groupings of the Cranbrook evidence illustrate what happened there in practice. Figure 5.1 shows that, of the 507 examples of first marriages in the Cranbrook area, 69 ended within four years or less, and 274 within 15 years; in other words, rather more than half of all marriages, 54 per cent, were over in less than 16 years, with the inevitable result that most children of those marriages must have lost one of their parents before they reached the critical age of 13 or 14 years. Less than a quarter of couples survived for 25 years together.

Figure 5.2 shows that the effect of remarriage (67 instances of husbands who married for a second time, and nine who married for a third time) was to reduce to 52 the family unions which ended within four years, and to 233 those which ended within 15 years. This represents a slight improvement, with rather less than half the combined marriages in the survey, 46 per cent, ending within 16 years. Nevertheless, these statistics support the contention that there was a real problem at this time in terms of bringing up children in a stable family group.

Numbers of Children per Marriage

If we now turn to the numbers of children known to have been born, we can begin to assess the impact on families of premature parental death. There are three stages in the consideration of child numbers, each of which takes us nearer to a realistic view of the problem of orphanhood at the time. Figure 5.3 illustrates the simple pattern of the numbers of children born to the 583 marriages which make up the Cranbrook evidence. As can be seen, large families were comparatively rare; 19

Figure 5.3   Number of children from 583 marriages, Cranbrook region, 1650-99

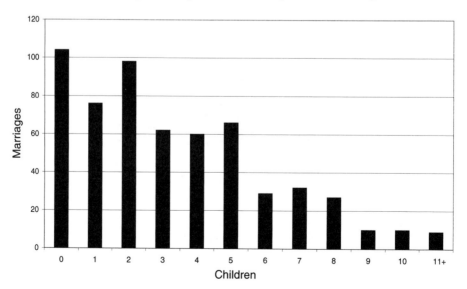

marriages produced numbers of children running into double figures (of which nine had 11 children or more, viz: 18, 16, 14, 12 and five had 11). The most common (modal) result of marriage was for the couple to have no children at all, and the second most common was for two children. Just under half (47.7 per cent) of all the marriages in the sample yielded two children or less, and 80 per cent of all children were in families of five or less.

The families with more than ten children were not confined to any one social or economic group within the parishes. Most were comfortably off, to judge by the known Hearth Tax assessments, and certainly the concentration was towards the upper end of the social bracket, but one widow was so poor that she had to be buried on the parish. It is remarkable, at a time when medicine was rudimentary and hygiene often non-existent, that wives continued to reproduce at fairly regular intervals for 20 years or more and, in most instances, outlived their husbands.

Stage two recognises that showing the number of children born to each union of husband and wife is less relevant than analysing the number of children accruing when remarriages are also taken into consideration. The motivation for such remarriages could be simple or complex. A widower may have desired more children, or children after a childless marriage; maybe he had been left with young children to bring up, and was looking for someone to care for those children; maybe he was looking for companionship, or had fallen in love a second time; it may have been a combination of two or more of these factors. Whatever the motivation, the second marriage could easily result in more children within the family.

The end result of these second, and, in some rare cases, third marriages can be seen from Figure 5.4. The most dramatic effect is the reduction of childless families

Figure 5.4   *Numbers of children from 507 families, Cranbrook region, 1650-99*

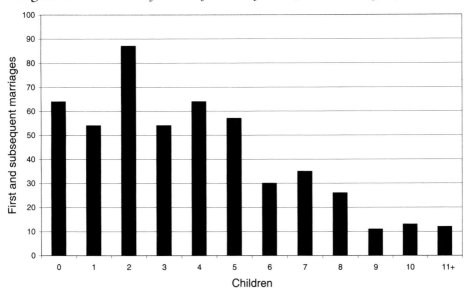

by 40 to only 64, a drop which is paralleled by a reduction, albeit less dramatic, from 76 to 55 of those who had hitherto had one child born to them. There is a corresponding rise in the number of couples with larger families. Now the most common size of family is quite clearly two children, and the percentage of families with six or more children has risen from 20 to 25 per cent.

The third stage of analysis reflects the fact that these figures still do not provide us with an accurate impression of the number of children in a typical family in the Cranbrook region between 1650 and 1700. There were other limiting factors. Of these the foremost must be the high number of infants known to have died within a year of birth. In overall terms, within the 583 marriages under consideration, there are records of the births of 1,947 children of whom at least 334 died as infants (17 per cent) and another 252 (13 per cent) before they attained the age of 10; at least 30 per cent of the children of the sample families, therefore, were dead before they could reach their tenth birthday.

This figure is not as high as the overall figure for child deaths given in Table 4.2, page 80 (34.9 per cent), because of the need to eliminate from the present sample those families which contained children simply referred to in the registers as 'child of'. In addition, the Hawkhurst burial figures for children are so low as to suggest that the registrar failed to register many, if not most, deaths of unbaptised children in that parish (page 81). The figure of 30 per cent is therefore very much a minimum.

Figure 5.5 shows the profound effect on family size of the removal of children known to have died in infancy or at latest before the age of 10 years. We can now see the number of offspring for whom parents actually had to take responsibility; the profile of children per marriage union approximates to that indicated in Figure 5.3, except that the largest families have almost disappeared. The stark conclusion is that the most common state, affecting just over 20 per cent of the families in the Cranbrook region at this time, was to end up childless.[3] The next most frequent state, affecting just under 20 per cent of the whole, was to end up with two children who lived at least to the age of ten. More than half of the families (some 56 per cent) in the Cranbrook area ended up with two children or less, and large families with six or more children now made up less than 13 per cent of the whole. Ultimately the effect of these factors, which so reduced family size, may well have been to render the remaining children that much more precious in the eyes of their parents.

We have therefore established that, while few families in the Cranbrook region had large numbers of children at any one time, many of those children could expect to lose at least one parent before they reached the age of 15 years. The picture is perhaps best illustrated by the statistics in Table 5.1, which shows the pattern of parental loss parish by parish among the 1,947 children. They show that, with the exception of Biddenden which appears to buck the trend, between 40 and 50 per cent of children lost at least one parent; this corresponds with the picture provided by Figure 5.1 which shows 54 per cent of first marriages ending within 16 years. What is possibly even more remarkable is that the number who lost both parents at roughly the same time was comparatively small at 144 (7.4 per cent).

Figure 5.5   *Effect on family size of infant and child mortality,*
Cranbrook region, c.1650-99

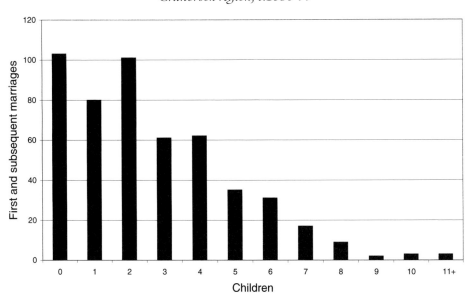

Table 5.1   *Children under 15, alive and 'orphaned' by the death of one parent,*
Cranbrook area, 1650-99, as a proportion of children born

	total children	losing 1 parent	%	losing 2 parents	loss caused by death of		
					mother	father	both
Benenden	424	182	42.9	31	14	55	14
Biddenden	499	131	26.3	20	25	35	14
Cranbrook	486	222	45.7	52	30	57	24
Hawkhurst	429	173	40.3	33	23	40	16
Staplehurst	109	55	50.4	8	10	14	4
Total	1947	763	39.2	144	102	201	72

Note: Figures taken from the analysis of the 583 marriages used as a basis for all the material in this chapter

Strategies for Caring for Surviving Family Members

Cranbrook evidence reveals several solutions to the problem of children who lost one or both of their parents. Surviving fathers or mothers might decide to bring the children up themselves, or remarry. Those who anticipated death by leaving wills invariably made specific provision for their wives and children as appropriate. All but the poorest in society could take a young person into service as the necessary extra pair of hands to help with the youngest children. If the surviving parent were poor, the parish might arrange for the child or children to go into service, or to be farmed out to foster-carers, who received a small sum of money to help with their upkeep (page 140). If both parents were dead, guardianship was a natural consideration, using kinship links or other relationships, with apprenticeships arranged for the older children (page 141ff).

That only 144 (7.4 per cent) of the 1,947 children in the sample were left without the protection of at least one parent or step-parent underlines the efforts to which parents went to care for offspring whom they clearly saw as a prime responsibility. Among that 7.4 per cent is the family of Christopher Dive; he could not have anticipated that he would die within a year of his wife's death, leaving six children under 13; they became the responsibility of his brother Thomas. Another Benenden parishioner, Walter Springate, had been married for 18 years when both he and his wife died in 1704, leaving five young children; maybe his brother, Stephen, stepped in. Such large groups of orphaned children were, however, exceptional; of the 144 orphaned children across the whole region, the vast majority were the youngest of several siblings of whom the oldest could often have exercised some protective care.[4]

Men, left with young children by the deaths of their wives, frequently remarried, though rarely in haste.[5] Richard Burcham's experience is typical of numerous families in the Cranbrook region. At the time of the death of his first wife, he was a labourer, living in a two-hearth house but exempt from tax, and later appeared working part of a 39-acre parcel of land called Babbs, owned by Simon Henden, gent.[6] His first marriage had lasted 14 years, and he was left to look after four children: two sons, aged 13 and five, and two daughters, aged 10 and eight. His elder son may have acted *in loco parentis*; maybe he was old enough to help his father in the fields, and the role of parent-substitute passed to the 10-year-old daughter Mary. Richard is unlikely to have been able to afford to take someone into annual service.

He married again 16 months later, to Mary Oxenbridge, who had been a widow for nearly two-and-a-half years. She was of similar social standing; her husband had been exempt from tax on a one-hearth house and was 'poore' at burial. She had been left with three children of her own, then aged 14, 11 and five. It may well be that, when she married Richard Burcham, part at least of the motivation was to join their families together for mutual protection. If so, this second marriage satisfied both parties; they lived together for 24 years until Mary died, by which time both sets of children had long been of age. He died four years later, referred to in the registers as an 'aged man, pore'. They appear to have been successful in caring for their children, possibly helped by the fact that Mary's two daughters were old enough to go into service rather than living with their step-father.

The case of Richard Burcham can be reduplicated many times, with a father of under-age children remarrying, possibly with the prime intention of securing the care of those children. The yeoman, William Gutsole, illustrates another possible motive. He had only been married two years when his first wife died, and they had no children; by marrying again he achieved the family which had eluded him in his first marriage. His second wife bore eight children in 11 years, including triplets

13. This early 17th-century yeoman's cottage, now dated to 1609, has three rooms downstairs, and three upstairs, with an entry lobby leading either side of the central brick chimneystack. This was in situ from inception, providing flues for two rooms downstairs plus a bread oven, one upstairs room and a heated drying-chamber.

14. This rear view shows the original outshot. Despite its 17th-century build, the house had unglazed windows, upper rooms open to the rafters, and wattle and daub interior partitions.

of whom two survived for a year. On the other hand, Richard Curd, a blacksmith, may well have married his second wife, Susan, for mutual comfort and support; his two eldest were already 18 and 16 years of age, and Susan had been a widow for 14 years. Together they saw their respective families through to maturity.

The evidence of the reconstitution leaves one with the strong impression that one of the main considerations of widowers in remarrying was to ensure the care and upbringing of their children. Admittedly, few marriages were contracted in less than twelve months. On the other hand, remarriage was common,[7] and the evidence of contemporary wills shows how concerned parents were to care for their offspring. If the preservation of the family was a major motive, then usually the remarriage process worked admirably; sometimes it failed. Sometimes, indeed, it compounded the problem because a second marriage to a woman who was still nubile could so easily end in the production of yet more children.

Such a case was that of the mercer, Walter Jones. At the death of his first wife Walter found himself with four children under ten. Within a year he married a young widow, Elizabeth, and their marriage lasted seven years before his death in 1680. By this time his sons by his first marriage were 17 and 16, his daughters 12 and eight, but to them had been added another daughter of four and a son of one. It was now Elizabeth's turn to have regard to the children; in 1684 she married John Pankhurst and by the time of her death in 1700 had seen all the children to maturity; her only child by John Pankhurst was stillborn. The cases of Richard Curd and Walter Jones begin to underline the crucial role played by widows in the protection of their offspring, and thus bring us to consideration of the distaff side.

Table 5.1 shows that fathers were twice as likely as mothers to die prematurely, thereby leaving the widow to cope with the children. She would not necessarily marry again; especially if her children were over 15 years of age, she might wish to enjoy independence from a husband. Widows could hold land in their own right, and as the inheritors of their husbands' property they could, and frequently did, lead independent lives. They could also be a powerful economic factor within the parish. As such, they might well prove to be an attractive proposition in the marriage stakes not so much because of any personal allure but because they might bring with them considerable wealth.[8]

Remarriage of Widows

It has not been possible to quantify the proportion of widows remarrying. Details of the subsequent lives of 321 widows in the survey are lost, often because of the difficulty of tracing through the distaff side, but at least 146 of them either had no children at the time of their bereavement or had seen their families to maturity. Enough is known of 52 remarrying widows, however, to draw some general inferences.[9]

Elizabeth Brandford, for instance, was widowed in 1665 after 11 years of marriage and was left with a 10-year-old son. Her clothier husband John had been one of the wealthier men in Benenden, paying tax on five hearths and leaving goods and chattels to the value of £329 even after his expenses and debts had been honoured. Elizabeth was therefore a widow of substance, made all the more attractive because her husband had looked after the financial welfare of his young son by bequeathing his lands to him, together with an income of £18 per annum. 'Widow Brandford' duly appears in the churchwardens' accounts, as holder of what had been her husband's land, in 1666 and 1667, but by 1668 the holder is 'Mr Hope', reflecting the marriage in July 1667 of Elizabeth to Richard Hope of Cranbrook, gentleman. The Hope family, from which Elizabeth had originally sprung, had brought her fortune back home. Her son John's protection was assured, but the process of assuring it had economic implications as well as social ones.

Sometimes inter-relationships became very complex. William Playford, labourer, died after just seven years of marriage, leaving his widow Elizabeth eight months pregnant and with a son of three to look after. Three years later she married Henry Roots, another labourer, and had three more children. When Henry died, Elizabeth, with a son of four and a daughter of one to add to the son of 16 and daughter of 12 by her previous marriage (neither of them necessarily at home), married a third time, to William Clarke, who already had six children of his own aged 15 or more at the time of this marriage. By the time of his death in 1698, however, all his own, and his wife's, children had long since come of age.

The results of remarriages were not always so beneficial, as exemplified by the complex marital career of Elizabeth Pratt, her husbands and their wives. Thomas Pratt of Benenden was a 'poor carpenter'; in January 1681 he died after 13 years of marriage leaving his widow Elizabeth with six children aged 11, 10, eight, seven, five and three; his eldest daughter, a 'maid of 12', was buried with him. Two years later, in February 1683, Elizabeth married Thomas Baker, who had three children by his first marriage, then aged 14, 10 and seven. Elizabeth appears to have died shortly afterwards as in June 1684 Thomas Baker married a third time, to Dorothy Hatcher, widow of William Hatcher, yeoman of Benenden.

This Dorothy had inherited the yearly profits for life of her deceased husband's house and lands provided that she should not remarry. If she did marry again, then those profits were to be used 'for the education and upbringing of the children until Henry is of age 21'; in fact she brought two sons and two daughters with her, aged from five to 14. By her remarriage Dorothy forfeited her share of the goods and chattels, which were to go to the daughters.

Discouragement from Remarrying

William Gouge, writing in 1622 of the 'Christian rule: Love me and love my child', advised, 'Let widowers and widows that have children seriously think of it beforehand and be the more circumspect in taking a second or a third husband or wife.'[10] The attempt by William Hatcher to persuade Dorothy not to remarry was neither unique nor the norm.[11] In 138 of the 304 wills available for analysis, the wife of the testator figures as a legatee; in 21 (15 per cent) of those wills there are phrases discouraging her from remarrying which provide interesting insights into relationships.

The circumstances in which such discouragement occurred varied from family to family. John Leigh, gentleman of Cranbrook, for instance, was a wealthy man who left his wife Katherine the use of his household stuff and the profits from several properties, but stipulated that these were to go immediately to his sons and daughters at her death or remarriage. The children were already of age and his wife in her late sixties.[12] Similarly Richard Beale, clothier of Biddenden and another wealthy man, left his loving wife Mary the use of properties in Biddenden '... while a widow unmarried'.[13] She was 64 at the time of this stipulation, with no under-age children to consider. The restrictions expressed in these wills, therefore, were designed to keep assets within the family rather than to protect under-age children. There was always a danger that, in the event of any remarriage, the new husband and his heirs and assigns might secure control of those assets and that they would be lost to the testator's own family.

Others, like Robert Pattenson, yeoman of Biddenden, clearly did have their children in mind when they made their wills. He left his house to his son William with the proviso that he pay his mother £12 per annum 'while she remain my widow', but only £8 per annum 'if she remarry'. At the time of the writing of the will, William was not yet 10 years old, and he had nine sisters who ranged in age from Margaret, who was 18, to Phyllis (variously Finis) who was as yet unborn. Robert's widow did remain unmarried, and eventually died in 1692, by which time she had seen all her children (bar one who died aged seven) come to age, and most of them married.[14] In similar fashion Richard Vincett, husbandman of Cranbrook, died leaving a young family and attempted to restrict his wife's freedom to remarry.[15] Neither Robert Patterson nor Richard Vincett stipulated that their widows were not to remarry, but they did adjust the size or nature of the bequest should such a remarriage take place, and this was the most common form of discouragement as expressed in the wills.

Among those who attempted to discourage their wives from remarrying, approximately half had under-age children. In virtually every case they made the point that their widows should use rents and profits for the education and maintenance of those children.

Kinship, Guardianship and the Duty to Care for the Young

Parental attitudes, and relationships within and outside the family circle, are well illustrated by the wills of fathers of families who had already lost their wives, and by those wives who had been widowed. The main avenues open in such cases were to turn to brothers and sisters who might take responsibility for their orphaned nephews and nieces; or to older siblings if they were of an age to take such responsibility; or to look beyond the kin link to a friend, a neighbour or a colleague; and to ensure that the resources to fund that care were available. Guardianship was seen as a function to be kept within the nuclear family if possible; otherwise, recourse was made to in-laws and other kin.

Older children looked after their younger brothers and sisters. When Anne Latter, widow of Adam, yeoman of Hawkhurst, died just two years after her husband in August 1674, their eldest son, Samuel, was already old enough to become administrator of the estate and guardian to his younger siblings. He charged to the estate the costs of the maintenance of his brothers Peter, aged 11, and Andrew, aged seven. Samuel claimed £10 for his costs 'for the space of one whole yeare with meate drinke apparrell and educacion' for his two brothers. He went on to claim another £30 'to further provide for and mainteyne in dyett clothes and educacion of the aforesd Peter and Andrew Latter till such time as they are able to be placed out to apprentices or otherwise provided for', and actually charged his mother's estate £20 for two-and-a-half years' wages at a rate of £8 per annum.[16] On this evidence it would be difficult to question his competence to look after his brothers and sisters!

Walter Viney, thrice-married butcher of Staplehurst, neatly illustrates the problem of remarriage and attitudes to children. He appointed his eldest son (by his first wife), Walter, as executor; he was then 36 years old. This younger Walter was to keep

15. This reconstruction of a 17th-century bedstead and hangings illustrates the items so frequently met in inventories – bedstead, mattress, curtains, valences, bolsters, pillows and coverlets, and highlights the tensioning pegs for the ropes which supported the mattress which enable the sleep to 'sleep tight'. The doorway beyond leads to a smaller bedroom.

16. This reconstruction shows how the truckle bed could be wheeled out from under the main bedstead; beyond can be seen the low doorway which links to the room beyond the fireplace.

an eye on his full sister, Sarah, aged 30, and his half-brothers by his father's second marriage, who were then aged 24, 22 and 20. He was also charged with bringing up his father's five younger children by his third wife Mary, then aged 17, 14, 11, 10 and seven years, until the youngest reached the age of 14, and 'afterwards to do for them as his own love and discretion shall lead him'.[17] This last clause seems to encapsulate the love and concern for their children which parents showed by the provisions they made for their welfare at this period.

The oldest child was not always of an age to take responsibility; in such cases recourse was to the testators' own brothers or brothers-in-law. Christopher Dive, yeoman of Benenden, kept arrangements for the care of his six children firmly within the family: 'My brother Thomas Dive to be my sole Executor to take account for the upbringing of my children and to give a perfect account to my children and to my overseers, and I do entreat my very good uncle Thomas Hickmott and my brother-in-law Silby to be their overseers.'[18]

Jane Taylor, a widow of Staplehurst, entrusted her children to her 'loving sister Anne Dymand and loving kinsman John Scoones' (1681).[19] John Chandler and his wife Margaret, buried on the same day (1683), entrusted their only surviving child to William Jeffery whose wife was the boy's aunt.[20] Relatives by marriage were frequently selected to carry on the work of protecting the children. Stephen Vincett, clothier of Staplehurst, entrusted his daughter to the care of his mother-in-law, Jane Batcheller,[21] and Thomas Stedman, blacksmith of Biddenden, left responsibility for the upbringing of his three children to his brother-in-law Robert Dibly.[22]

Testators who had no immediate family sometimes helped with the care of more distant relatives. George Smith, clothier of Staplehurst, still a bachelor when he died in 1685, arranged for his executors to put the bulk of the money accruing from his estate into interest, 'that interest to go to my sister Phebe Kent until Jane and Hannah [her daughters then aged six and one] come of age ... towards the education of Hannah and Jane'.[23] Thomas Kingsnorth of Frittenden left £10 'for the use of bringing up my kinswoman Patience Blundell until she is 18', excusing his wife from paying the legacy if she were willing to undertake the task herself.[24] Peter Combes, yeoman of Cranbrook, required his wife to look to the education of their own sons (aged four and one) and that of his cousin George Combes, who was to receive lands and property in Tenterden.[25]

Guardianship beyond the Immediate Family

Only two of the Cranbrook area wills specify provision of guardians beyond the family circle. Richard Walter, tailor of Staplehurst, required that, if his wife remarried, 'his loving friend' Robert Furby of Staplehurst was to take the three children. John Bailey, husbandman of Staplehurst, stated that he did not want his well-beloved wife and executrix Dorothy to be 'overburdened by maintaining and bringing up my two children'. Accordingly he empowered 'his well beloved friends and bretheren in the Lord', George Weldish of Goudhurst, Francis Cornwall of Marden, Thomas

Kingsnoth of Frittenden and Richard Kingsnoth the younger of Staplehurst 'to be overseers of the disposal of my goods and the bringing up of my children', and made them responsible for his children if his executrix should die.[26]

The second example provides a strong clue to the first. The guardians appointed are known to have been four of the leading Baptists of the area. Richard Walter's will shows that he had several children who do not appear in the baptismal register, and Robert Furby's family is known only from burials; they also had strong nonconformist links. In some cases, therefore, co-religionists might provide a substitute for kin in looking to the welfare of their brethren.

The majority of people at this period died intestate, thereby leaving no testamentary direction to determine guardianship of any under-age children.[27] No doubt in most cases the family stepped in anyway. In situations where an individual died intestate and owing debts greater than the value of his goods and chattels, the court might appoint the principal creditor to be guardian, with the title 'tutor or curator' of the minors specified in the introduction to the account. Thus when Thomas Smith, bellowsmaker of Cranbrook, died of smallpox in 1679, Richard Botting of Cranbrook, principal creditor, was appointed tutor or curator of his son, and James Groombridge was similarly appointed guardian of the son of John Brooker, tanner of Staplehurst, in 1681.[28]

On other occasions leading men of the parish took on the role of guardian and in some cases this reflects a form of service to the community rather than a kinship choice or an arrangement by a court (page 138). For example, James Bunce was the 'tutor and curator' lawfully assigned to the two young children of Peter Lewkner, a poor clothworker of Biddenden, who died intestate in 1675. Peter's widow Anne appears to have given up the administration of her late husband's goods and with it the guardianship of the girls. There is unlikely to have been a kin relationship between James Bunce and Peter Lewkner or his wife; on the other hand James Bunce was a very wealthy parishioner who, at this time, had lost nine of his ten children in infancy and was to bury his third wife just five days after Peter Lewkner's burial (page 89).[29]

Several probate accounts provide an insight into the costs of guardianship, and that of Solomon Ware does so in detail.[30] He was a husbandman and miller of Cranbrook, twice married, with children by both marriages. On his death in 1662, soon after his second marriage, his brother Robert was appointed tutor or curator of Solomon Ware junior, then aged 13 years. Robert duly charged the account £14 2s. 5d. for keeping Solomon junior in 'eate, drinke, apparel, lodging, schooling and all other necessaries' for a year and five weeks, and another £2 0s. 11d. for board, lodging and schooling with Mr John Buckland of Staplehurst for 16 weeks. It cost another £10 4s. to have Solomon, then 15 years old, taken on as an apprentice for seven years by the same Mr Buckland. Robert had also taken responsibility for providing board and schooling (but not lodging) for his nieces, 19-year-old Judith Ware (£4 1s. 11d.) and 17-year-old Elizabeth (£7 10s. 10d.), even though they were quite old enough to go into service themselves, and in the process he neglected his own business for which he charged £15. Guardianship was not a responsibility to be lightly assumed.

Other probate accounts provide us with variations on the theme of guardianship. When George Moorcocke's brother John became guardian to his two nieces, he passed the buck, paying Charles Hodge, a gardener of Cranbrook, £50 'for meat, drink, washing, lodging and apparrell until they reach 18'.[31] Similarly John Sharpey, testamentary guardian and probably kin by marriage of John Longley's son, boarded him out with John Afford, the Quaker mercer of Cranbrook (page 190). Sharpey paid £4 (2s. 6d. per week for 32 weeks) for board and schooling for the six-year-old up to 24 April 1675, and another £3 1s. 8d. to cover from 24 April to 2 October at the same rate but to include 4s. 2d. for 'stockens, shooes and a hatt'.[32] At least most of these costs could be charged against the estate.

Education and Apprenticeship

Testators were anxious for their offspring to have the best start in life: to be educated, to compete in the market place, to earn their living and, in particular, to master a trade. Henry Jenkin, gentleman of Biddenden, and George Humphrey, saddler of Cranbrook, for instance, required their wives to take care of the education of their children.[33] Such education might mean schooling with a schooldame, or in the parish 'petty' school (page 17) or with a private tutor, or maybe in one of the endowed Grammar Schools like those at Biddenden (founded 1566) or Cranbrook (1573).[34]

Apprenticeship, usually lasting seven years and tying master and apprentice by contract, was an essential qualification for those wishing to establish themselves in skills or crafts.[35] Entry to such agreements was normally at age 14 or thereabouts, although apprenticeship with the London guilds tended to be rather later, and was in no way limited to specific groups. Between a fifth and a third of those entering the grocery, drapery and haberdashery trades, for instance, were sons of knights, esquires and gentlemen.[36] Many testators in the Cranbrook region provided for the training of their offspring: John Bennet, a Staplehurst yeoman, set aside £5 each for his sons, as yet aged three and four, to be apprenticed; another yeoman, Robert Pattenson of Biddenden, mentions the £20 given to his son William by his uncle John to cover his apprenticeship; and Richard Worsley, a Hawkhurst butcher, neatly underlined the normal apprenticeship pattern with 'my desire is that £14 be deducted from the estate and given to Anthony at 40s. per annum for seven years, it being my desire that he should be bound apprentice'.[37] At the other end of the scale, Alexander Groombridge, a very wealthy landowner in Cranbrook, left £100 to his son Alexander for putting him out to be an apprentice, and £100 more at age 21 (he was eight at the time).[38] Wealthy householders from the Cranbrook area might well send their sons to London to be apprenticed with the companies there.[39]

Masters could, incidentally, take on their own kin as apprentices, as indicated by the will of Richard Mills, gentleman of Frittenden, whose son Charles Mills 'says he will take my son [i.e. Charles' own brother] John Mills apprentice to his trade'. Charles was 26 at the time, and John, at 13, on the threshold of training.[40] However, formal apprenticeship within the family was unusual; of the 24 apprentice-master relationships revealed by probate documents, only five definitely involved a kin relationship. Only one is as close as the brothers noticed above; cousin, kin and relationship by marriage mark the other examples. In more than one example the apprentice had started off in the host's household as a youngster in service before being given the more formal contract. Kinship was not, therefore, the major factor in arranging apprenticeship indentures, although it did have a part to play. One cannot say whether the parents' relationship with the apprentice master, when they made the arrangement, was that of friendship, or neighbourliness, or simply a business one assisted by third-party contact.

Provision for Surviving Family Members

It was customary for testators to make generous provision for their wives and children, trying thereby to cover every eventuality according to their means.[41] The remarkable variety of scope and provision in the wills available, however, reinforces the point that there was no typical family, and no typical testator. For instance, of the 89 yeomen of the Cranbrook area for whom wills have survived from 1660-1700, only 19 (21 per cent) represent the typical nuclear family with a wife and at least one son and daughter at the time of their decease. Within those 19 examples there are considerable variations, from the basic one wife, one daughter and one son (James Willard), to one wife, one daughter, two sons and 16 grandchildren (Thomas Merriall). Each family was a unique institution. Some testators had lost their wives, some had grown-up families, some had very young children to provide for, some were widows; some had no surviving sons or daughters, but could pass their possessions to grandchildren, others were bachelors or spinsters who looked beyond the immediate family for their bequests. Some had much to give, some very little indeed. That being said, some relationships do show a pattern.

The bequest of property to sons was standard practice where property was owned freehold, and occasionally the lease of rented property was passed on to the next generation. Provision for the widow for life from the yield of the property was also a standard practice, often linked with a request for the upbringing of the children. Provision for daughters was more often in cash than in property, and it was normal to expect the legatee to wait until she was of age (sometimes 18, sometimes 21) or married, whichever should come first. The patterns of these relationships with wives, sons, daughters and other family members can ideally be illustrated by a few examples.

In June 1677 Jervase Morelen, yeoman of Benenden, made typical provision for his wife and young family of three sons and two daughters when he made his will.[42] He arranged for his eldest son, aged six, to receive the 12 acres of land adjoining his house in Benenden, together with the house itself, while his wife was to receive the rents and profits of that land 'for the education and maintenance of my said sons and my other children'. To his younger sons, aged four and one, he left jointly 20 acres of land in Benenden, hoping that it would not be necessary to sell it off to pay his mortgage, with the proviso again that his wife should receive the rents and profits until the children were 21 years of age. To his wife and two daughters he left 'all and every my goods and chattels and household stuff' to be divided equally between them, and the girls to receive £50 each at the age of 23; they were aged nine and seven at the time. Jervase had therefore provided his sons with land, his daughters with their jointures, his children with their maintenance and his wife with an income for life. As it happened he lived on for another 12 years as head of the family.

Testators of the Cranbrook area who had more than one son or daughter generally treated the sons equally, and the daughters similarly, irrespective of age, in keeping with the basic principles of partible inheritance; in practice such even-handedness was not always achievable. Not all were as highly principled as William Ellis, butcher of Biddenden, who left his property jointly to the grandchildren of his son William and his daughter Susanna, 'my mind being that a female heir shall enjoy as much as a male heir';[43] nor as practically even-handed as Thomas Luckhurst, brickmaker of Cranbrook, who left one shilling each to his two brothers, his three brothers-in-law and his four sisters, with the residue of the estate going to his widowed mother.[44] Some, like Samuel Hunt, yeoman of Benenden, had already passed on their property to their sons who were of age, and were content to leave their daughters sums of money for their dowries.[45] Others, like Stephen Langford, had no children, so he arranged for the sale of all his lands and disbursed the proceeds as cash, with his brothers and sisters receiving five shillings each, and their children, his nephews and nieces, larger sums of £25 per family to be enjoyed at the age of 21. He made provision for his wife, and appointed her executrix of his will.[46]

Many testators looked further afield for their bequests because they had no immediate family to benefit. One such was William Kipping, yeoman of Benenden, who chose to divide up his cash and lands between seven cousins, and made his spinster cousin Elizabeth Kipping, 'who lives with me', his sole executrix.[47] Another, William Page, clothier of Staplehurst, left sums of money to 11 named kinsmen and kinswomen and his land and personal property to a twelfth.[48] Widows, bachelors and spinsters provide an especially rich picture of inter-family relationships, with bequests to brothers, sisters and cousins, and many of those married or unmarried made a point of including sons-in-law, daughters-in-law, brothers-in-law and sisters-in-law (these last often as 'brother' or 'sister') among their beneficiaries.

Parents were therefore willing to go to great lengths to secure the proper care of their under-age children. It was almost a matter of course for a widower with young children to remarry, but it was husbands who died young more frequently than wives, and widows who bore the brunt of providing for their children. Despite the comparatively short duration of so many marriage unions, more than 90 per cent of children in the sample were cared for until they reached their majority.

In providing for their children, the first call of parents was on kin, with siblings sometimes called upon to act *in loco parentis* for their brothers and sisters. Guardians could be appointed; sometimes these were close friends, sometimes co-religionists, sometimes even principal creditors (who, as will be seen, might therefore have had a kinship relationship). Sometimes leading men of the parish, with charitable intent, might take on the role of carer. At every turn the impression is one of a desire on the part of the parents to care for their offspring, and to do so even-handedly.

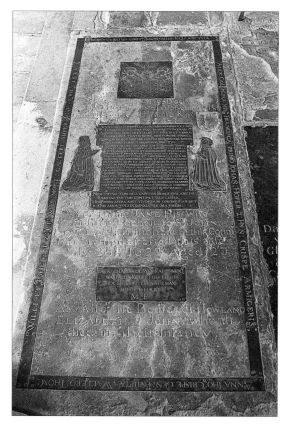

17. The main slab commemorates the burial of Sir Thomas Roberts of Glassenbury, Bart., who departed this life Nov: 1706 aged 48, and Dame Jane, his wife, daughter and coheir of Sir John Beale of Farningham, Bart, who departed this life July 25th 1692 aged 27.

18. Close-up of the Latin inscription, which commemorates an earlier Sir Thomas Roberts (died 1627), Knight and Baronet, and his wife Frances, daughter of Martin James Esq., and their family of eight children, with the two contemporary mourners.

Chapter 6

The 'chiefer sort'

Commentators on late 17th-century English society, both contemporary and modern, have remarked on its profoundly hierarchical structure. Indeed, in his *Scheme of the income and expence of the several families of England* (1688), Gregory King epitomised the social pyramid by ranking people according to their economic contribution to, or drain on, society.[1] Recently some have questioned whether such divisions, which subordinate social status to economic factors, accurately reflect post-Restoration society; they would prefer to use 17th-century terms—'better sort', 'middling sort', 'vulgar sort'—to distinguish groups in society.[2]

This chapter looks at those who, by their status, transcended the parochial scene, and at those who devoted themselves to local parish administration. In all this the most important concept was the term 'gentleman'. As Wrightson says, 'gentlemen stood apart, and the possession of gentility constituted one of the most fundamental dividing lines in society'; as he goes on to suggest, however, that line was a 'permeable membrane'.[3] Examination of that permeability will help us to understand a major aspect of village societies.

Baronets: Relationships beyond the County

The highest stratum of society in the Cranbrook region was occupied by three hereditary baronetcies; Baker of Sissinghurst and Roberts of Glassenbury already enjoyed that position in 1660; Guldeford (Guildford) of Hemsted was promoted in 1688. All three families had home estates which lay within Cranbrook or Benenden parishes, as well as estates in parishes elsewhere. As major landowners they leased out farms to local yeomen and husbandmen, but their contact with tenants was limited because they conducted their affairs through stewards, themselves gentlemen, who were responsible for the management of the estates and for relationships with those who worked the land.[4] They were also involved in local affairs, especially as justices of the peace, and this provided some contact with parishioners.

All three families had been settled in the area for many generations. The Bakers had settled at Sissinghurst in the parish of Cranbrook in the 1490s. In 1664 they were assessed to pay tax on 38 hearths (for the house and associated buildings), and their Cranbrook estate alone extended to some 300 acres. The Roberts family, in the area since 1103, had acquired the Glassenbury estate by marriage in the 14th century. In the 1470s they had built the house which they were still inhabiting in the 17th century; Lady Roberts was assessed to pay tax on 32 hearths. By 1650, however, the official value of the Glassenbury estates, loaded with debts, was just £1,000.[5] Meanwhile, Edward Guldeford Esq. lived at Hemsted in Benenden, the estate where his family had been settled since 1388, and on which he was assessed to pay tax on 17 hearths. He was the leading landowner and wealthiest man in that parish.

The pattern of relationships of upper gentry families such as these normally transcended parish and county boundaries; in this respect, however, the Bakers, Roberts and Guldefords look almost parochial. When Sir John Baker died in 1661, he left no male heir. The reduced state of the family's fortunes is subsequently highlighted by the fact that the four surviving co-heiresses each married an esquire rather than into other baronetcies or the lesser nobility, and that only two of them married husbands whose estates lay beyond the county boundary. These daughters were brought up under the protection of their mother Elizabeth, Lady Baker, who continued to live on at Sissinghurst until her death in 1693, and to manage the estate through Mr Hooker, her steward.

Lady Roberts was also widowed by the premature death in 1661 of her 27-year-old husband, Sir Howland; she proceeded to bring up her daughter and two sons, the elder of whom, Thomas, was less than three years old when he succeeded to the baronetcy. She ran the estate through her steward, Peter Sharpe,[6] and continued to have a major say in affairs until her death in 1706 at the age of 81. By 1684, however, her son, Sir Thomas Roberts, had taken over responsibility for the estate, and, at the latest in 1688, he took on a senior administrative position locally as justice of the peace; thus he did have contact with local people. Sir Thomas married Jane Beale, the 18-year-old daughter and coheir of Sir John Beale of Farningham in Kent; his brother Jocelyn married the daughter of a merchant tailor of London; and their sister, Bridget, married Mr Edmund Trench, a nonconformist minister, confirming the nonconformist predilections of the dowager Lady Roberts (page 183). None of these marriages was auspicious in terms of inter-relationships and family fortunes, but the family had not looked far afield in earlier generations. Sir Howland's father had married a bride from London, and his grandfather and great-grandfather had found their brides in neighbouring Brenchley and Smarden.[7]

The star of the Guldefords, on the other hand, was rising again. As the grandson of a knight, and with links to the nobility through his mother Catherine, daughter of the Hon. Thos. Petre, and grandmother Lady Elizabeth Somerset, daughter of Edward, Earl of Worcester, Edward's contacts went far beyond the Kentish Weald.[8] He had married Ann Throckmorten, daughter of a Buckinghamshire baronet, and his sisters married husbands with estates in Shropshire and Hertfordshire. Edward died in 1678, but his wife survived him, living on until 1710; in that year, she was included in the list of papists resident or having estates in Kent,[9] a circumstance which helps to explain the provision in 1685 of a baronetcy for her son by a sympathetic James II. The Guldefords' steward was Mr John Throckmorten (variously Frogmorten), almost certainly one of Edward's wife's relatives;[10] contact with local people, even their tenants, was therefore at one stage removed, and their involvement in administration at parish level was certainly very limited.

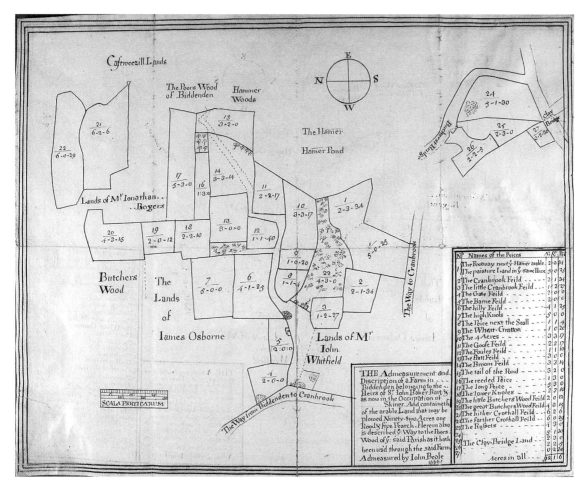

19. Map of a Farm in Biddenden belonging to the heirs of Sir John Baker, Bt., 'now in the occupation of — Skiner', 1666, as measured by John Beale. The man whose name escaped the map-maker was Isaac Skinner, yeoman of Biddenden, son of Golding Skinner of Frittenden; Isaac worked these lands throughout the 1660s. Golding died 1666, Isaac 1670.

Knights and Esquires: Relationships County-wide

Between baronets and gentlemen in the social hierarchy came the knights and esquires from whom the Lord Chancellor customarily appointed Justices of the Peace. Their role had traditionally been to maintain law and order in the king's name throughout the countryside, and they continued to perform this role in the period under scrutiny. A single justice could impose a variety of punishments for minor misdemeanours, from a whipping or consignment to the stocks, to distraint of goods or even imprisonment. He could also require people to enter into recognizance by which they promised to act on pain of forfeiting a sum of money. More serious misdemeanours required two justices to work together; such meetings became known as petty sessions. Important crimes, or appeals from earlier judgements, were referred to the quarter sessions and Assizes; the former consisted of justices as a body, the latter of the sovereign's judges.[11]

So successful had the justices been in co-operating with local communities in the judicial role that, long before the second half of the 17th century, they had also been given responsibility for the supervision of local government, and this work now occupied the bulk of their time.[12] They worked closely with, and in some cases supervised, parochial officers such as churchwardens, overseers of the poor, constables and surveyors of the highways. Among the parish officers, the churchwardens were appointed by the incumbent and the parishioners, but the justices met annually to appoint the overseers nominated by parishes, and, after 1691, the surveyors of the highways.[13] They checked and countersigned all the overseers' accounts, sanctioned changes in the value of a man's property and heard appeals against assessment for church rates. They worked very hard, and related to people of all levels, both the parish officials and the humblest individuals, whether male or female, making their petitions or giving their testimony.

In Kent at this period there were between 80 and a 100 justices active at any one time, covering 63 hundreds and 413 parishes.[14] Cranbrook and its adjacent parishes formed only part of a petty sessional district which extended over a wider area. It was bounded to the west by Tonbridge, to the north by Bearsted, and to the east by Ashford; to the south lay Sussex. In 1680 and again in 1704 this large area was represented by just six justices at any one time.[15]

Because the petty-sessional district of Cranbrook was larger than the area covered by the parishes which have been reconstituted, not all the justices who operated in the seven parishes at any one time figure in the reconstitution. Of the six justices of 1667-8, for instance, Samuel Boys, John Horsmonden, Sir John Henden and Richard Kilburne were local to the seven parishes, but Edward Finch was from Kenardington parish and Richard Hulse from Chartham; all the justices were expected to cover any parish in the district.[16] Table 6.1 summarises those from the seven parishes who bore the brunt of the work during the period, and gives some idea of the length of the periods over which they operated.

These men were already pre-eminent in their neighbourhoods because of their family backgrounds, and wealthy enough to have had legal training through the Inns of Court, owing their title 'esquire' to their subsequent appointment as justices of the peace.[17] John Horsmonden and Anthony Fowle of Goudhurst, for instance, were registered at the Middle Temple and Grays Inn respectively, and assessed on nine and 10 hearths; the former came from an ancient Wealden family, the latter from Sussex. Richard Kilburne of Hawkhurst, historian and author of a *Survey of Kent* (1659), acted as a lawyer as well as justice of the peace;[18] he also was an incomer, having settled with his wife in Hawkhurst in the 1630s. Sir John Henden's family had been clothiers, but in recent generations they had found their living through the Law. In 1662 he inherited the estates of his cousin, Sir Edward Henden, Baron of the Exchequer, and was assessed in 1664 on 24 hearths for his family home of Biddenden Place at the south end of the parish, the third largest house in the Cranbrook region. Finally, Samuel Boys of Hawkhurst took over the role of justice from his father William, and his own son William was a justice in the 1690s. Samuel was also an attorney at law, and belonged to an ancient Kentish family with numerous branches throughout the county.

Table 6.1   Long-serving local JPs, Cranbrook petty sessional district, 1660-99

		1660	1670	1680	1690
John Horsmonden, Esq.	Goud.	pre-1660 --------------- 1667			
Richard Kilburne, Esq.	Hawk.	pre-1660 ----------------------------------- 1678			
Sir John Henden, Kt.	Bid.		1662----------------------------- 1683		
Anthony Fowle, Esq.	Goud.		1663------- 1672		
Samuel Boys, Esq.	Hawk.		1667 ------------------------- 1687		
William Campion, Esq.	Goud.			1676 ------------------------→	
Sir Thomas Roberts, Bart.	Cra.				1688------→
William Boys, Esq.	Hawk.				1692--→

Sources: mainly signatures from overseers' accounts, settlement certificates and apprenticeship indentures.

Despite their contact with all strata of village society by virtue of their office, justices tended not to mix socially with those below their status, arranging their marriages at county level and beyond. John Horsmonden's father had married the daughter and coheiress of William Austen 'of Burrs', and he himself married in turn Grace Shoyswell and Elizabeth Aynscomb of Sussex, both families recognised by the Heralds in their Visitations. Sir John Henden married (1660) Northamptona, daughter of Sir William Haward, Knight, of Tandridge, Surrey, and the marriage of their eldest surviving son, William, to a daughter of Sir Nicholas Toke of Wye, Kent, confirms that their inter-relationships were at knightly level. Samuel Boys' mother was Cordelia, daughter of Sir John Wildegos of Eridge in Sussex, and he himself married Philadelphia Parker, daughter of a baronet, also from Sussex; William Campion also married the daughter of a knight.

Gentlemen: Relationships Locally and Beyond

In 1640 the Kentish gentry consisted of some 800 to 1,000 individuals from about 170 families sharing about 81 names.[19] This concentration of gentry families was greater than in any other county in 17th-century England, forming a 'community of gentry knit together by ties of neighbourhood, landownership and marriage'.[20] While a small knot of these closely related families dominated county affairs, most confined themselves to parochial rather than county matters, and did not aspire to parliament or even to be justices of the peace. The gentry of Kent also differed from those in other counties at this time in that a remarkably high proportion of them resided in the county, on their estates, and had a relatively low proportion of their total estates in other counties. This led to a high degree of kin-relationships between the families.[21] The evidence from the Cranbrook region suggests that these characteristics were even more pronounced in this part of the Weald than in the county generally.

In the present discussion, definition of who was a 'gentleman' is of crucial importance, but the term is far from easy to define in practice. William Harrison (1577) included those who merited the status because of their education and profession, such as lawyers, university graduates or physicians; and those who had sufficient resources, usually in land, to enable their families to live without them doing manual work. Gregory King, on the other hand, distinguished between 'gentlemen', 'persons in greater or lesser offices', 'persons in the Law', and 'eminent' and 'lesser clergymen' as if they were distinct groups. The Poll Taxes 1641-1699, and the Marriage Duty Act of 1695, likewise distinguished between a gentleman or reputed gentleman with estate of £300 and former or present aldermen, doctors of physic and doctors of Law, who were taxed at a higher rate.[22]

At its most restrictive, it might be said that only those who were armigerous had the right to call themselves gentlemen. Registrars and scribes, however, commonly prefaced a person's name with 'Mr', or appended the term 'gent.' after it, to signify that they regarded these people as gentry. This raised them above the level of the vast majority of their fellow parishioners who were customarily addressed merely by their forename and surname with the occasional interpolation of the label 'Goodman' to indicate that they were people of some substance. The only effective way to define the term is to see how it was used, and ideally how it was acquired, in the context of Kent, and of the Cranbrook region in particular.

Michael Zell has identified the clothiers who were active in the Weald between 1539 and 1640,[23] of whom 42 were living in Cranbrook and four of its adjacent parishes in the generation before 1640.[24] The succeeding generations of about three quarters of these men can be traced over the following six decades via the reconstitution, thereby providing a picture of changing status.[25] Table 6.2 provides extracts from his list, and indicates the value of each man's probate inventory. Although inventory totals include neither real estate nor debts owed by the deceased, they do give a feel for a man's wealth, and it is clear that those in the top third of the list were very wealthy men, who outstripped in material resources all but the wealthiest of the local gentry.[26]

While he found 'no predictable pattern' of successful clothier-landowners deserting manufacturing for the life of a petty squire, Zell did note their tendency to enlarge their freehold estates, and a movement into the ranks of the gentry which was becoming more common towards the end of the 16th century.[27] The subsequent family history of those in Zell's list now shows conclusively that, as the 17th century progressed, such men were more and more willing to put aside their work as merchants and to live as gentlemen off their estates. The increasingly parlous state of the woollen industry encouraged change. Analysis highlights four factors which enabled individuals and families to pass through Wrightson's 'permeable 'membrane' to gentry status: wealth, marriage, education and changing ethos.[28]

Wealth was a prerequisite to gentry status because, without wealth, aspiring gentry could not develop their holdings sufficiently to support themselves and their families. Unless a man could live off the unearned income of his estates, he could not expect to be recognised as a gentleman. All but one of the wealthiest clothier families in the list, interpreted as those with personal property valued at over £1,000, experienced a transition to gentry status, and in all but two that transition applied to most of the sons of the second generation. Among those with less that £1,000, such a transition was rare.

Table 6.2   *Cranbrook region: change in status among clothier families during the 17th century*

	scene pre-1640			scene post-1660		
Name	Parish	death	value	status/occup.	HT	marriage alliances
Sharpe, John of Staplehurst		1613	£2689	gent/clo/yeo	4<10	local gent /clo. /yeo
Taylor, Walter of Cranbrook		1613	£2207	clo→ gent	11	London/Beds gentry
Ginder, Stephen of Benenden		1617	£1923	clo→ gent	10	local gentry
Bigge, Smallhope of Cranbrook		1638	£1823	Esq./yeo		(mainly Rolvenden)
Holden, John of Cranbrook		1623	£1075	clo→gent/clo	6<10	local clothiers
Draner, Ambrose of Biddenden		1621	£1043	clo→gent	8	county-wide/moved
Colvill, Josias of Cranbrook		1631	£1027	clothier	5<7	local clo.,[*Quaker*]
Weller, Alexander of Cranbrook		1612	£858	clo→innkeep	4<6	local, husbandman,
Hunte, Edward of Benenden		1616	£852	yeomen	13	local vestry
March, Joseph of Cranbrook		1626	£740	clothier	2	local clothiers
Weller, Richard of Cranbrook		1611	£732	thatcher		
Chittenden, John of Hawkhurst		1633	£632	one gent/clo	1x<4	local and various
Basden, Walter of Benenden		1618	£561	clo→yeomen	4	local vestry
Weller, Alexander of Cranbrook		1631	£575	carpenter, tailor		
Fowle, Francis of Cranbrook		1633	£450	yeoman	1<4	local vestry
Courthop, Richard of Cranbrook		1616	£440	gent /clothier	3<4	local gt/yeo/clo [*Quaker*]
Chittenden, Nathan.l of Hawkhurst		1623	£433	some carpenters		mixed fortunes ...
Usborne, John of Staplehurst		1615	£404	clo. / yeo etc.	2<7	local yeo / clo etc.
Chittenden, William of Hawkhurst		1632	£332	husbandmen		
Parks, Richard of Cranbrook		1629	£317	broadw/husb	1x<2	local miller, husb.
Holnes, Robert of Benenden		1627	£312	clothiers	2	local clothiers
Henden, Edward of Benenden		1625	£261	gentlemen		[already gentlemen]
Bennett, John of Hawkhurst		1633	£258	clo / yeo / hus	1x<4	local, [*Qua & Bap*]
Knight, Thomas of Cranbrook		1615	£223	clo→gent		local, 1 Maidstone
Kidder, John of Cranbrook		1633	£179	clothier		
Couchman, Thomas of Cranbrook		1612	£162	clo. (lots), +	2x<6	local clo./yeo.
Weller, John of Cranbrook		1623	£158	kersimaker etc		
Couchman, Edward of Cranbrook		1618	£155	yeo / broadw.		
Wood, Thomas of Hawkhurst		1637	£119	clothier		local husbandman
Sacrye, Richard of Benenden		1611	£?	yeo / husb		local marriages

Source: Zell (1996) 687-91; (1994) 221ff;

Note: HT = Hearth Tax returns March 1664, showing range where appropriate

clo = clothier   husb = husbandman   yeo = yeoman etc.

clo→gent signifies transition from family of clothier status to one of gentleman status 1640-80;

clo / yeo / gent implies different members of the family achieving clothier or yeoman or gentleman status at the same time.

20. The earliest part of this house was probably built about 1610 by John Bigg, a Cranbrook clothier. John's son, Smallhope Bigg, figures in Table 6.2 as a wealthy clothier.

Marriage was a major factor. When an alliance was made with an influential county family, the transition to gentry status was dramatic. Wealth, of course, played its part too; without wealth such a match would never have been made. In other cases the transition was more gradual and the marriage alliances more local, as was the custom of those who lived in the Weald. Sometimes alliances were with the local gentry, sometimes with other leading clothier families who were on a par, or nearly so, financially. The effect of gentry alliances was to gentrify the clothiers, while alliances with other clothier families, which were also going through a similar process, in no way impeded the transition.[29]

Education might be a factor associated with gentility, but it was not a prerequisite. While a university education was a required route for anyone to become an Anglican minister or a schoolmaster, their status thereby was not gentry *per se*. Nor was the lawyer, educated at one of the Inns of Court, *ipso facto* a gentleman either, although he was likely to come from a gentry family. In reality, because education via the Inns of Court was beyond the purse of all but a wealthy few, wealth was again the essential concomitant. The qualified attorney would expect to make money, and was likely to be termed 'gentleman', but was unlikely to achieve appointment as a justice of the peace unless his family was already well established.

Finally, a change of attitude is discernible, at least in the Cranbrook region. The Restoration brought with it the reinstitution of a hierarchical social structure and concomitant overthrow of the levelling forces of the republic; as a result there was a tendency for scribes and the compilers of monuments to be increasingly liberal with their use of the title 'Mr' or 'gentleman'. As a result of these changes in attitude, men who played a leading role in their communities, and who were of reasonably substantial means, were increasingly treated by their fellow parishioners as gentry even if it might be argued that neither their wealth, nor their marriage alliances, nor their education, deserved it. Men who but a generation before would have simply been referred to as yeoman, or clothier, or victualler, now found themselves called 'Mr', or 'gent' as a matter of course. It is a phenomenon also noted by Stone, and highlighted by French who, speaking of parish elites, says they developed a tendency in the late 17th century to describe themselves as 'gentlemen'.[30]

These points can be illustrated by the history of some of Zell's clothier families from Table 6.2. Walter Taylor of Cranbrook, for instance, left a messuage and land to each of two sons, together with cash bequests totalling £1,250 to them, their brother (£350) and their two sisters (£200 each).[31] Marriages were contracted with families of similar substance, but not of gentry status at the time: Ramsden, Sharpie and Couchman. Despite the family's wealth, however, there was no question of Walter being a 'gentleman'. The second half of the 17th century then saw an interesting transition. Walter's son Robert Taylor, who died in 1662, is referred to as 'clothier' by the assessors in his probate inventory, as 'yeoman' in the registers, and as gentleman in his will by himself.[32] When Robert's own daughter Joane married Richard Parratt in 1654 the register refers to her father as 'Mr Robert Taylor, clothier'. He therefore neatly epitomises the dilemma faced by anyone attempting to categorise people at this time.

The distinction between yeoman and clothier is not a real one because, with his land-holding, Robert was entitled to be referred to as 'yeoman' while at the same time he was clearly still involved in the wool trade. The courtesy 'Mr' may well reflect how his daughter saw him, while the term 'gent' in his will indicates how he saw himself. Robert Taylor's son, also Robert, died prematurely in 1676 at the age of only 33 and after only two-and-a-half years of marriage; the assessors saw him as 'clothier' in his probate inventory, but again in his will he refers to himself as 'gentleman'.[33] Robert Taylor was assessed on 11 hearths, so the family continued to enjoy its wealth, but it would be presumptuous to refer to them as gentry.

Ambrose Drayner, on the other hand, married Elizabeth Twysden, of the same ancient Wealden family as Sir Roger Twysden, Knight of the Shire of Kent in the Short Parliament, and archetypal 17th-century scholarly squire.[34] When one married a Twysden one married the Twysden family and, through them, into many other of the leading families of the county which were interrelated by a complex web of marriage alliances.[35] Their son, Robert, made a similarly impressive match; in 1627, at the age of 23, he married Margaret, the daughter of Giles Master, Esq., leading burgess of the city of Canterbury, and Mary née Hales, the family with the largest land-holding in Kent. At that time Robert was still referred to simply as 'clothier'.

When Margaret died at the early age of 36, Robert Drayner went on to marry Susanna, daughter of Edmund Stede of Biddenden, gent. (1642), and this time was referred to as 'gentleman' rather than 'clothier'. By 1642, therefore, Robert Drayner was recognised by others as a 'gentleman'. This change in recognition must have been influenced by the marriage alliances formed by his father and himself with the county gentry, which were in turn helped by their great wealth. Edmund Stede was a considerable landowner and one of the leading gentry of Biddenden, paying tax (with his son Edmund?) on houses with nine and eight hearths; to judge by his will he was a lawyer by training.[36] By 1674, Robert's own will shows the dispersal of considerable parcels of land in Biddenden, Frittenden and Staplehurst, but no hint of continued clothmaking activity.[37]

Someone with clothier connections but not in Zell's list was Bernard Randolph, who arrived in Biddenden in the 1580s and married Jane Boddenden, of an old local family and heiress to the Lassenden estate. Of their surviving four sons, two remained in Biddenden, two found their fortunes elsewhere. The registers do not refer to Bernard, or any of his sons, as 'Mr' or 'gent.' before 1640, but on his funerary inscription in the church, dated 1628, he is 'Bernard Randolph, Gent.'. This is consistent with a discernable tendency to be generous in terms of status on funerary monuments. One of his sons, William Randolph, referred to himself as 'clothier of Biddenden' in his will (1641) but was 'William Randolph, Gent' on his brass in the church; he had married Elizabeth Curtis from a leading Tenterden gentry family. Two other sons, Herbert and Edmund, had a university education and married daughters of Giles Master Esq., of Canterbury; Edmund was one of that elite group, a Doctor of Physic. The fourth son, John, was 'of the City of London, gent'. Wealth and advantageous marriages figured strongly in the rise of the Randolphs to established gentry status, and education was an important component. On the other hand it is clear that their status was not absolute, and that during the period of transition, recognition of gentry status was in the eye of the beholder.[38]

Even more telling is the transition of William Beale to gentry status. His father, Richard, was a Biddenden clothier, and was referred to as such through to his death in 1691 at the age of 72, as was his uncle John, who died in 1667. When he married Elizabeth Newenden in 1665 William was referred to as a grocer of Biddenden, and, as 'William Beale, grocer', he figured in many probate accounts and the Churchwardens Accounts. Throughout the baptisms of his children (1667-79) he was plain William, and similarly when he married his second wife, Sarah Kadwell, widow, he was still William (1686). On her death in 1690, however, he was referred to in the registers as Mr William Beale, and at the time of his third marriage, to Audrey Giles in 1694, the licence referred to him as William Beale, gentleman of Biddenden.

William Beale's transition from 'grocer' to 'gentleman' had nothing to do with his university education; he had none. He was certainly a man of substance by the late 1680s, and may well have had sufficient wealth to be able to retire from his daily grind and live off his estates; he was, for instance, lending money on bond by 1692. More to the point, he had married the widow of a Kadwell, and thereby joined the gentry family circle of the late justice of the peace George Kadwell Esq., of Rolvenden. The most important factor in William's change of estate, however, may well have been that by the end of the 17th century people were more liberal in their use of the term 'gentleman'. Such a transition is mirrored among numerous of William's contemporaries in the Cranbrook region.

Clothier families which fell below the thousand-pound mark in Zell's analysis can be quickly surveyed. The Hendens rose higher than any of their contemporaries by their training as lawyers and their support for the royalist cause; several were knighted, and they sought their marriage alliances well beyond the county boundary. The Courthops had long been among the wealthiest clothier families of the Weald and some in the 1670s were 'gentlemen'. What is surprising is the number of Courthop(e)s who remained as clothiers, although this lack of social striving might well have a lot to do with the Quaker sympathies of several of the family in the generation after the visit by George Fox in 1655 (page 187).

Of the other families the majority still figured as clothiers in the period between 1660 and 1700 even though the industry was in decline. Some did diversify; Dence Weller, clothier at marriage (1652), was referred to as 'innkeeper' by 1657, and his brother Thomas Weller, also 'clothier', is shown as innkeeper of the *George* in 1662 and was still running the inn in 1673; he was more innkeeper than clothier.[39] Samuel Hunt senior and junior of Benenden became wealthy yeoman farmers, the elder paying tax on 13 hearths; they were very involved in the Benenden vestry, and married locally, but there is no hint of them becoming 'gentlemen'. Similarly the Osbornes of Loddenden in Staplehurst concentrated on farming and married local equals, but there is no indication of a change of status even though they were wealthy enough to pay on six hearths.[40] The move to gentleman status, which meant giving up whatever lucrative trade one had been following and living purely on unearned income, was a transition in which some might not wish to indulge.[41]

Not all did so well; the Chittenden family, for instance, had mixed fortunes, and the descendants of Richard Parks ceased to be clothiers, ending up as husbandmen and broadweavers exempt from the Hearth Tax. Those who prospered, however, almost without exception, married within a group of families with comparable wealth who lived in the immediate circle of Kentish Wealden parishes, and made occasional forays across the county border into Sussex. Together with those who had made the transition to gentleman status, and under the nominal leadership of the Anglican incumbent, they formed the administrative groups which ran the parishes and served their fellow villagers as constables, churchwardens and overseers of the poor. This was their social milieu, and these are the people who now merit examination.

Parish Administrators: Minister and 'Vestrymen'

As the titular heads of the parishes and chairmen of the vestry, Anglican ministers were key figures within the communities,[42] but their social standing varied according to the value of their benefices and, more importantly, the families into which they married. Moses Lee, for example, was already in his 50s when he was appointed to the parish of Biddenden by the King himself in 1660;[43] the following year he married by licence Elizabeth, widow of Mr Jonathan Rogers, gent. In this way he came to live in Castiswell, one of the great houses of the area, and had to pay Hearth Tax on two houses, one with nine hearths, and one (the parsonage) with eight. Castiswell subsequently passed to his wife's son Jonathan in 1681.

In 1682 Dr Giles Hinton succeeded Moses Lee, but his domiciliary experience was less happy than his predecessor's. The year after his arrival he reported to the Archbishop that 'the parsonage house was ... a most ruinous and dreadful spectacle, ... soe ragged and unclean that I never saw any building stand more in need of a lustration. ... I was not borne in a pigstie though I may die in a worse place ...'. He went on to point out that, for the 51 years from 1609 to the appointment of Moses Lee, no rector had been resident in the parish, and that no-one had lived in the rectory for 73 years.[44] Hinton did his best to repair the ravages of time and it cost him dear (above £300) so that in May 1685 he was gaoled in 'the common place of confinement in Maidstone'. Nevertheless he soldiered on in the parish with his wife Dorothy until his death in 1702; he did not benefit from a brilliant marriage.

Table 6.3   *The Anglican incumbents of Cranbrook region parishes 1660-1700*

	1660	1670	1680	1690	1700
Benenden	Nicholas Monyman --- ➤				
	Sept. 1662, vicar				
Biddenden	Moses Lee -------------------------------------- ➤ Giles Hinton --------------------- ➤				
			1682, rector		
Cranbrook	John Cooper Charles Buck-- ➤				
	1662, vicar July 1668, vicar				
Frittenden	Robert Clarke Robert Newton -- ➤				
	Jan. 1666 vicar				
Goudhurst	Edward Thurman ------------- ➤ James Fen--- ➤				
	1662, vicar 1676, vicar				
Hawkhurst	Jonathan Pleydell --- ➤ Benjamin Horner ➤				
	Sept 1662 vicar			1691	
Staplehurst	Stephen Sowton --------------------------------- ➤ Joseph Crowther ----------------- ➤				
	Nov. 1662 rector		Aug. 1684 rector		

Source: largely Venn & Venn (1922)

John Pomfret did marry well. Originally a schoolmaster, he became rector of Newchurch near the Kent coast, but continued to live in Biddenden where he had married Elizabeth Rogers, daughter of the now widowed owner of Castiswell who had earlier married Moses Lee. On his wife's death Pomfret further secured his position by marrying Jane, daughter of Vincent Quilter of ancient lineage, by whom he acquired the old house which had belonged to Edmund Steed, gent.[45] Similarly the young vicar of Hawkhurst, Jonathan Pleydell, son of a Gloucestershire gentleman, made a good match four years after his arrival in 1662. At the age of 25 he married by licence Mistress Alice Leigh, the 24-year-old daughter of John Leigh, gent., of Cranbrook. Her father and her grandfather had been attorneys in the public eye, her mother a Courthope, and one of her uncles had married into the influential Roberts family of Glassenbury.

Nicholas Monyman exemplifies the process of social advancement. His father, a Norfolk carpenter, managed to send him to Cambridge whence he was appointed as a schoolmaster at the Grammar School in Cranbrook in 1658. After his appointment by Sir John Henden as vicar of Benenden in September 1662 he combined teaching with parish duties for a few months; he was to serve the parish until his death in 1700. When he took on the benefice he was already married to Hannah, the young widow of Henry Edmonds, a schoolmaster colleague at Cranbrook. He is frequently referred to as 'Mr Nicholas'; his son Henry, firmly established as a gentleman, married Susanna Woolball from one of the leading Biddenden clothier families, and two of his daughters married sons of local gentry, Thomas Freebody, gent., and Richard Sharpe, gent. A third daughter married a millwright from Ashford in Kent.

The Anglican clergy, therefore, were on the fringe of the gentry scene in the Cranbrook area parishes, and those who settled, married well locally, and had their families there, were regarded as gentlemen. It is significant that in the Hearth Tax returns the assessors refer to Mr Robert Clarke (Frittenden), Mr Edward Thurman (Goudhurst) and Mr Stephen Sowton (Staplehurst), but to Moses Lee, clerke (Biddenden) and John Cooper, clerke (Cranbrook). The distinction appears to have been at the whim of the scribe.

It has been possible to build a picture of those who were active in the parishes of Benenden, Biddenden, Cranbrook and Frittenden by listing signatories to the churchwardens' and overseers' accounts. These were the men who ran the parishes, the officers of 'the only popular assembly, other than the House of Commons, which had the right to impose compulsory taxation',[46] and they were therefore genuinely important. That they knew their own importance is borne out by the use in the Cranbrook churchwardens' accounts of that telling phrase in which they claimed to be the 'chiefest gentlemen and yeomen of the parish'.[47] They provided the parish officers, the churchwardens, overseers of the poor, constables and surveyors of the highway, and, whether in office or not, met regularly as an unofficial vestry group in each of the parishes. The inter-relationships between the families of these men provide the key to where power and responsibility lay within the parishes.

Those who held the office of churchwarden in Benenden in the first ten years after the arrival of the new incumbent are fairly representative of the signatories at parish meetings. Six were yeomen, five were gentlemen (of whom two were alternatively mercer and clothier), two clothiers and one, to whom no status is ascribed, probably best fits the description husbandman. Most of these men lived in houses with a hearth tax assessment of between three and six hearths; three of them paid on two hearths and one, who almost certainly had his main dwelling in Tenterden, on one hearth. Moreover, with the sole exception of John Cryer, who seems already to have passed his farms to the next generation, they were all assessed on lands held in Benenden (not necessarily their own land; they could have been renting it from others) which had a rental value of between £18 and £29 per annum for the yeomen, more than £30 for the gentlemen, and rather less for the mercer and the clothiers; even the presumed husbandman was assessed on land valued at £14 10s. per annum.

Table 6.4 *Kinship and other links between Benenden churchwardens, 1663-73*

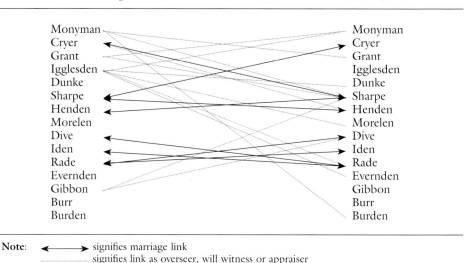

Monyman	Monyman
Cryer	Cryer
Grant	Grant
Igglesden	Igglesden
Dunke	Dunke
Sharpe	Sharpe
Henden	Henden
Morelen	Morelen
Dive	Dive
Iden	Iden
Rade	Rade
Evernden	Evernden
Gibbon	Gibbon
Burr	Burr
Burden	Burden

Note: ⟵——→ signifies marriage link

.... signifies link as overseer, will witness or appraiser

The comparative wealth of these men is supported by the evidence of inventories, probate accounts and wills. John Henden's goods and chattels were worth £126 (£16 after payment of debts) and John Burr's were worth £164 (down to minus £34). In his will John Dunke left £220 to his daughter as well as his lands;[48] Peter Sharpe (inventory value £210) left a 20-acre farm to his daughter, another farm to his wife to yield £20 per annum for another daughter who also received a £60 lump sum, and £100 to his grandsons. Jarvice Morelen (£153) left his son a 12-acre farm and dwelling; Christopher Dive (£285) left a farm in Rucking and another in Cranbrook to his two sons; and Thomas Rade (£140) disbursed £15 each to three grandchildren, £20 each to three daughters and a 12-acre farm to his son. None of these is a huge sum or large holding; they do indicate a comfortable prosperity on the part of the vestrymen.[49]

Wealthier men than these appear among the early vestry signatories but did not take office as churchwardens at this time. They include Richard Sharpe, who paid on six hearths and bequeathed £350 in lump sums besides several farms in Sandhurst, Hawkhurst and Benenden and at least another five houses and associated grounds; Stephen Ginder, a clothier, who lived in a ten-hearth house and paid assessment on lands worth more than £50 per annum; and Samuel Hunt, who paid tax on a 13-hearth house and had lands with a rental value of £32 per annum.[50] A rare example of a socially less distinguished signatory is James Turner, who is variously described as husbandman (at his marriage in 1659) and labourer (at his death in 1674); who is recorded as being paid 1s. 2d. for a day's work in the churchyard in 1671-2; who paid tax on four hearths; and who was married to Susan Dive, widow, whose previous husband must have been a yeoman. James Turner is another salutary reminder that human beings cannot be put into neat categories; life is not like that.

The inter-relationships of the Benenden churchwardens of the first ten years after the Restoration have been worked out, as far as they are known, from the reconstitution, wills, probate accounts, churchwardens' accounts and the like. The resultant survey shows just how complex and far-reaching their social relationships were; they are so inter-twined as to defy analysis. In many cases the relationship was cemented by marriage, often between the offspring of churchwardens; it was not just a question of the men meeting together several times a year, but of a more substantial intermingling of families which led to such marital arrangements. Stone reflects the situation well when he says 'Intermarriage was very commonly used as social bonding among parish gentry families within the county in the early 17th century'.[51] Table 6.4 attempts to represent these links diagrammatically.

The kin link is of paramount importance; it is stressed in wills, and has economic overtones as it leads to the movement of goods and land between one family and another while keeping them within this restricted community. Almost as profound are the links created and maintained through friendship and trust, by which the vestry signatories acted as overseers, and to a lesser extent witnesses, of each other's wills. Where a will had been made, the executor(s) or executrix was normally the heir or heiress, a family member and often a principal legatee. The role of overseers of wills (page 147), could only be entrusted to the most trustworthy of friends. Two examples from the available profiles will give a flavour of the evidence.

John Cryer, yeoman of Benenden, was churchwarden 1662-3; in 1666 he witnessed the will of Stephen Leeds, cordwainer of Benenden, whose niece Mary married John Basden, clothier of Benenden and signatory to the accounts, in 1670.[52] The will of his brother, Richard Cryer, yeoman of Benenden, shows that Richard's daughter Martha was married to Richard Sharpe, gentleman of Benenden, and that John Brandford, clothier of Benenden, and the testator's cousin Richard Cryer the younger, yeoman of Benenden, were to act as overseers of his will. All three men signed the Benenden accounts over the following years, and were therefore part of the inner clique; Richard Cryer the younger went on to be churchwarden 1677-9. It is no surprise, therefore, to find that Richard Cryer's will was witnessed by Samuel Hunt, yeoman, Richard Grant, mercer, and John Basden, clothier, all of Benenden and all frequent signatories of the accounts.[53]

Jarvis Morelen, yeoman of Benenden, signatory in 1665/6/70, and churchwarden 1667-9, paid tax on six hearths; he made his 'loving friend' Richard Igglesden, gentleman of Benenden and churchwarden 1663-5, sole overseer of his will to help his wife and her brother as executors. His brother Samuel's will refers to Samuel's sister Martha, who was wife of William Butler, husbandman of Benenden, signatory 1669/73 and sidesman 1673.[54] He farmed land owned by Richard Sharpe, gent., signatory in 1664/5/6/8/71, who had as overseers of his own will 'my loving friend' Nicholas Monyman (the vicar) and Richard Grant, mercer of Benenden.

All the evidence suggests that the pattern of parish administration and inter-relationships at Benenden is mirrored in the other parishes. At Biddenden, for instance, five gentlemen, four clothiers and a yeoman figure among the 12 churchwardens who held office 1661-71. The two who did not fall within those categories were a grazier (assessed on three hearths, and working land with a rental value of £50 per annum) who was a wealthy and influential villager in his own right, and a barber (assessed on two hearths, with land worth £2 per annum), who was a remarkably faithful member of the vestry group and, incidentally, wrote up the churchwardens' and overseers' accounts. Eight of the others were assessed on five hearths or more, and they all worked land with substantial value. Richard Beale, clothier, and William Picks, gentleman, both very wealthy and distinguished men, were the first men appointed at the Restoration in 1660.

Table 6.5   Kinship and other links between Biddenden churchwardens, 1661-71

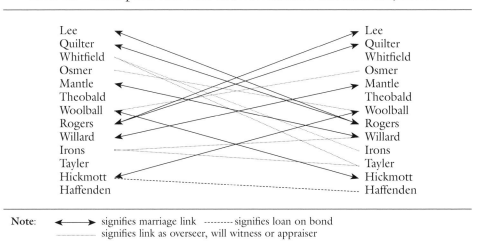

Note: ◄─────► signifies marriage link   ---------- signifies loan on bond
                    ·················· signifies link as overseer, will witness or appraiser

At Cranbrook the churchwardens of the 1640s and 1650s were men of very considerable status within the parish, and included justices of the peace and landlords with substantial estates. John Rabson (1643) and William Boys (1647/8) were esquires; Harman Sheafe (1644/5), John Courthop (1652/3) and Richard Holden of Branden (1656/7) are just three examples of the very wealthy men who dominated the administration during these decades. The immediately post-Restoration scene in Cranbrook, therefore, represents something of a change in approach. Richard Kingswood, Thomas Brooke, Thomas Weston, Richard Fowle and Thomas Daniell do not compare in wealth or prestige to most of their predecessors. It is less easy to see any close relationship between the holders of office; only after 1665 does one find the sort of inter-relationships which featured in the other parishes, and which continued thereafter in Cranbrook. Even then, the pattern of relationships is more distant than that found in Benenden and Biddenden, possibly thereby reflecting a less close-knit society in the market town than in its satellite parishes.

Table 6.6 *Kinship and other links between Cranbrook churchwardens, 1662-72*

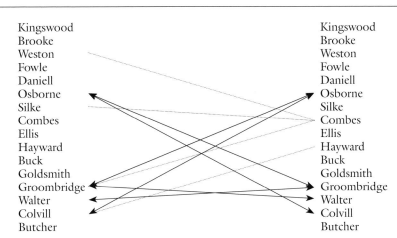

Kingswood	Kingswood
Brooke	Brooke
Weston	Weston
Fowle	Fowle
Daniell	Daniell
Osborne	Osborne
Silke	Silke
Combes	Combes
Ellis	Ellis
Hayward	Hayward
Buck	Buck
Goldsmith	Goldsmith
Groombridge	Groombridge
Walter	Walter
Colvill	Colvill
Butcher	Butcher

Note: ←——→ signifies marriage link .... signifies link as overseer, will witness or appraiser

Despite its comparatively small population, Frittenden managed to provide a complete run of two churchwardens for every year from 1661 to 1699. The pattern parallels that for Benenden and Biddenden both in terms of senior and junior churchwardens and in terms of the social status of those involved; of the 18 for whom the occupation is known, four were gentlemen, seven yeomen, two clothiers, two husbandmen, one a carpenter, one a butcher and one a tileman. These last, therefore, found themselves among the 'better sort' of the parish. All these men tended to find their relationships within their peer group in the parish and its environs. They witnessed each other's wills, appraised each other's property, met to ratify the church accounts, stood or were elected to offices of considerable power and prestige within the parishes, and were bound to each other by mutual ties in a complex web of inter-relationships. As they frequently cemented those relationships by marriage, they increasingly enjoyed a kinship relationship with each other.

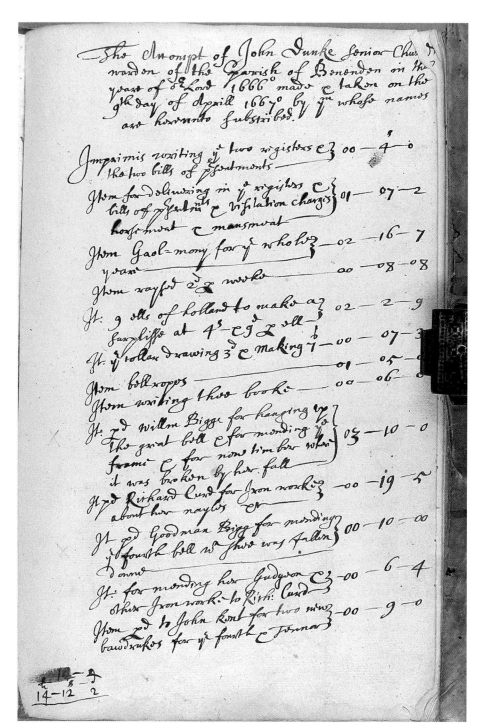

The Acompt of John Dunke Senior Churchwarden of the Parish of Benenden in the yeare of oʳ Lord 1666 made & taken on the 9th day of Aprill 1667 by yᵉ whose names are hereunto subscribed.

Impaimis writing yᵉ two registers & the two bills of presentments — 00 — 4 — 0

Item for delivering in yᵉ registers & bills of presentmᵗˢ & visitation charges & horsemeat & mansmeat — 01 — 07 — 2

Item Gaol=mony for yᵉ whole yeare — 02 — 16 — 7

Item rayled aᵈ yᵉ weeke — 00 — 08 — 08

It: 9 elles of holland to make a surplisse at 4ˢ — & 9ᵈ yᵉ ell — 02 — 2 — 9

It: yᵉ rollen drawing 3ᵈ & making — 00 — 07 — 3

Item bell ropes — 01 — 05 — 0

Item writing this booke — 00 — 06 — 0

It: pᵈ Willm Bigge for hanging the great bell & for mending yᵉ frame & for new timber where it was broken by her fall — 03 — 10 — 0

It pᵈ Richard Curd for Iron worke about her nayles & — 00 — 19 — 5

It: pᵈ Goodman Bigg for mending yᵉ fourth bell wᵗ shee was fallen donne — 00 — 10 — 00

It: for mending her Gudgion & other Iron work to Rich: Curd — 00 — 6 — 4

Item pᵈ to John Kent for two new bawdrikes for yᵉ fourth & former — 00 — 9 — 0

14 — 12 — 2

21. The account of John Dunke, the senior of the two Benenden churchwardens 1666-7, provides a cross-section of payments for work about the church and churchyard, and is typical of the clarity of the Benenden Accounts. (CKS P20/5/1)

Chapter 7

The 'other inhabitants'

It was common practice at this time to refer to those who were not included among 'the chiefer sort' as 'other inhabitants', 'poor inhabitants' or even the 'meaner' or 'poorer sort'.[1] Such apparently pejorative terms reflect the fact that most contemporary comment was by those with wealth and social standing; they do not necessarily reflect disdain by these people for the less and least wealthy in the community. Wills, probate accounts and even inventories tend to apply more to those in the upper tiers of the social and economic pyramid, while lists of parishioners who were charged tithes and rates by the churchwardens and overseers of the poor cover all those above the poverty line. Of their nature these sources omit the poor who figure as exempt in the Hearth Tax lists and who made up between a third and a half of the local population (Table 2.10, page 44), and they say little of husbandmen, craftsmen and retailers. On the other hand, the details provided by the overseers of the poor, in their accounts of disbursements to those in real need, do paint a comparatively full picture of the care and concern shown for the welfare of the poorest in the parish.

Day-to-day Contacts: Services Rendered

Any parish or group of parishes provided a market by which those with particular skills could earn their living by putting them at the service of others. Because of the nature of the sources, some craftsmen tend to stand out from their fellows, but they provide a flavour of work generally. Richard Curd, the Benenden blacksmith, provided much of the iron work around the church and churchyard, and his brother-in-law Simon Neeve increasingly took over as the man responsible for the bulk of this work from the 1670s to the end of the century. Richard also figures in several probate accounts as being owed for smith's work, and appraised the goods of the yeoman Thomas Dive for his inventory. Another craftsman, the bricklayer Henry Miles, was very much engaged on the church in the 1680s and 1690s, and John Grinstead, the mason, is mentioned as looking after the stonework, tiling and leads of the church over a 34-year period from 1663 to 1697, the year in which he died.

Craftsmen such as these were not limited by parish boundaries. Thomas Alibon used to come over from Cranbrook to look after the glazing at Benenden, and also appears in the Frittenden accounts glazing the church there. James Tapley was a Biddenden glazier who figured every year from 1665 to 1680 as doing some work on the windows in his parish church, and Robert Stedman and his son did much of the

129

iron-work at Biddenden. Thomas Honas was the main source of brickwork repairs and John Hills did a lot of carpentry work there. Richard Newball of Cranbrook was that rare individual in the region, a bricklayer who wrote a will;[2] he had inherited four acres, together with a house and lands in Cranbrook and 'elsewhere in Kent', from his father William, who was also a mason and bricklayer, and a remarkably successful one![3] Richard left his wife the annual rent of £5 per annum from his lands in Biddenden, together with free use of their present dwelling and one cow. He is mentioned (1665) as working on the stonework of Frittenden church, and in 1683 his son Henry was doing the same. These men clearly earned enough to keep themselves well above the poverty level. The going rate locally for a carpenter or mason was 1s. 9d. per day, with another 9d. per day for 'the boy' who helped them with their jobs. The Biddenden churchwardens' accounts actually record an agreement that 'no Churchwarden heareafter shall pay for a bricklayer & a boy above 2s. 6d. for one day's work'.[4]

Work recorded in the churchwardens' accounts shows that wealthy members of the parish were closely involved with these craftsmen. In the 1660s, for instance, when a great deal of work had to be done on the roof and steeple of Benenden church to repair the neglect of the Commonwealth period, Mr Throckmorten, steward of the Guldeford estates, provided the shingles which Thomas Payne fixed using nails provided by the blacksmith Richard Curd. The yeoman Richard Bigge supplied boards and planks, Mr Roger Goldstone 250 bricks, and Richard Grant, gentleman, mercer and Goldstone's brother-in-law, was paid for new ropes for the shingler to use, as well as for nails, pitch and tar. In fact these 'chiefer sort' were the mainstay of the craftsmen's livelihood, and frequently died owing them for work done. Again, parish boundaries proved no bar. The clothier, Robert Wightwick, and the yeoman, John Bishoppenden, both from Biddenden, owed John Grinstead of Benenden for masonry work,[5] just as Peter Courthope, clothier of Cranbrook, died owing Goodman Coleman of Biddenden for carpentry work.[6]

Of the 234 surviving probate accounts, 45 refer to unpaid wages, sometimes to servants, sometimes for services rendered, and for 35 of these the occupation of the deceased is known. Fourteen were yeomen, four were clothiers and another four were gentlemen; if one also includes the two widows, of a clothier and a yeoman, then more than two-thirds of the wage-paying group came from the upper status groups within the parish. The remaining third covered a considerable variety of retailers and craftsmen: two millers, a butcher, a blacksmith, an innkeeper and the widows of a brewer, a carrier, a tanner, a cordwainer and two husbandmen.

Some interesting relationships emerge. John Bishoppenden, yeoman of Biddenden, was in effect employing his 22-year-old stepson, Stephen Chittenden, as an apprentice. As with almost all these debts for wages, the time-span is not known; it is therefore not possible to work out whether Stephen was being paid per month or per quarter, but the fact that he was owed £5 suggests that his wage was not ungenerous.[7] In similar fashion, Samuel Latter was paid £8 a year by his mother Anne, who was two and a half years in arrears with his payments! As administrator of the accounts of both his parents, Samuel paid himself for working the farm from the time of his father's death (May 1672) until Michaelmas 1674.[8]

Mary Water, the daughter of John Water, yeoman of Frittenden, who was owed 20s. in wages, was actually doing service in her own household. Another 'yearly servant', Thomas Kettle, was owed £8 5s. by William Hoadley, husbandman of Hawkhurst. Hoadley's wife was born Kettle; in other words he provides a perfect instance of service being arranged within the kin relationship. Robert Batcheller's link was different; he took as a yearly servant a relative of the owner of the land he was working.[9]

Care of the Sick

One area of human activity in the parishes which illustrates inter-relationships is care of the sick and dying. Death being no respecter of wealth or social standing, the evidence comes from a variety of sources which range from probate accounts to the overseers' accounts and testimonies to burial in woollen.

For those who had the financial resources, two local men stand out as providing medical help: Mr (Dr) John Relfe and Mr William Silke. John Relfe had already established a practice in Cranbrook when, at the age of 38, he married a young girl of 18 from nearby Sandhurst. His funerary inscription, dated 1683, refers to him as a 'practitioner of Physicke in Cranbrook for the space of 33 years'. During this time he had a practice which was wide-reaching; ten references to him visiting and administering physic, dating from 1664 to 1683, show him attending patients in Cranbrook (3), Benenden (1), Hawkhurst (2), Biddenden (1), Frittenden (1) and Goudhurst (2). Those patients mostly came from the wealthier strata of local society, including one gentleman, three clothiers, a yeoman, a gunsmith and a husbandman. Charges varied from between £2 and £3 for several visits including physic, to between 3s. 6d. and 10s. for the physic alone; in every case Relfe seems to have administered the medicine in person.[10]

Despite the fact that in every one of these instances the patient died of the illness, the probate accounts almost invariably display a certain warmth, as 'for his pains in visiting', or 'his divers visits'. One such was Stephen Sharpey, yeoman of Benenden, who seems to have run the full gamut of medical provision at the time.[11] Not only did he owe 'Dr Relfe of Cranbrooke for physick by him administered, 7s.', but he also left debts of 6s. to 'Thankful Tharp of Hawkhurst for chirurgery', 6s. 6d. to 'Mr Thomas Kencham of Cranbrook, Apothecary, for sirropps and other things', and another 40s. 'for attendance upon the said deceased in the time of his sickness and for other necessary charges layd out uppon him'. Thankful Tharpe was a barber-surgeon operating in the area in the early years of the period; he died in 1670, but his son of the same name carried on the tradition as one finds him attending Thomas Thornton of Hawkhurst in the 1680s.

The second major medical figure, the chirurgeon Mr William Silke of Cranbrook, spanned an even greater period than Dr Relfe, from before 1660 to 1698. He is first encountered tending to Mr Samuel Hovenden of Cranbrook, gentleman, whose administrator paid 40s. 'for searcloth wherein to inclose the said deceased dead corps and for doeing the same hee dying of the smale pox'. Over the following 40 years he administered physic to patients, almost invariably in Cranbrook itself; being of lower standing than the physician he covered a wider range of occupation than Dr Relfe, including a hammerman, two widows, a carrier, a ripyer and a blacksmith. Inevitably, because of his relationship with the sick, he was frequently asked to witness his patients' wills (page 153).

Other practitioners were active in the area. John Bing of Biddenden, for instance, died owing 46s. 6d. 'to the several chirurgeons who administered phisicke', but does not name them. Peter Master, mercer of Cranbrook, owed 'the Apothecary for a debt due for physick, 8s.' and was attended by a Dr Hatley, as was Henry Carey, a victualler, also of Cranbrook.[12] There is mention of a Mr Ockenden, physician, and a Dr Groombridge who was active in the last years of the century providing physic to Thomas Dive, yeoman of Benenden, as well as James Blackamore, referred to in the registers as chirurgeon and living in Biddenden from 1684. Even the poorest widows and children of the parish received medical assistance paid for by the parish: thus in 1659 the chirurgeon examined widow Wimble's daughter for 2s. 6d., and two years later her operation cost the parish £1 7s.[13]

Not all practitioners were as qualified. Mr Richard Theobald, for instance, was still an active clothier in the 1660s, living in an eight-hearth house with his wife Phoebe. They both tended the sick and injured of Biddenden, apparently with some skill. We find the overseers of the poor paying Richard fees ranging from 10s. to £2 for surgery, and in particular for 'cureinge Jude Bluets childs bodie which was broke'. Mistress Theobald was equally in demand, curing John Coltman's leg (£1), setting widow Springet's arm (10s.) and, in each of three years, being paid for several cures done for the poor. Alexander Homsby, a yeoman farmer, is found 'letting blood'; more surprisingly, John Powell, the Biddenden sexton who was paid a quarterly salary of 6s. 8d., and more every time he dug a grave or rang the knell, is also found practising minor surgery on old Richard White in 1660 (5s.), and lancing and dressing Elizabeth Gaskins' neck two years later (1s.).

Nursing was an integral part of the care provided for the sick and dying, and another area in which some were clearly skilled. Henry Parkes, a weaver of Cranbrook, and therefore of slender means, succumbed to smallpox in February 1680. His probate account records 'to Nurses and tenders who looked after and watched with the said deceased in his sickness whereof he dyed, being the smale pox, and for the charges otherwise occasioned, 40s.'[14] Widow Boorman was paid 5s. per week to nurse John Chandler and his wife in Biddenden in May 1683, and was joined there by Christopher Amis' wife who helped out for 12 days. Earlier she had nursed David Russell of Cranbrook (December 1672), charging 30s. for six weeks' nursing, again a rate of 5s. a week. She had then been supported by Mary Marten, who was paid 8s. for two weeks' attendance on the dying man. When Richard Harvey, ripyer and warrener of Cranbrook, was dying he employed the services of 'Peter Reynolds and his wife for their attendance on the said deceased in his sickness whereof he dyed, 18s.'. Laurence Willard, yeoman of Biddenden, owed his kinsman, James Willard, 10s. 'for attending him at time of sickness and for his pains'.[15]

Often it fell to friends and neighbours to fulfil this nursing function, and this was nowhere more true than among the really poor. Widow Wyborrow, for instance, nursed John Maynard when he and his children had smallpox (the parish paid out £1), and, when he had recovered, John Maynard in turn nursed Mary Weller 'she being sick of the small Pox' (14s.). The actions of Joseph Downe's wife and widow Chandler in looking after Elizabeth Wimble when she was unwell (10s.), or of Goody Shelly 'washing & tending Goody Gram' (1s.), or of Gutsole's wife being paid 5s. 'att 3 severall times to relieve her husband beinge sicke' are merely typical examples of a caring and self-help culture which permeated the parishes, and was supported by payments from the overseers' funds. Frequently medicines were provided on the parish, and joints of meat for those really sick; entries such as 'Beere for Robert Stedman when he had ye Pox' also suggest a certain empathy with the patient.

Support of the Very Poor

This brings us naturally to a consideration of the very poor in the parish. Their survival was dependent on the application of the poor laws which, for the period under examination, means those of 1598 and 1601 supplemented by 1662.[16] They provided that vagabonds were to be whipped by order of a justice or of the parish officers and sent with a passport to their place of birth or last dwelling for a year (their place of settlement). In this way parishes lessened the burden on their own assessment money. The Act of Settlement of 1662 allowed for the removal of newcomers to a parish if a complaint was made within 40 days and they were renting homes worth less than £10 rental per annum. By the end of the period one's settlement could be established by paying rates, serving an apprenticeship or doing a year's service.

Some contemporary settlement certificates have survived from Cranbrook and Frittenden which confirm the concern felt by parish officers about people who might become a drain on their finances. For instance, the churchwardens and overseers of Biddenden, worried that Edward Pierce's servant (and incidentally relative by recent marriage), Thomas Robins, might become a parish charge, contacted their counterparts in Frittenden; the latter confirmed that he was indeed 'last legally settled as an inhabitant of the parish of Frittenden', and that they would receive him back. Such settlements followed a standard format, and were countersigned by the justices.[17] Equally standard are the examples of removal orders which sent individuals back to their respective parishes because they had not 'taken a tenement there of the yearly value of tenne pounds, nor hath given or delivered notice in writing of the house of their abode to one of the churchwardens and overseers'. In most cases the home parish was nearby.[18]

The legislation also required churchwardens and overseers of the poor to tax those inhabitants and occupiers of lands in their parish who were over a certain wealth level, and gave them the power to distrain the goods of any who refused. At approximately six-month intervals, the churchwardens and overseers of Biddenden, for instance, met at the *Lion* or the *Chequers*; there they listed those parishioners who had the necessary resources to contribute to the sesse, as it was called, and recorded the rentable value of the land they occupied or the value of their stock in trade. They then set a rate of so many pence in the pound for the purpose of making 'a Sesse for the relief of the Poor of the Parish of Biddenden and putting out of Children whose Parents are not able to maintain them according to the Statute in that case made and provided'. These lists were signed by the officers and other leading parishioners.

Every month the overseers and churchwardens met in their respective parish churches and itemised the details of those to whom payments should be made.[19] This was a complex operation, no doubt honed over years of experience, but nevertheless requiring a fine balance between income and anticipated expenditure. Not only did the officials provide monthly payments to the established recipients, but they also provided relief on a monthly basis as need arose. Besides this, they had to allow for half-yearly payments for clothing and rent for those in receipt of regular payments, and for exceptional one-off payments to apprentice young people and to cover emergency repairs to the housing stock. In the 1660s, the Biddenden sesses were designed to yield between £100 and £150 per annum, and the annual accounts, scheduled for April or May of each year, and countersigned by at least two justices of the peace, regularly achieved an approximate balance. Cranbrook, as befitted its size, had a budget of over £400, Goudhurst more than £300, Staplehurst rather less.

The most obvious feature of the overseers' accounts is standard payments of cash to the really poor, most of whom were widows; these sums were hardly large, ranging from 1s. to 4s., exceptionally 6s., per month at a time when the standard local rate for a bricklayer per day was 1s. 9d. (page 130). On the other hand, the bricklayer was probably earning for his whole family, whereas the pauper was receiving support for him or herself alone. Gregory King's average pauper household income of £6 10s. per year implies £2 per person per year, or 3s. 4d. per month, so the sums given to the very poor would certainly have gone a long way to help them make ends meet.[20] Such parish relief must not be seen in isolation; many paupers were partial wage-earners, and the parish officers would take their circumstances into consideration when allocating funds.[21] In Biddenden in any given month this subsistence might go to 20 individuals in a parish of 182+ householders (11 per cent), of whom 69 (38 per cent) were exempt from Hearth Tax payment (Table 2.10).[22] These monthly payments were long-term commitments by the parish which, once commenced, would literally continue for life. Elizabeth Bristow's husband, for instance, was buried in October 1656; thenceforth, until her death in May 1668, Elizabeth received a monthly subsistence allowance of 2s. 6d. rising to 3s. 6d. which supplemented her earnings as a midwife (page 140). The list of payees varied from one year to the next as some died and others were added because of personal circumstances.

22. This page of the Biddenden Overseers' Accounts for May 1664, written by Thomas Irons who succeeded John Beale as the main scribe, shows how the parish listed its contributors alphabetically by Christian name and, like the Churchwardens, calculated by rental value and value of goods. (CKS P26/12/1)

Most of the regular recipients were widows, but some were men or women caring for children and some were spinsters. Mercy Brissenden, for instance, was in regular receipt of 1s. 6d. per month during the 1660s, as well as Mary Blist (6s.) and Jude Bluett (varying sums from 1s. to 2s.). Judith Bluett had long figured in the registers of Biddenden as mother of successive illegitimate children; at her burial in 1669, the registrar was quite open in recording her as 'an old whore who died of smallpox'. Yet the parish supported her, and occasionally made good use of her services by paying her to care for elderly, sick or dying neighbours despite her earlier anti-social tendencies.[23]

Almost as numerous in most months were payments which came under the category of 'Relief', and were occasioned by circumstances as they arose. Often these led to recurring payments; in other cases they might last for a month or two until the recipient had recovered. Thus Goodwife Masters was paid 2s. 6d. in August and September 1663 'her husband being sick'; he was a sawyer, and the couple normally gave a home to 'Wacher's girl', for which service they were paid 3s. per month. Robert died that October, and thenceforth his widow received the 3s. for Wacher's daughter's keep. About the same time, Margaret Bigg was paid for looking after Margaret Norwood and Mary Blist, both of whom were sick; Margaret Norwood was a regular recipient of monthly support, and died in September 1664, but Mary Blist recovered. Christopher Gutsell was paid 'relief' while his wife was 'lying in' early in 1664; he and his wife suffered a series of infant deaths between 1664 and 1667, at which time she died of the plague.

These occasional payments show that the overseers had constantly to be aware of the circumstances of the poor within the parish, and that they acted on that knowledge. An entry in the Cranbrook accounts under the year 1666 provides a nice example of instant decision-making. Seven named parishioners were fined 5s. or 10s. each for attending a nonconformist conventicle; an eighth man was found guilty of profane swearing. The churchwardens, in possession of fines totalling £3 13s., distributed the money, in gifts of a few pence and shillings each, to a considerable number of their poor, and included a large donation of £1 'towards the relief of the poor visited at Heselden Wood', and 5s. to Edward Beale and his family who were suffering from smallpox. The justices confirmed their action.[24]

Those who received assistance monthly also had their rents paid every six months, at Lady Day and Michaelmas. As with the sums paid out in subsistence, there was a wide variation in the amounts paid by the overseers for the housing of their charges. In the payments of Lady Day 1664, for instance, which are contemporary with the Hearth Tax assessment, one wonders what it was about Mercy Brissenden, or the accommodation provided for her by John Chadwick, which merited a payment of only 2s. 6d. when Widow Bristow's accommodation with Richard Holman cost six times as much. Did the discrepancy depend on the needs of Widow Bristow or the quality of the accommodation provided? Widow Wimble's rent of 12s. was paid to Richard Lucas, Ann Gason's rent of 2s. 6d. to John Burden. Richard Woolball received 15s. for 'Gutsell and Mercy Barr', and another 15s. for Widow Clarke and Joan Pott, whilst Mr John Mills received 12s. for Widow Sims and Widow Harper.

The Hearth Tax returns shed some light.[25] Mercy Brissenden, for instance, does not figure in the Hearth Tax lists; she was therefore presumably living with the husbandman, John Chadwick and his wife Alice, who paid on a one-hearth cottage, and may have helped around the house, thus earning part of her rent. Both John and Mercy succumbed to the plague. Widow Wimble, on the other hand, is listed as living in a one-hearth cottage and exempt. She was not, therefore, lodging with Richard Lucas, but living in a cottage belonging to him, for which the parish paid Lucas the rent. Indeed, out of 27 individuals for whom rent was being paid in April 1664, 13 are readily identifiable as living in exempt properties which were therefore owned by the persons receiving rent from the parish. Variations in amount paid might therefore reflect the quality of the accommodation as well as other sources of income.

Table 7.1 reflects the broad cross-section of people in the parish who took in the poor and the indigent. Widow Stevens, for instance, is known from the Hearth Tax returns (HT1 exempt), and had 'Old Widow' [Margaret] Beard living with her. As Margaret had married in 1625, she was now in her late 60s or early 70s, and by 1664 she had been widowed 14 years; she died in August 1668. These housing arrangements, therefore, contributed to the welfare both of those accommodating and of those providing accommodation. John Wilkins senior, tilestriker and

Table 7.1   *Paupers' 'landlords' by Hearth Tax value, April 1664*

HT	name	rental value	Occupation	other
6	Mr Richard Mills	£34	gentleman	O/p '62
5	Richard Woolball	£30	clothier	O/p '63, Chw
5	Alexander Hornsby	£24	yeoman/mercer	'vestry'
?	Richard Holman	£24	(not in HT; bur 1675)	
4	Edmund Crotwell	£20	clothier	
4	William Whitney	£16	(not in reconstr)	
4	Mr John Mills	£5	gentleman	'vestry'
3	Widow Bennet	£22	of yeoman	
3	Richard Bateman	£18	clothier	'vestry'
3	John Iggleden	£9		
2,1x	Thomas Caffinch	£11	butcher	O/p '63
2	John Wilkins jnr	£5	brickmaker	
1	John Willard	£6	clothier	
1	John Chadwick	£4	husbandman	
2x	Richard Lucas	£3	tailor	
1x	John Wilkins snr	£11	brickmaker	
1x	John Burden	n/a		
1x	John Sherwood	n/a	labourer	
1x	Widow Stephens	n/a		

Source: Biddenden Overseers' Account for April 1664

brickmaker, was said to be 88 years old when he died in 1669; he was exempt from tax on a one-hearth house, and consistently had two women staying with him and his aged wife, for which he received ten shillings a half year. The probability is that their lodgers assisted them in their infirmity, providing care in the community, and received housing themselves.[26]

John Sherwood, poor labourer, who in 1664 was living with his wife and child in a one-hearth cottage exempt from tax, received 7s. 6d. from the parish for widow Morgan's rent, but she also appears in the Hearth Tax in an exempt one-hearth house. The implication is that John Sherwood owned both houses, and rented one out via the parish to widow Morgan. She was buried in December 1666, and the overseers' accounts record the standard procedure for the burial of a poor person on the parish. In November she received relief (1s.) and help while she lay sick (2s. 6d.), and in December another 2s. 10d. Then a coffin was provided for her at a cost of 5s., and John Powell the parish clerk was paid 2s. for digging the grave and ringing the knell. Widows Stone and Hovenden, both in receipt of support themselves, were paid 3d. each for 'socking' her and 6d. each for laying her forth and four men were paid to carry her to her grave at a total cost of 1s. 4d.; finally 6d. was paid to 'Wid: Morgans Girle'. The actual burial process cost the parish a little more than 10s.

Table 7.1 shows that householders who lived in large properties also provided accommodation. Richard Woolball, for instance, was a wealthy clothier, who paid on five hearths. He married in 1662, and already in 1664 was being paid rent for Christopher Gutsell, Mercy Barr, Widow Clarke and Joan Pott. Of these, Widow Clarke is recorded as occupying a one-hearth house in March 1664, but the other three do not figure in the Hearth Tax returns, implying that at the time they were lodging with Richard Woolball. Why, one wonders, should a young and wealthy couple, with a baby son, bother with the old and the impoverished?

The answer lies in Richard Woolball's position in the parish. In 1663-64 he was overseer of the poor, and from 1664 to 1667 he was churchwarden for three years. As one holding such offices he was, in a sense, duty bound to take a lead in making provision for the poor. Here was a man who, despite his wealth or because of it, and certainly because of his upbringing, saw it as part of his role in society to be of service to those less fortunate than himself. He also acted as bondsman and witness on many occasions, was parish constable in 1676-7, and was a signatory to church accounts in most years until his death in 1684. The register specifically refers to his brother Peter as 'a very honest religious bachelor'.

Similarly, Mr Richard Mills, Mr John Mills and Alexander Homsby, yeoman, were paid rent by the parish for accommodating paupers in the early 1660s. All three men were closely involved in the running of the parish, had held office during the 1650s and continued to attend meetings and sign accounts. It is no surprise, therefore, to find Richard Dibly (HT6), overseer 1671-2, and John Jennings (HT3), overseer 1678-9, both of them very involved in administration, providing accommodation for the poor later in the decade. These were the sort of men who supported the local free Grammar schools financially, and left money in their wills for distribution to the poor; 25 of the 304 extant wills refer to such legacies, some of them by wealthy widows, with bequests ranging usually from £2 to £5. In one case Edward Stringer, gentleman of Goudhurst, left specified sums totalling £50 to the poor of Goudhurst, Cranbrook, Hawkhurst, Staplehurst, Marden and Horsmonden.[27]

Sometimes help to the needy was occasioned by emergencies, and the most dramatic one of the whole 40 years, for Biddenden, fell in 1667. The register names the 12 individuals who were buried in Bettenham Woods in June of that year having died of the plague: they included three Packhams and their maid Susanna Woolball; three Gutsells who were living in Richard Woolball's house there; and John Chadwick and Mercy Brissenden. Twelve others are reported to have had plague sores but recovered.

The overseers' account shows that the Gutsell and Brunger families both lived in houses in Bettenham Woods, and the area rapidly appears to have become an isolation unit; anyone who showed symptoms of the plague appears to have been sent there to join them. Over the following three months Thomas Mount is recorded frequently as the supplier of meat, and John Mayham, then in his 60s, was paid to take it to the sick in the isolated area: 'a neck of mutton', 'a leg of mutton', 'more beef', 'two necks of veal'. John Marketman, a poor man himself, took 'a bundle of straw in for Goody Brunger', and Mercy Brissenden received milk and butter. These items were paid for by the parish, as were the parishioners who took the awful risk of approaching the Wood.

Over the next two months a continuous flow of food and other goods was taken in, organised by the officers. Robert Sampson was the carpenter paid to make the coffin for Mercy Brissenden, but no other coffins are specifically mentioned; William Day, not a pauper himself, carried in faggots for the use of the sick, and was commissioned to buy a handbarrow to bring the dead bodies out; Mr Thomas Rogers, churchwarden at the time, took responsibility for funeral arrangements. Succour was provided by the parish throughout July, August and September. By October the account can speak of items 'given to the visited at Bettenham Wood', as if contact was now freer, and by November all mention of sickness was over.

The plague incident provides a dramatic example of the parish pulling together for its own protection and attempting to make life reasonable for the sick and dying, but it is an isolated incident on a grand scale. There were similar practical expressions of support for the very poor every month, apart from the provision of cash benefits. In April 1660, for instance, Simon Tanner was paid for masonry work 'about the poors houses'; more comprehensive was the work done on 'Millses house', a cobbler recently deceased, by Thomas Southernden. The overseers were looking to secure its roof in June 1666, and to this end purchased 200 'withs', 200 'priggs', 100 'latts', 'thatch wood', and 'eight cop of straw'. Clothes were a constant need, and readily supplied. In September 1662, for instance, every child in care, and most of the adults, received new shoes. Suits, coats, breeches, waistcoats and petticoats were ordered, made and delivered, as well as kersey or other material for home manufacture. Cards were supplied to enable people to work from home prior to spinning, and wood, in the form of faggots as fuel for cooking, was a costly winter provision for every adult being cared for. Those to be apprenticed normally received a set of new clothes.[28]

Care of Children

One of the most important responsibilities of the parish was the care of orphaned children and those illegitimate children born within the parish who had no declared father. The quarter sessions provide useful insights. For instance, under May 1667, they record how Elizabeth Lackenden of Biddenden accused Richard Clements of Cranbrook, labourer, of repeatedly having 'carnel knowledge' of her at the house of Richard Venos in Biddenden, as a result of which she was pregnant. Subsequently, Martha Morlen of Biddenden, the wife of John Morlen, clothier, who assisted at the birth of the child in September, testified that, in the pain of labour, Elizabeth had confessed that the real father was Thomas Purchen of Biddenden, clothier, and that she freely discharged Richard Clements of all blame. Widow Bristow, acting as midwife, also heard the confession, as did Mildred, wife of William Clarke, clothier of Biddenden. They both bore witness to the truth of Martha Morlen's testimony. The verdict of the justices was that Thomas Purchen was the real father, and that he should pay the churchwardens or overseers of Biddenden 10s. to defray the costs of keeping the child thus far; that he should pay Elizabeth Lackenden a weekly sum of 1s. 2d. towards the child's keep and maintenance for eight years; and that when the child attained the age of eight he should pay £5 for putting it out as an apprentice.[29]

In a male-dominated society this case tells us a lot about relationships. It was the potential mother who accused the supposed father to the justices; women journeyed to Maidstone subsequently to give testimony. The registers indicate that Elizabeth had already had an illegitimate son baptised in January 1665, and went on to have another son, baptised in May 1669, and a daughter, in July 1674. This disgraced mother was nevertheless supported at the birth by a midwife and two women whose husbands, as clothiers, were men of substance in the parish.

The overseers regularly paid out money to villagers who cared for orphaned or illegitimate children, and thereby acted as foster-parents. In the early 1660s in Biddenden, for instance, there were regular payments every month for the support of Pepper's children, Wacher's boy, Potter's children, Eason's girl, Tar's daughter, Fuller's children, Stedman's boy and Gaskin's girl. As a matter of course, and as implied by the quarter sessions judgement above, it was standard practice to care for these children until they were old enough to be apprenticed. Because they were children 'on the parish', that age was low, sometimes as low as eight, more normally ten. Until that time, money was furnished monthly to the people with whom they lived. Thomas Marketman sometimes housed several children at a time; in the latter months of 1662 he was receiving 7s. each for one of Pepper's children, for Wacher's boy, and for Woolball's daughter.

Few of these fostered children were settled with one carer for long. In this respect, the experience of Pepper's three children was not unusual, although their circumstances were. The family does not figure in the reconstitution; one, at least, was an illegitimate child by Laurence Attwood, and their mother abandoned them all early in 1662 and ran away to London. They appear in the overseers' record in December 1661, split two and one, and within two months one had been moved; by April 1662 all three were being housed separately, none with their original carers. They remained settled for the rest of that year except that from October only two were in care because the eldest girl had been apprenticed to Jeremy Coultman, a general handyman, in that month. From March 1663 the second child disappeared from the lists. The remaining child, a boy, changed home three times in 1663 before finding a more settled home with James Willard. He moved to join Goody Sampson in April 1667.

The work of the overseers in providing for children in this way shows concern for those for whom there were no ready guardians or willing kin. It could hardly have brought much profit to those who took the orphans into their homes because the allowance, which ranged from 4s. to 7s. per month, would barely cover the cost of board and lodging. Relief in the form of clothing was provided by the parish, but, for most of the children being farmed out in this way, it must have been a miserable experience, as no doubt they were expected to contribute to the family with whom they were staying by grinding hard work and strict obedience. Much of the accommodation would have been utterly basic. Edward Stone, James Willard, Thomas Marketman and widow Downe, who fostered children in the 1660s, were all living in one-hearth houses on which they were too poor to pay tax. Other carers may well have offered better accommodation: William Whitney, for instance, paid tax on four hearths, Richard Collins and widow Boone on three hearths, widow Salter on two hearths and William Hopper and widow Masters on one hearth. Mary Salter had inherited her two hearths from her husband, who had been a haberdasher; she may well have carried on some sort of retail business as we find her supplying loaves for the Communion Table. Potter's girl, for whom she was receiving 6s. per month in 1664, was with her from the death of her mother Anne in 1658 right through to 1668 and beyond. Similarly, Jane Marrian was fostered by the labourer Thomas Marketman until his death in July 1664, and thereafter she stayed with his widow Mary, for exactly the same fee, until 1668 and beyond. Few, however, were settled with one carer for so long.

Apprenticeship on the Parish

In most years there is record in the Biddenden overseers' accounts of apprenticeships being arranged for children hitherto subsidised by the parish, but the bald statements provide no details. The most intriguing fact to emerge is that the men who took on these orphans as apprentices tended to be either members of the vestry group, or men who anyway worked for the church or the poor as a matter of course.

The churchwardens and overseers were therefore making use of their own people, and helping them in the process.[30] For greater detail one has to turn to the 15 apprenticeship indentures from Frittenden, dated between 1663 and 1699.[31] In each case the two churchwardens and the two overseers of the poor negotiated terms with an individual willing to take on the child, and the arrangement was ratified by two or three of the local justices of the peace. In each case the placement of girls was until the age of 21 or marriage, and of boys until the age of 24. This was a major commitment on the part of the apprentice master; all but two of the eight children for whom the ages are clear were aged 10 or below, the exceptions being 11 and 14 years old. The adult was therefore contracting to take a child into his or her household for at least ten years.

Two probate accounts from other parishes show how difficult the resulting relationship might be. On her husband's death, Joannah Bird of Hawkhurst asked for an allowance of £10 from the estate 'for the maintenance and clothes of Priscilla Harmon, a servant maide whom the said deceased tooke as an apprentice from the parish and is bound to maintayne for a certain time yet to come and she is a very hopeless person and a great charge to this Accomptant'. Thomas Bird was a yeoman farmer, and overseer of the poor of the parish of Hawkhurst at the time of his death.[32] A similarly charitable approach is suggested by the case of Thomazine Austin, 'a lame girl and unfitt for service'. Robert Holnes, clothier of Benenden, had taken her on from the parish; at his death, his widow, Mary Holnes, found herself bound to maintain 'one Thomazine Austen, aged about 14 years ... till she comes to 21 years of age'.[33]

At Frittenden it was the duty of the parish at any one time to have 40 poor children placed with masters who would accommodate them and teach them a trade. A minority (six out of 15) of the placements known were to households within Frittenden, the others being to adjacent or nearby parishes. At least four of these six children had recently been orphaned. Robert Payne, yeoman, took two and John Pullen and John Russell took one each; as churchwardens and leading vestry members they shared responsibility for arranging such placements. Robert Payne and John Pullen also happened to be kin by marriage. The other two masters, Thomas Merchant and William Grayling, were both yeomen with strong family ties to contemporary churchwardens. Within Frittenden, therefore, it was those of yeoman status, with a social conscience like that suggested for Thomas Bird of Hawkhurst above, who took on the responsibility. With the exception of John Russell, who undertook to teach his charge 'to ritt and read', no specific training is mentioned. It is therefore probable that these children were really providing masters with cheap labour or domestic service, as was the common practice for poor-law apprenticeships.[34]

The one clear exception to this practice was the apprenticeship of William Shoesmith, then aged eight, to Thomas Mercer, a Hawkhurst tanner, who undertook to teach and instruct him 'in arte and skill of tanning by the best means he can'. Indeed, the poor Frittenden apprentices who were placed in other parishes may well have fared better in terms of learning a trade; they were taken on by a bricklayer of Cranbrook, broadweavers in Biddenden and Cranbrook, a clothier in Biddenden and by Sir John Henden, the Justice of the Peace. One of the masters, John Shelly of Biddenden, was himself a comparatively poor man, exempt from Hearth Tax on his one-hearth house in 1664, and referred to as a labourer in the indenture. He took on Peter Hyland just after the death of the boy's father, no doubt because his own wife was a Hyland; in this way he received Frittenden parish funds to help to care for his own nephew. In only one case has it been possible to pursue a child beyond the moment of apprenticeship. In the late 1650s, John Caselden was apprenticed to Golding Skinner, yeoman and overseer of the poor at the time. Golding died in 1664. His son, Isaac, in his will dated 1670, left 30s. to 'my servant John Casselden', showing that the 'apprentice' of the 1650s had stayed on as a servant with the family.[35]

As with the Biddenden examples, there was no standard payment for placements, sums ranging from £2 10s. for Sara Hyland and £3 for her brother Peter, to £14 for Stephen Smith and £10 10s. each for the Jennings children. The largest payments tended to be to Frittenden masters; the median payment was £7. Possibly to assist the parish in managing its very limited funds, and possibly to ensure a steady income for the person taking the child into their home, larger payments were not all paid at once. Thus Robert Payne was to receive his £14 in six instalments, with £4 at Easter 1683, and £2 each successive Easter until 1688.

Conclusion

The evidence from the Biddenden overseers' accounts, which echoes very closely that from Cranbrook, Goudhurst and Staplehurst, shows that parish officers took seriously the duty to care for the poorest in their society. It closely parallels Newman Brown's findings in Aldenham, Hertfordshire, for a similar period, where 'the humble officers facilitated agreements and mutual respect between the 'ranks' and 'orders' of parish society'.[36] They were prepared to remove from their locality those who had no claim on them, and equally prepared to use the resources at their disposal to ameliorate the lot of their parishioners. The aged and infirm, especially widows, were consistently supported, and those in need of relief were helped. The poor were encouraged to care for each other, which thereby fed extra resources through to those in need; vestry members helped the poor in a practical way, even to taking them into their homes.[37] This was all the more true when it came to placing young children who had reached the age of 10 or 11; the 'chiefer sort' were willing, not just to provide for, but to accommodate, the indigent. The craftsmen and retailers of the parish contributed by meeting needs, and being paid for their efforts; many of them anyway contributed money through the assessment process.

Lest this should appear to be too rosy a picture, two cases reinforce it. In April 1672 a plea for clemency was made to the Justices by the parishioners of Benenden for the release of Joan Laycock, who had been committed to the 'house of correction' six months earlier. Some of the parishioners who had visited her in gaol certified that she was in 'a very calamitous condition, very sick and lame'. The petition was signed by virtually all the leading parishioners of the time, led by the vicar, Nicholas Monyman. Presumably they were successful as she was buried in Benenden towards the end of the year; all this effort was directed to rescue the single mother of an illegitimate daughter, Ruth, who had been baptised two years earlier.

Six months later the parishioners were back again, this time appealing for the release of James Tampsett, a poor linenweaver of Benenden, from recognizances reimposed by the justices at Maidstone because he had left the court without permission, arguing that, 'being a stranger, from sixteen miles distance, he had no-one to help him'. His supporters spoke of Tampsett's journeys to and fro, which had already cost him dear in time and money, and made the point that this was 'to the great hinderance and damage of himself, his poor wife, and many helpless children'. They closed by certifying that the petitioner 'is a very poor man and hath great charge of wife and children'.

As with the first appeal, the petitioners were again the 'chiefest' parishioners of Benenden, and they were appealing on behalf of a man of lowly position, someone who was buried on the parish in 1699 as 'linenweaver, poor'. Nevertheless, he did have powerful friends. As a legatee of the will of Mary Holnes in 1687, he is referred to as 'my kinsman'; her late husband, Robert Holnes[se], clothier, was signing churchwardens' accounts at the time of this appeal in the early 1670s. This is not just an instance of the great and the good supporting the poor, therefore; it may be an example of kinship, even distant kinship, proving remarkably strong.[38]

Chapter 8

Support across Village Societies

We have now explored in general some of the ways in which different village societies pursued their own social contacts within and beyond the parishes, and have begun to look at ways in which there was interplay between those societies. The time has come now to explore the available evidence more deeply, and see whether the impression of contact across social and economic groups, highlighted by the overseers' work with the poor, is strengthened or weakened in other key moments in the average parishioner's life-cycle.

Allegants, Testifiers and Bondsmen

The normal method of announcing a forthcoming marriage was by the publication of banns, but it was possible for applicants to obtain licences or dispensations which waived this requirement by entering a bond that they had their parents' or guardian's consent.[1] Such consent was standard practice if either the bride or groom was under age. Licences for Cranbrook and its neighbouring parishes 1660-1700 specify the names of 38 allegants or testifiers who confirmed that a person had such consent, and in 143 cases provide the name of a bondsman. When Samuel Bridgeland of Biddenden sought a licence to marry Martha Hopper of Smarden, for instance, allegation was made by his brother James Bridgeland of Cranbrook, clothier; and Vincent Bateman of Biddenden, clothier, acted for his sister Jane in her marriage to Thomas Beeching.

One would expect that the intimate nature of an oath confirming that parents or guardians agreed to a marriage would naturally come from kin of the couple to be married, but this does not appear to have been the case. Only a third of allegants/ testifiers can be shown to have been related to them; relationships by marriage, however, can defy the researcher, and this might account for some of the instances where the link in unknown. Thomas Albourne of Cranbrook, for instance, allegant in the marriage of Richard Hope of Cranbrook to Ann Barham in 1675, happens to have been married to Richard's sister Susanna née Hope.

Sometimes non-kinship links can be deduced. When John Pomfrett, clerk of Biddenden and later rector of Newchurch, sought a licence to marry Elizabeth Rogers, the allegant was also a clerk, Francis Drayton of Tenterden; the link was clearly the Church. Clothiers acted for fellow-clothiers, and also predominate in the list of testators or allegants for whom there is no obvious kin or occupational link; in most of these cases the link would appear to be comparable status, with clothiers acting for gentlemen and yeomen. There are however some strange combinations: it is not clear why John Smither, gentleman of Biddenden, should have been allegant for a husbandman from Biddenden, Thomas Goodwin, or his wife-to-be Mercy Lincke; nor is it easy to explain why the palemaker Robert Wybrow of Staplehurst should have acted as allegant for Richard Doe, an innkeeper. This small sample of allegants and testifiers serves to show that relationships were far more complex than being simply the result of kinship links or even social equals.

Kinship was also the most common link in the choice of bondsmen, but it was far from the only one. Indeed, a fifth of those seeking a licence (28 of 143) seem to have chosen their bondsmen in Canterbury itself. While one can show that in two instances the couple were using an acquaintance who happened to live in Canterbury,[2] it seems more likely that these bondsmen were being asked to perform a ritual process, rather than offering themselves as guarantors because of some long-standing relationship with either the bride or the groom. This impression is confirmed by the identification of four of these bondsmen as Canterbury innkeepers, and a fifth as an ostler. One of the couple seeking the licence was presumably staying in the hostelry for the night and paid those on the spot to act for them. Cowper noticed that such men were 'ready to give a bond for £40, £100 or £200 according to period; and that they had degraded what was intended to be a security into a trade'.[3]

In cases where a link can be established, the majority of bondsmen (40 of 56) were kin to one of the couple, usually a sibling or relative by marriage. Thus when Lucy Kadwell of Rolvenden, daughter of George Kadwell, Esq., J.P., sought a licence to marry Thomas Moyse, tanner of Benenden, her brother Thomas acted as bondsman; and Henry Monyman acted as bondsman when his sister Hannah was licensed to marry Richard Sharpe, gentleman of Benenden. Some kin relationships were more remote. Thomas Post, broadweaver of Biddenden, was bondsman for Ann Buckhurst and James Busse in 1661; both Ann and James had been married before, James to Thomas Post's sister. Sometimes cousins acted as bondsmen; when Michael Barnes of Cranbrook acted for Hannah Couchman the link was a Couchman-Beale marriage and a Beale-Barnes marriage. Possibly most complex of all was a joint application for licences by a mother and daughter. Mary Sceeles, a widow of Biddenden, and her daughter, Sarah Sceeles, still a spinster of 18, both sought licences on the same day. The mother was a Lindridge by birth; a relative, Alexander Lindridge, acted as bondsman for her daughter in her request for a licence to marry William Lanes, while he (William Lanes) acted as bondsman in the licence request for his mother-in-law to be!

Sometimes the kinship link was paralleled with an occupational or status link. Partridge Russell was bondsman for Edward Kingswood in his marriage to Alice Besbeech in 1667; both men were yeomen of Cranbrook as well as being related by marriage, Edward's brother having married Partidge's sister. There was a similar double link between Alexander Burden of Headcorn and Samuel Bayley of Staplehurst when the latter sought to marry Mary Waters of Cranbrook by licence; both men were again yeomen, and kin by marriage.

While kinship accounts for the majority of bondsmen where a link can be established, 16 of the 56 cases suggest an occupational or status link alone. Richard Andrewes, clothier of Staplehurst, acted as bondsman for John Wellars of Staplehurst, clothier, when he sought to marry Anne Hewes of Staplehurst, widow of a clothier; and John Grant of Hawkhurst, millwright, acted as bondsman for Stephen Stephens, miller of Hawkhurst. Similarly, in each of his marriages John Danes, tanner of Staplehurst, had tanners as bondsmen, one from Frittenden (1663) and one from Biddenden (1673) when he married a local tanner's widow.

These occupational links act as a useful reminder that people moved in several different spheres, only one of which was their own kin, and that a close relationship with those who shared the same occupation was only to be expected. Those for whom no obvious link can be identified may be examples of kinship links yet to be established, or simply neighbourhood relationships or friendships established in the course of everyday life. Thomas Freebody, gentleman of Benenden, for instance, sought licence in 1688 to marry Elizabeth Monyman, the vicar's daughter; Richard Hope of Benenden, clothier, who stood as bondsman, was a benefactor of the church and a member of the vestry group, and therefore closely linked with Elizabeth's father. It is also noticeable that three of Thomas' relatives, Richard Freebody, Anne Freebody senior and Ann Freebody junior acted as witnesses to Richard Hope's will in 1691, which may suggest an even closer connection.

Other bondsmen, however, apparently fall outside such naturally-developing groupings. Why, for instance, should a lathmaker, John Yates of Halden, act as bondsman for a Biddenden yeoman, Stephen Chittenden, and Margaret Bayden of Leeds; or a limeburner, Francis Speed of Charing, act for Peter Sharpe, gentleman of Cranbrook and Hannah Wilson, a 21-year-old orphaned spinster from Cranbrook. There is a clear discrepancy between the lathmaker and the yeoman farmer and between the limeburner and the gentleman which, when taken together with the evidence suggesting that bondsmen could be 'picked up' on the spot on arrival in Canterbury, does raise the question of precisely how seriously their role was taken.

Executors and Overseers of Wills

It was almost universal practice for each testator to appoint a close relative, wife or son if possible, as the executor or joint executors of his or her last will and testament. They, it was assumed, would honour the wishes of the deceased. In cases of wills with a great deal of real estate to be settled, or wills complicated by multiple provisions designed to prevent the break-up of the estate subsequent to the deaths of legatees, overseers were also appointed, to supervise the executors of the will; 138 are named. They were persons of considerable social standing, often chosen from kin (41 per cent) or from close friends (36 per cent) or from those simply linked by status or occupation (23 per cent), a pattern which closely parallels Wrightson's findings in Terling.[4]

Thus, for instance, Edward Roades, yeoman of Goudhurst, chose Peter Parris, gent., a kinsman and 'loving friend', and his 'loving friend' John Streater, gent., while John Brissenden, a Biddenden yeoman, chose his 'loving brother' Robert, and his friend, James Harding of Biddenden.[5] Sometimes only one overseer was chosen, as when Jarvice Morlen, yeoman of Benenden, selected his 'loving friend' Richard Igglesden, whereas Richard Hope, a Benenden clothier, had three overseers, all of them kin by marriage.[6] Usually there were two. Isaac Walter the elder, clothier of Cranbrook, chose his two brothers, Abraham and James, to oversee his will, whereas Richard Sharpe, gentleman of Benenden, chose his loving friend Nicholas Monyman, the vicar of Benenden, and the mercer Richard Grant.[7] Alexander Groombridge, the very wealthy Cranbrook yeoman, chose John and Stephen Stringer of Goudhurst to act for him. He left them £5 each 'as an earnest of his love'; such a gesture was not uncommon, usually accompanied by some such phrase as 'for their pains' in carrying out their duties.[8] In practice it appears that, in choice of overseer, *gravitas* was deemed as important a quality as kinship, and that close friendship was also very important.

Table 8.1 shows that kinship links covered the whole spectrum, from son to the generic 'kin', with a preponderance of brothers and brothers-in-law. Members of the nuclear family played little part in this role, but, as most executors came from the nuclear family, the overseer had to be at one step removed. It is also noticeable that in-laws and kin provided that detachment which the testator required.

Table 8.1   *Kin-relationship of overseers to testators, Cranbrook region, 1660-99*

nuclear family	wives, sons	2	3.6%
at one remove	brothers, sisters	14	25.0%
at two removes	uncles	1	1.8%
in-laws	brothers-, sisters-, sons-	19	33.9%
kin	cousins, kindred	20	35.7%

The proportion of 'friends' was almost as high as the proportion of kin involved in the overseeing process, and the fairly constant repetition of the epithet 'loving' in terms of these friends serves to reinforce the importance of relationships outside the purely family ones. In terms of status such friends were almost invariably on a par with, or slightly higher than, the testator himself. Thus yeomen and clothiers tended to use other yeomen or clothiers, or gentlemen, as their overseers, while the Biddenden butcher William Ellis used Robert Wood, another butcher, and John Carley, a Biddenden victualler, used William Beale, the local mercer.[9] Rather less than a quarter of the overseers of wills neither had an obvious kin relationship with the testator, nor were referred to as friends.

The case of Stephen Langford hints at other links. He was a relatively humble Cranbrook weaver, paying tax on one hearth in 1664; he made his dear and loving wife Elizabeth executor of his last will and testament, and because there were no children of the marriage, the children of his brothers and sisters were to benefit.

He entrusted the task of selling his land, and helping his wife with her affairs, to two Cranbrook clothiers, Mr Harman Sheafe and Josias Colvill.[10] Harman Sheafe, who figures in the Heralds' Visitations of 1663-8, was a very wealthy and influential man in Cranbrook, assessed on eight hearths, which might reflect his ownership in the 1660s of *The Bell Inn*. Josias Colvill was taxed on a five hearth house and had married Sibilla Boys, daughter of the Hawkhurst Justice of the Peace of the previous generation, who paid on 21 hearths. Stephen Langford, therefore, was so far below the social standing of these two men that one wonders how he could consider asking them to act on his family's behalf.

Two clues present themselves. Langford's probate account shows that his total assets amounted to £18 11s. after debts and expenses had been paid, and confirms his comparative poverty while indicating that he was not in penury.[11] When his wife died two months later, Josias Colvill took on her role as executor and administrator of Stephen's estate. It is probable that Stephen Langford had been one of the broadweavers to whom Josias Colvill had farmed out work, and that the clothier was fulfilling his Christian duty of caring for his worker's affairs after death; he certainly acted as witness to other weavers' wills. Such charitable roles have already been met (pages 105 and 138). It is also apposite that John Colvill, Josias' brother, was a leading Quaker and that he and his brothers shunned baptism, as did his wife's family. Harman Sheafe, the other overseer, had actually been imprisoned at the Restoration because of his nonconformist sympathies.[12] Although there is nothing to link Stephen Langford with nonconformist tendencies, it may well be that Josias Colvill's approach reflected both Christian virtues and care of a fellow nonconformist.

That shared nonconformity could be a powerful link in choice of overseer is borne out by the case of Stephen Bennett, Quaker supporter and yeoman of Staplehurst. He appointed his well-beloved friends, Thomas Scoones and Robert Kite, as overseers of his last will and testament.[13] Scoones was a Staplehurst bricklayer who, together with his two brothers, occupied land belonging to Thomas Burren, whose brother Peter's house was licensed as a nonconformist meeting house in 1672; Kite was a prosperous Staplehurst mercer (he paid tax on six hearths) whose house was used as the Quaker meeting place in the period before 1680. The nonconformist link, therefore, was an important factor binding individuals together in mutual support (page 186).

Will Witnesses

Thus far we have seen that kin, friendship, shared occupation and common religious persuasion all featured in varying degrees of importance as relationships which led people to support each other in seeking marriage licences and selecting those who were to be responsible for their affairs after death. Another area, and one which has received considerable scholarly analysis in recent years, is the relationship between testators and those invited to witness their signatures. It has been suggested that, at a time when individuals were often under considerable emotional strain with death approaching, 'testators generally selected their witnesses quite deliberately, basing their choices upon personal friendship and social respect'.[14] Others, while accepting that viewpoint, would caution that 'very occasionally, an odd witness was merely a passer-by pressed into helping', and that, at least for the parish they were examining, 'it was not only kin but neighbours who joined together across very substantial economic divides in the intimate circumstances of death and inheritance'.[15]

Table 8.2   Cranbrook region; testators by occupation as known, 1660-99

gentlemen	25	clothiers	32	yeomen/graziers	90
manufacture	17	husbandry	14	wives/widows	45
retail	12	craftsmen	38	bachelors/others	9
spinsters	8			[total 290]	

The 304 wills from the Cranbrook area parishes for 1660-1700 show that the testators' signing and sealing was normally witnessed by three individuals, but there are instances of four witnesses, two witnesses and, in four cases, just one witness. There are therefore 304 wills with 862 witnesses, most of whom can be identified. They show that, while there is evidence for kin relationships in the will-witnessing process, kinship was not the main criterion in choosing witnesses, and such relationships were sometimes remote. Peter Henden, for example, clothier (sometimes 'gentleman') of Benenden, had three witnesses, each of them on a social standing approximating to his own. They were John Saxby, a newly-married yeoman of Cranbrook, his wife Martha, and Elizabeth Silcock, wife of a wealthy grazier (sometimes 'gentleman') of Tenterden; Elizabeth alone was kin, a Sharpe by birth and therefore related to the testator by marriage in the previous generation.[16]

When it comes to Isaac Walter senior, a Cranbrook clothier, his choice of witnesses may betray the place where his will was signed.[17] He selected John Boorman, either the clothier of Cranbrook or the beerbrewer 'of the Town'; Thomas Weller, clothier and innkeeper of the *George Inn* at Cranbrook at least from 1660 to 1673; and Richard Kilburne, Esq., of Hawkhurst, author, lawyer, justice of the peace and one of the leading thinkers and writers of his day. The likelihood is that these men witnessed Isaac's will at the *George* rather than at his house, especially as the justices used to hold their petty sessions there.[18]

The majority of wills, however, display a mixture of social levels among the witnesses which supports the proposition that people co-operated across the social and economic spectrum. It is especially remarkable that, in many wills made by those at the lower end of the social scale, one at least of the witnesses was of high standing. Thomas Munn, a Cranbrook woollendraper,[19] had as witnesses Thomas Weston, clothier, and Samuel Birchet, gentleman. Susanne Hubbard was merely the servant of a Biddenden weaver, Thomas Kemp, but her mark was witnessed by Robert Drayner, clothier and gentleman, a man who paid tax on eight hearths. The link here,

Vera Effigies Richardi Kilburne Armigeri : : Topographiæ Cantianæ Authoris : : Ætatis suæ 52 · 24 · Septemb 1657 · J. Crose sculp

23. Line engraving (1659) by Thomas Cross of Richard Kilburne Esq. of Hawkhurst, Justice of the Peace, lawyer and author of *A Survey of Kent.*

however, is known; Thomas Kemp was Robert Drayner's tenant, a nice example of a landowner doing his tenant a favour.[20] James Willard, a Biddenden labourer, had his will witnessed by Thomas Stede, gentleman, together with Stephen Colvill who could not write his name. Similarly, John Godsmer of Biddenden, a bricklayer, had as witnesses the rector, a clothier and a lawyer.[21] Conversely, Margaret Pattenson, a wealthy yeoman's widow from Biddenden, included James Tapley, the local glazier, and Robert Foster, the local carpenter, among her will witnesses. Maybe they were doing some work for her about the house when she came to write her will?[22]

Oral wills are useful for shedding light on how witnesses to wills were chosen. When William Silke the surgeon visited William Woodwin of Cranbrook, he was told that his patient had not made a will. John Ballard and widow Elizabeth Ballard, relatives of the patient's wife, were summoned, and they, together with the doctor, witnessed the deposition.[23] This surgeon neatly matches Margaret Spufford's category of 'passer-by'. John Buckland of Staplehurst died 'at the home of Mary Alday, widow, where he then lodged' before he could make his will. He entrusted his last wishes to Thomas Smith the schoolmaster, Mary Alday his landlady, Ann Weller, probably the wife of John Weller of Staplehurst, and Tobias Ferrall who does not figure in the reconstruction. Where the last two of this hastily assembled congregation came from cannot be told, but the presence of Mary Alday, who witnessed with her mark, shows a willingness, or necessity, to use people who happened to be on site.[24]

Using as a witness someone who happened to be in the house at the time of the signing of the will was a common practice in the Cranbrook area at this time. Joseph Paule, for instance, a gentleman of Hawkhurst paying tax on five hearths, used two wealthy neighbours, clothiers of almost comparable standing each paying on four hearths, to witness his will together with Mary Badcock 'my now servant', who made her mark.[25] The witnesses for Samuel Morlen, yeoman of Benenden, were John Cooper, the vicar of Cranbrook, together with his wife Jane, and Rose Juge who made her mark.[26] Rose Juge does not figure in the reconstitution, and was probably a servant in Samuel's household. Just so, Elizabeth Shereings of Cranbrook used her maid Judith Cecil to make her mark.[27] If these were isolated cases one might assume a special relationship between master and servant, but the evidence is that such crossing of the social divide was standard practice.

Because the burial registers give the date of burial of almost every one of the 304 testators, and most of the wills provide the date on which they were written, one can see that few parishioners anticipated their death by more than a year or two, and many left the will-making process until the last moment, possibly fearing to tempt providence.[28] Most parishioners, in fact, died intestate. Because burial was normally between three and five days after death (page 5), wills written less than ten days before the testator's burial were in effect death-bed wills. Of the extant wills, 56 (18 per cent) were made on, or virtually on, the testator's deathbed. In such circumstances one might expect a certain haste about the writing and witnessing process, but that does not necessarily mean that preferred witnesses were not present. These wills account for only a marginally higher than average number of witnesses who were unable to write. The most remarkable example of a rushed will is that of the Cranbrook brickmaker, Richard Boorman, who wrote it on 20 April and was buried on 24 April.[29] He made his mark, which was duly witnessed by his kinswoman, Susan, 'by her mark', and by Robert Iney, 'by his mark'!

The majority of testators were not on their death-beds when they made their wills, and were therefore presumably able to invite in as witnesses those whom they wished to have present. This included professionals. Yet 161 witnesses (19 per cent) ratified the testator's will with a mark; in other words almost a fifth of the witnesses in the sample were unable to write their names. In a prosperous region, and with most testators literate, this is too high a proportion to suggest that all will witnesses were normally friends, or kin, or on an equal social footing with the testators. Even allowing for the fact that wills made in haste on the death-bed account for 37 of these 161 witnesses, it still leaves 124 illiterate witnesses who were presumably chosen at leisure and for good reason.

Some parishioners were serial will-witnesses; in this the Cranbrook evidence parallels that found recently at St Albans.[30] Four men between them signed 82 (27 per cent) of the 304 wills. One specialised in Hawkhurst, one in Goudhurst, one in Cranbrook, and one largely dealt with Biddenden. Thomas Curtis, gentleman and attorney-at-law from Biddenden, featured in 33 wills between 1659 and 1692, mostly from his own parish but also from Cranbrook [4], Benenden [3] and Frittenden [6]. He also figures very largely in the probate accounts of the parishioners of Biddenden, wrote inventories for leading Biddenden yeomen, and was owed payment for 'journeying to make the will' of Thomas Dive of Benenden.[31] He worked closely with Jeremy Botting, the foremost lender of money on bond in the area (page 178), and no doubt formulated the legal documents which accompanied such transactions. His legal training must have greatly benefited prosperous householders when they bequeathed their lands and houses but he also witnessed the will of a bricklayer, a weaver and a husbandman, and acted as scribe for the wills with which he was associated. He was present as a will witness because of his legal skills.

Samuel Birchet of Cranbrook, another gentleman and attorney-at-law,[32] witnessed 25 of the 304 wills, almost exclusively for his fellow parishioners. His presence was also as a professional; for instance, on her death in May 1671 Mary Friend's brother James paid Sam. Birchett 2s. 6d. for 'drawing up the deceased's will into form'.[33] The other two men who each witnessed ten or more wills were John Foord of Hawkhurst, who accounted for 14 of the 30 wills from that parish, and James Besbeech who witnessed 10 of the 22 from Goudhurst. John Foord was the local schoolmaster and James Besbeech a gentleman. Others, like John Avery of Cranbrook and John Barnden, the Cranbrook parish clerk who was also a very frequent witness to burial in woollen, witnessed several wills, and one can be sure they were present to help with writing them and apportioning property rather than because of any family or purely neighbourly relationship. Schoolmasters were generally in demand, with Thomas Smith of Staplehurst and Robert Hatley of Cranbrook covering another ten wills between them, and John Streater of Goudhurst, who appended 'scriptor' after his name, another five. These men were present as part of the will-making process rather than as kin, friends or neighbours.

Others were also present for professional reasons at the time of the making of wills, and happened to be witnesses. Thus John Relfe and William Silke each witnessed wills on more than one occasion; in their roles as physician and 'chirurgeon' they were present to tend the dying, and therefore on the spot. In at least 114 (37.5 per cent) of the wills, therefore, one witness was simply there for professional or semi-professional reasons.

One can therefore conclude that, while kinship, personal friendship and social respect were considerations when testators invited people to witness their wills, there was also a major category of will witnesses who were present at the signing because there was business to be done; these were mainly the lawyers and writers of wills. Nor were witnesses necessarily important or relatively important people in the testator's life; too many were present at the process simply because they were part of the household as servants or apprentices, and, because of the extreme haste in which some wills had to be completed, witnesses were called in almost from the highways and byways. It is not possible to see any discrete religious groupings among will witnesses; the evidence for specifically nonconformist groupings is there, but, whenever one delves further, their exclusivity melts away. What comes over most strongly is that there clearly was co-operation across social and economic divisions. In example after example one finds a remarkable mix of social status among the three or four witnesses to any will. Not only did wealthy members of the community witness will-signing by their much poorer neighbours, but comparatively poor, not to say illiterate, parishioners joined the social and economic *élite* to witness their signatures.

Witnesses to Burial in Woollen

Further insight into inter-relationships is provided by the detailed register of burials in woollen maintained by the Rector of Frittenden, Robert Newton, from 1 August 1678 to 8 April 1696.[34] Newton was meticulous about securing a certificate to establish that every deceased person in his parish had been buried 'according to the requirements of the Act' (page 4). The first two certificates hint at the complexity of the relationships within and across local parish boundaries which such a simple bureaucratic exercise might entail:

> September 15th 1678: That then a Certificate was brought to me under the hand of Sr. John Henden Kt, Justice of the Peace &c. that the said Mris Dorothy Bayly was buried in woolen according to ye aforesaid Act wch was testified upon oathe by John Whitfeild of Biddenden and Robert Freebody of Frittenden

> Novemb: 7th Mem. Then a Certificate was brought to me under the hand of Richard Kilborne Esq that the said Mr Thomas Cox [citizen of London] was buried according to the aforesaid Act, wch was testified upon oath by Lucy Mishingham of ye parrish of Cranbrooke, and under

24. The signatures of three justices of the peace open the page, ratifying the entries of the previous year, and there follow entries for 1683 in Robert Newton's immaculate script. CKS P152/1/1

the hands and seales of Elizabeth Thunder of Cranbrook and Thomas Bourner of Frittenden.

These first two Frittenden affidavits alone involved five different parishes. In terms of socio-economic groupings they covered a very wide spectrum from the two justices of the peace, busy and important men living in very large houses (25 and 12 hearths respectively), via two gentlemen of substance, both of whom paid tax on seven hearths, to a member of a clothworker's family (Missingham) and a carpenter (Bourner) each of whom was exempt from tax on a one-hearth house.

Table 8.3 provides an insight into the complexity of cross-parish communication generated by this one small requirement. It also shows that for the first eight years of the operation of the Act it was the justice of the peace Sir John Henden who bore the brunt of the workload. During that time there were 98 Frittenden burials of which 52 passed through Sir John's hands for certification. The fact that during those same years, in his own parish of Biddenden, 203 burials took place most of which would presumably have come to him, makes clear just what a vast amount of paperwork was generated by the Act. From the early 1680s, however, certification passed increasingly from the justices to the local clergy, working for each other, until by 1686/7 they had taken over the role completely.

Table 8.3   *Sources of affidavits for burial in woollen, Frittenden, 1678-96*

name	parish	office	period of responsibility	number of mentions
Sir John Henden	Biddenden	JP	1678-86	52
Richard Kilburne Esq.	Hawkhurst	JP	1678	1
Samuel Boys Esq.	Hawkhurst	JP	1679	1
Sir Francis Clearke	(Boughton Malherbe ?)		1680	1
Walter Pemble Esq (Major)	Tenterden		1689	1
Samuel Whetstone	Headcorn	vicar	1681-95	28
Stephen Sowton	Staplehurst	rector	1681-83	3
Joseph Crowther [a]	Staplehurst	rector	1686-96	17
Charles Buck	Cranbrook	vicar	1682-92	15
Dr Giles Hinton [b]	Biddenden	rector	1685-96	11
John Pomfret [c]	Newchurch	rector	1688-96	7
Thomas Crowther	Newchurch	curate	1692	1
and again	Cranbrook	curate	1693-95	6
Benjamin Hollinsworth	Staplehurst	curate	1692-93	5
John Davies	Staplehurst	curate	1685	2
Benjamin Horner	Rolvenden	vicar	1683	1
Abraham Walter	Tenterden	curate	1683	1
George Amhurst	Marden	vicar	1695	1
James Mede	Bobbrisden (?)	curate	1695	1

Notes: The person before whom the affidavit was sworn is specified in 155 of 179 burials.
[a] Joseph Crowther took over from Stephen Sowton in August 1684;
[b] Giles Hinton, appointed to Biddenden 1681, in effect took over from Sir John Henden in 1685/6;
[c] John Pomfret, although the incumbent at Newchurch, lived in Biddenden.

25. Another page of affidavits for burial in woollen, this time ratified by two justices, 1687. (CKS P152/1/1)

Affidavits were invariably ratified by the local justice or one of Newton's fellow Anglican ministers, all of whom belonged to the upper levels of village society, but usually three other people were involved in the process. They were the person who swore the oath before the justice or the minister, that the deceased had been buried in woollen, and two others who simply witnessed that swearing process. The oath-takers had to have been present at the preparation of the body for burial or at the burial itself, while the other two merely witnessed that the oath had been taken; they did not need to have been present at the funeral.

One might expect that those taking the oath would be relatives of the deceased person, like Margery Burden who testified to the burial of Martin Burden, widower and poor inhabitant of Frittenden. Of the 112 records which provide the names of these people, however, only 22 can be identified as definitely kin of the deceased, and most of them were parents acknowledging the proper burial of their children. In fact most of the remaining oath-takers were women, and, as we have seen (page 138), it was standard practice for poor women of the parish to prepare bodies for burial; the younger Samuel Bayly of Cranbrook, in compiling the probate account for his father, notes 'to two women for laying the said deceased forth, two shillings'.[35] Margery Burden, mentioned above, figures as oath-taker on six other occasions, and was herself buried as a 'poor single woman'. She is typical of the pauper earning a pittance by such work while yet being entrusted with the swearing of the oath before the justice or the vicar.

Margery Burden was far from alone in appearing as 'oath-taker' more than once. Martha Burton, mother of a base-born child, figures five times, as does Rebecca Caffinch who reported each time to the rector of Cranbrook; Anne Drayner of Frittenden appears five times, Katherine Leaper of Frittenden seven times, and Katherine Saxby of Frittenden seven times. In all cases these women, and/or their husbands, can be identified in the reconstitution as paupers being supported on the parish.

Not all who swore the oath fit into this picture. Mary Ellis, for instance, swore the oath for Thomas Brooker, a widow's son, in 1683 at a time when her husband was churchwarden. Henry Bourner, the carpenter, or his wife or other members of the family, swore the oath on eight occasions between 1679 and 1689, no doubt enabled to do so because Henry was making the coffins. In the case of a child of William Waterhouse, it was Ann Amhurst, the wife of the vicar of Marden, who took the oath. Nevertheless there is a clear pattern whereby the oath was sworn either by the parents in the case of the death of infants or very young children, or by those poor women of the parish who earned a meagre remuneration by tending to the bodies of the dead.

The status of those who witnessed the taking of the oath is more consistent. In 48 cases before Sir John Henden one of the witnesses was Richard Greenway. In 18 of those 48 cases the co-witness was Thomas Murgin or Morgan, and in another 13 cases it was Richard Finch. Greenway and Murgin do not feature in the reconstitution, but a Mr Richard Finch did settle down and start a family in Biddenden before the turn of the century. Justices of the peace commonly had clerks, and there can be little doubt that these witnesses were members of Sir John Henden's staff who were customarily called upon to perform such tasks; as such they would not necessarily feature in the registers.[36] By the 1680s, with Anglican ministers taking over the role from the justices, their wives (and occasionally other members of the family) witnessed the oaths: Elizabeth and Dorcas for Charles Buck in Cranbrook, Dorothy for Giles Hinton in Biddenden, Elizabeth for Samuel Whetstone in Headcorn, Jane for John Pomfret in Newchurch and Grace for Joseph Crowther in Staplehurst.

The deceased who were the occasion for these oaths to be sworn came mainly from Frittenden but some were brought from Staplehurst, Headcorn, Biddenden and even Rye in Sussex. Many witnesses lived in Frittenden, but even more lived in the parish of the incumbent to whom application for the oath was made. One such was John Barnden, the parish clerk of Cranbrook, who witnessed to the oath for seven individuals, in each case before Charles Buck the vicar; all seven were Frittenden residents. Elizabeth Bayley probably lived in Headcorn; she acted as witness to the oath for six Frittenden people before Samuel Whetstone between November 1682 and March 1683. So close was the relationship across the parish borders between Frittenden and Headcorn, and Staplehurst and Frittenden, that several families quite clearly spanned the parishes. In the Cranbrook region, parish boundaries were no bar to social or any other intercourse.[37]

Appraisers of Probate Inventories

The appraisal of the goods and chattels of a deceased person was the responsibility of the executor or executrix, or, in cases of intestacy, of the next of kin, a tutor or curator of any minors, or the principal creditor, appointed by letters of administration. They chose the appraisers. By identifying appraisers in Cranbrook area parishes we can draw further conclusions about social interaction in the region, and judge to what extent the region matches the accepted pattern: that appraisers tended to be creditors, legatees or next of kin, or, failing that, 'two honest men', who provided the expertise to value different parts of the estate and to write up the inventory. 'Inventories were usually made carefully, and the goods valued appropriately.'[38]

Probate accounts occasionally provide an insight into the inventory process. Rebecca Dive, relict of the Benenden yeoman Thomas Dive, simply paid 'Mr Springet and Simon Neeve for apprizing the deceased's goods, 8s.'.[39] The former was either George or Stephen Springate whose family, like the Dives, was traditionally involved in parish offices; the latter was the local blacksmith who consistently did work around the church. By contrast, the task facing Thomas Yorkton and Thomas Kipping, principal creditors and administrators of the estate of Robert Kite, the Staplehurst grocer, was a far more complex one, with 'to John Leigh, 5s., to Robert Delton, 15s., to Edward Baker 10s., for their paines and trouble in apprizing the said testator's goods, the same consisting in wares that took up much time'. They also paid Thomas Smith, the local schoolmaster, 9s. for 'copying out the names of the said Testator's debtors in two parts and for writing', and for 'attending a whole day at the sale of the said testator's goods'.[40]

Although the Cranbrook evidence generally supports the contention that the inventory and valuation were done with great care, one case proves to be an exception. Robert Ware was tutor and curator of his nephew, the son of Solomon Ware, husbandman and miller of Cranbrook, and therefore responsible for the probate account. He accused the appraisers, Thomas Bayly, Robert Marchant, John Chamberlain and John Ferrall, of over-valuing stock 'though the accomptant did his best'! He then itemised the losses incurred on the sale of 12 acres of wheat; on parcels of oats, pease, barley, hops, malt and tares; on livestock including horses; on the timber, the plough, the wagon and 'other husbandry tackle'; and on debts especially desperate debts.[41] As a result, Robert managed to persuade the court to reduce the appraisers' valuation from £570 19s. 9d. to £509 1s. 2d. Thomas Bayly was almost certainly the Goudhurst clothier and Robert Marchant was certainly from Goudhurst and a husbandman and contemporary of Solomon Ware; the implication is that the deceased had fields, and maybe stock, in Goudhurst. John Ferrall was a Cranbrook butcher who should have been able to appraise the stock accurately; John Chamberlain's identity is less certain, maybe from Cranbrook, maybe from Goudhurst.

By the 1660s, in the Cranbrook area, it was standard practice for two men to appraise the property of the deceased, with on occasions three or even four or five, and, very rarely, one, in which case he was invariably a relative and executor. The central decades of the 1670s and 1680s provide a sample of 510 inventories, and overseers' and churchwardens' accounts give a fair picture of the vestrymen of three of the parishes. The resultant analysis of the relationship between the appraisers and the deceased in these parishes can be seen in Table 8.4. This shows that there were occasions when kin helped with the inventory process. Alex Groombridge, for instance, assessed the goods of his father-in-law Isaac Walter, working with the clothier Thomas Weston, who carried out many other appraisals in Cranbrook. William Burden, with Richard Cryer, appraised the goods of John Basden who had married Agnes Burden; William Tilden of Staplehurst helped appraise his father's goods, and Richard Woolball alone appraised those of his son Peter, as did William Pix of Hawkhurst for the few belongings of his own father, also William. Such kinship contacts, however, appear in only a small minority of the inventories analysed.

Table 8.4 *Relationship between appraisers of inventories and deceased*

	No. of deceased	of whom vestry link	of whom kin link	No. of appraisers	of whom vestry link	No. from elsewhere
Benenden	28	8 (29%)	7 (25%)	69	44 (63%)	19 (28%)
Biddenden	36	8 (22%)	5 (14%)	73	44 (60%)	16 (22%)
Cranbrook	67	24 (36%)	9 (13%)	158	107 (68%)	19 (12%)

Note: kin represents a minimum figure. The pattern from the other parishes cannot be analysed as precisely, but mirrors the pattern in these three parishes.

Some occupational links present themselves. John Standen appraised the property of John Coleman: they were both blacksmiths. Similarly Simon Vredge, a cordwainer and himself a kinsman, and Henry Stephenson, a leatherdresser, appraised the goods of the cordwainer Richard Wood, of Cranbrook, and were joined in this process by Aaron Bowyer, barber/ gentleman, and Alexander Rimington, clothier/yeoman. One would expect yeomen, clothiers and gentlemen to be able to value goods in the house, in the yard and in the barn, and to put an accurate price on stock and crops in the field; they were all intimately connected with farming.

What is remarkable, however, is that a far higher proportion of appraisers than of the deceased themselves came from those who ran the parishes by supplying the churchwardens and overseers of the poor; in other words, appraisal was more a matter of status than of family relationship. The pattern is exemplified especially by the way in which individuals seemed almost to specialise in the appraisal process, even though, in some cases, they appear to have had little relevant expertise. In the following samples, HT indicates, where known, the numbers of hearths on which individuals were assessed for tax, and therefore gives some idea of their wealth.

In Benenden Nicholas Monyman, the vicar, was regularly involved, presumably as a concerned person of impeccable character; he figures in four appraisals between

1670 and 1679, three of them with Richard Iggleden (HT5), gent., and between 1680 and 1689 he appears another eight times together with other appraisers, Iggleden having died in 1679. Richard Iggleden himself carried out seven appraisals in the 1670s, in each case with vestry members as partners; in the second decade, Samuel Hunt and John Springett, took over much of the appraisal duty. In Biddenden the lead was taken by Richard Beale, clothier (HT4, 12 times), John Whitfield, gent. (HT7, 8 times), and Anthony Pigott (HT3, 8 times) between 1670 and 1689; John Jennings, cooper (HT3, 11 times) became increasingly involved latterly. In Cranbrook between 1670 and 1679 the main appraisers were Thomas Weston, clothier (HT3, 10 times), and Stephen Osborne, yeoman (8 times); several individuals like John and Alex Groombridge (the latter HT16, yeoman); John Avery (HT4); Robert Wood, butcher (HT3); Thomas Buttery, mercer (HT3); and William Peachy, gent., all carried out several appraisals. In the following decade Stephen Osborne figured in another seven appraisals, with Peter Couchman, clothier (HT4) and Richard Crottal, clothier (HT2) appearing five times each.

The pattern is repeated in the other parishes. In Frittenden, Thomas Kingswood, yeoman (HT2) appears five times, and Francis Cornwell (HT6), Nathaniel Taylor, yeoman (HT3), and Thomas Amery, clothier (HT4), three times each. Of these, Francis Cornwall was actually 'of Staplehurst', but the two parishes were very closely linked, and he appraised there as well (for his nonconformist links see page 184ff). In Staplehurst itself, the bulk of the appraisals of the 1670s were carried out by Edward Osborne, yeoman (HT3, 4 times, who died in 1672), John Stephens, yeoman (HT6, 5 times, died 1677) and Thomas Amery of Frittenden. In the 1680s, Richard Bridgland, clothier (HT3, 4 times), David Austen, yeoman (HT4, 4 times) and Peter Burren, clothier (HT8, 5 times) appear most frequently. In Hawkhurst, several parishioners appear several times, like John Springett, yeoman (HT3, 4 times), Thomas Mercer, clothier (HT4, 9 times), Robert Wakeline (3 times) and latterly John Foord (HT2, 4 times). In Goudhurst, John Streater, gent. (HT4, 10 times), John Groombridge (HT4, 8 times) and Thomas Bayly, clothier (4 times), feature most frequently over the two decades.

These 'chiefer sort' not only carried out the appraisal process for their own kind, the yeomen, clothiers and others of substance in the parish and their widows, but they also provided a similar 'service' for those of lesser status. For instance, John and Robert Leigh, both gentlemen, and the young newly-wed clothier Richard Hewes (or his father), all of them members of the Cranbrook vestry, appraised the goods and chattels, valued at £20, of the carpenter William Wenman; and Richard Hewes and Alexander Groombridge similarly dealt with the property of the woolcomber, William Brown. Indeed, Table 8.5 shows how these influential men took on the role of assessing the goods of those with the lowest valuation.

Finally one should note that, not infrequently, appraisers travelled from other parishes. Simon Evernden, clothier of Benenden (HT2), came to Cranbrook to appraise the goods of Richard Acton, clothier (HT6), joining James Parton, clothier (HT6) for the purpose; Simon had a kinship link as well as an occupational one. James

Parton went to Biddenden to appraise the goods of John Mantle, clothier (HT3), with Andrew Hills, clothier of Biddenden (HT5). In some cases the nonconformist bond was at work in determining appraisers.

Table 8.5   *Appraisal of the poorest in the parishes, Cranbrook region, 1660-99*

year	deceased	parish	£	occup	appraiser 1	appraiser 2
1672	John Hickmott	Hawk	2		Edward Batcheller, yeo	
1679	Thomas Newman	Ben	3	servant	Walter Jones, mercer, HT4	
						Francis Smith
1684	John Bennett	Hawk	3		Will Whatman, mercer HT5	
1683	John Piper	Hawk	4		Will Whatman, mercer HT5	
						Peter Crothall, clo. HT6
1671	William Marsh	Cra	6		Will March	
						John Munn, broadw
1676	Joan Warren	Hawk	6	widow	Edw. Plum, HT3	
						Andrew Skynner (chwd)
1684	Edward Couchman	Hawk	6	clothier	John Stone	
						John Evans, HT4
1670	Peter Walter	Goud	7	broadw	Edward Sibly	
						Thomas Kingsmill
1670	Peter Woolball	Bid	8	16 yrs	Richard Woolball, father	
1675	William Austen	Cra	9	broadw	William Parton	
						Fred. Couchman clothier
1672	Goodgift Matthews	Ben	10	widow	John Tharpe	
						Richard Illenden
1675	John Kadwell	Bid	10	servant	John Jennings, cooper	
						Rob Stedman, black, HT2
1675	Samuel Newman	Hawk	10	husb	John Springett, yeo HT3	
						Peter Crothall, clo. HT6

Kinship played a part, to a greater or lesser extent, in the process of choosing testators and legatees, of arranging apprenticeships and looking for bondsmen, but friendship, and identity of occupation and religion also played their part in such selections. What cannot be gainsaid is that, no matter which of these various areas one looks at, the evidence shows that there was support across the socio-economic spectrum at every turn. Servants witnessed their master's wills and the wealthy witnessed those of the poor; the wealthy carried out appraisals for the least wealthy parishioners and appear to have seen it as part of their right, or duty.

Chapter 9

Borrowing and Lending Money

The Wider Context

Over the last few decades it has become increasingly clear that, by the mid-17th century, the borrowing and lending of money was already a fully-developed feature even in relatively remote rural areas like the Cranbrook region.[1] The picture in Kent has recently been clarified by exploitation of the county's rich deposit of probate accounts, showing that 'Kentish, and indeed English, rural society at large was penetrated through and through with habits of formal borrowing and lending in the period immediately before the emergence of a country banking system there, and had been since at least the 1620s'.[2] The Cranbrook evidence confirms that being in debt was increasingly part of the way of life in Kent;[3] Table 9.1 shows that, by the post-Restoration period, 90 per cent of those with probate accounts were dying with debts, described as such, to be paid. A proportion of those debts was secured formally by 'specialty'.

Table 9.1 *Comparative analysis of types of debts from probate accounts*

	east Kent	Cranbrook
total of accounts	13586	234
dates	1569-1740	1660-1699
% with stated debts	81	90
% with 10+ debts	19	36
% with 20+ debts	4	14
% with specialty debts (a)	27	44.2
% with debts on bond	25.6	43.8
median no. of debts left	3	6

Source: Spufford, P. (2000) 215
Note: Because the Cranbrook percentages concentrate towards the end of Spufford's period one would expect them to be higher.
(a) Specialty includes bond, bill, book and mortgage, as well as the term 'specialty'.

The pattern of indebtedness of people in the Cranbrook region was very similar to that found by Muldrew among their near contemporaries in Hampshire (Table 9.2). There, in probate accounts dating between 1623 and 1715, 14 per cent of specified debts were for formal loans on bill or bond, whereas for Cranbrook the equivalent figure was 12.5 per cent; the figure derived from inventories is 13 per cent.[4]

Table 9.2   Debts: comparative figures, Hampshire and the Cranbrook region

	Hampshire 1623-1715		Cranbrook region 1660-1699	
sales credit, services, work done	1006	74%	1677	74%
bills and bonds	193	14%	285	12.5%
rents	90	7%	193	8.5%
wages	51	4%	49	2%
tithes	5		62 (a)	3%
mortgages	4		2	
heriots	3		7	
Total	1352		2275 (b)	

Source: Muldrew (1998) 105
(a) The higher figure for unpaid tithes may reflect the nonconformity of the Cranbrook region.
(b) The total of 2,275 lacks 148 debts which do not fit easily under Muldrew's headings, such as the 12 payments for apprenticeship, the 52 legacies which deceased individuals had yet to pay to those due to inherit, and the 23 'portions' owing to kin.

Because probate accounts list the sums owed by the deceased at death they provide unparalleled insights into the way in which people were habitually 'living in part on other people's money' in the 17th century.[5] Table 9.3 illustrates the known occupational coverage of the returns from the 234 probate accounts which have survived for the Cranbrook region of Kent between 1660 and 1700, and Table 9.4 analyses the reasons for which debts were owed by the deceased.

Table 9.3   Occupations of deceased from Cranbrook region probate accounts

barber	1	cordwainer	2	labourer	1	tanner	5
blacksmith	3	draper	1	locksmith	1	thatcher	1
bricklayer	1	innholder	2	mercer	4	victualler	3
broadweaver	6	dyer	1	miller	4	wheelwright	2
butcher	4	gentleman	12	rector	2	widow of brewer	1
cardmaker	1	grocer	1	ripyer	2	widow of blacksmith	1
carpenter	6	gunsmith	1	shopkeeper	1	widow of clothier	1
carrier	4	hammerman	2	spinster	1	widow of yeoman	2
clothier	27	husbandman	15	surgeon	1	widow	6
clothworker	1	joiner	1	tailor	4	yeoman	38

Table 9.4 is confined to debts owed at death to named individuals; it does not, therefore, include sums paid out for funeral arrangements, nor for the probate process; nor does it include general taxes and tithes, unless the individuals due to receive them were named in the probate accounts. In these areas it was rare to specify names. Most payments to named individuals fall under the generic heading of 'debts due', and those debts tend to be for goods received or services rendered. In most of them the sums owed are for unspecified purposes, but the reason for the debt is given in some cases, and can be deduced in others. In general (Table 2.7, page 38),

Table 9.4 *Entries in probate accounts of Cranbrook region, 1660-99*

Total number of named entries—2,651   Number in which purpose is specified—2,423

allowance	1	debt interest	1	promise	1
annuity	1	deed of sale	1	quit rent	1
apprenticeship	12	excise duty	2	rent	188
bill debt	8	heriot	7	schooling	1
bill obligatory	2	judgement	2	scot	2
bond debt	260	legacy (not on bond)	52	sesse	25
book debt	8	Lord's rent	5	specialty debt	6
chimney money	2	maintenance	16	surety	1
contract	1	mortgage interest	2	tax	6
costs	101	pest fine	1	tithes	62
credit	13	portion	23	wages	49
'debts due'	1560				

husbandmen owed less than labourers and weavers, and far less, as a proportion of their wealth, than yeomen and clothiers. Presumably husbandmen could not bear, or did not need, the levels of debt sustained by wealthier inhabitants.

Day-to-day Contacts: Retail Goods

Probate accounts help us to picture one aspect of daily life by specifying goods which have been received but not yet paid for; they tell us what each of the deceased owed for, and often indicate to whom it was owed. Such goods include grocery and mercery wares, tallow, items of clothing, a church rope, timber, bundles of faggots, coal, gloves, hemp, beer, meat, malt, laths, saddletrees, shoes, tobacco, wine and loads of wood. When John Longley of Cranbrook died in 1674, the guardian of his five-year-old son John had to pay off his debts for beer to three different people: 4s. 6d. to Robert Robotham, 15s. 6d. to William Reader, and 2s. to Henry Carey, victualler. John Longley lived in Cranbrook, but rented a shop just across the county border in Robertsbridge, Sussex, though what he sold from his shop is not known.[6]

James Rich was a yeoman who also had property in two parishes, Chart-next-Sutton and Staplehurst; he paid an annual rent of £43 10s. to Sir Roger Twysden for Chievny Farm in Chart, and Hearth Tax money there of 24s. which, together with the intriguing spread of his debts, might suggest responsibilities beyond merely family ones.[7] He owed five different butchers considerable sums for meat (5s., 11s. 10d., 19s. 2d., £1 7s. 2d. and £1 8s. 5d.) and William Ollive of Staplehurst for groceries. He owed Patience Mayo 5s. 'for two sheets for Richard Shaw', Robert Sabb 3s. 11d. for a 'frock for Edward Austen', and various people for gloves, leather 'beecher', and shoes. Most of those named were from Chart, but two of the butchers, Stephen Smith and Walter Viney, came from Staplehurst, and knew each other well, the former witnessing the latter's will.

Like most butchers at this time they probably kept the animals, at least for a time, behind their shops, slaughtered them and prepared the meat for consumption. Probate accounts show how common it was for people to owe for meat at the time of their death, with sums ranging from 1s. 8d. to 46s.; most owed 2s. or a little more. That customers did not pay such bills promptly is most graphically illustrated by the inventory of the goods and chattels of Thomas Smith, butcher of Cranbrook, dated March 1671, which exceptionally itemises sums due to him.[8] His belongings were valued at £176 12s. 8d., and another £51 14s. 3d. was owed to him in debts, both sperate and desperate, by 52 named individuals of whom 37 can be identified with some certainty; even this truncated list shows a wide range of people from different walks of life and a variety of parishes (Table 9.5).

This one retailer, therefore, was selling his meat in his home parish of Cranbrook and in five adjacent parishes, and dealing with the whole spectrum of economic backgrounds from gentlemen with nine or six hearths to weavers and artisans living in one-hearth houses and exempt from tax and owing a few shillings. While the average amount owed was 12s. 4d., the median, at 4s. 8d., provides a more realistic picture of the sums owed.

Of the 14 other butchers named in the probate accounts, those figuring most frequently are Robert Wood, active as a Cranbrook butcher from his marriage in 1663 to his burial in 1690, Edward Umanden (Omanden) of Hawkhurst, married 1654, buried 1703, and Stephen Smith of Cranbrook. Wood

26. Part of the Inventory of Thomas Smith of Cranbrook, butcher, March 1671, which, after listing his household goods, value £176 12s. 8d., goes on to itemise all the debts owing to him for meat at the time of his death in May 1670. (PRC 11/33/220)

Table 9.5   A Sample of the Creditors of Thomas Smith, butcher of Cranbrook, March 1671, assessed on 2 hearths (The Towne) and 3 hearths (Smithsditch)

Customer	£	s	d	parish	HT		identification
Mr Rich. weeb Ju	13	18	8	Frit	9	=	Webb, gent., bur. '91
Mr Francis Haydon	1	19	9	Ben		=	Heyton, young gent.
John Baker Carpinder		7	4	Cra	3		m. '47, *of Chittenden*
James Glasbrooke		2	1	Cra	1x		broadweaver, m '58, bur. '76
Richard Halden	1	9	8	Cra	6	=	Holden of Branden, clo
Christopher Peckham Ju	1	7	8	Cra	1x	=	Packham, mason, *of Milkhouse*
Rich. Spice Sen	1	2	9	Cra	2		broadweaver, of *Collyers Green*
Haslin Bathurst	1	14	0	Frit	4		bur. '75
John Young		1	3	Cra	2x		m. '42, husbandman
Tho. Bayly	2	17	4	Frit	3		yeoman, bur. '72
Samuell Kealsden	1	2	8	Cra	1x		broadw, *Milkhouse*, m'47 & '59
Stephen Chittenden		5	0	Cra	1x		carpent.,*Goldford*, m. '59 & '60
John Tolherst		13	8	Cra			m. '65, bur 1703
Tho. weller		9	9	Cra	6		innk.r of George m. '46 bur '74
Mary Ellis wid.		8	2	Cra	(4)		wid. of clo. bur. '70, *Milkhouse*
Robert Whightwick	3	8	4	Frit	6		clo, moved to Bid. bur there '71
John Dabs		2	1	Cra		=	Dabbes, yeo., m. '69 & '70
John Richeson		2	0	Cra	2x		broadweaver, m. '40s, bur. '87
Tho. Munk		4	8	Bid			m. '65, moved to Bid. '70
Allen Bryant		5	4	Cra	1		bur. '97
Andrew Hills		1	4	Bid	5+2+2		clothier, earlier Staplehurst
John Grove		2	8	Sta	4 + 2x		s. of Robert, clo. & wid Mary
Tho. wadman		4	0	Cra		=	Whatman, husb., *Hess W.* m. '57
wid Bassock		4	0	Cra	2x		Bridget, wid of Edw., broadw.
Richard Hadman		3	6	Frit	1x		bur. '80 as 'poor householder'
Mr Waterhouse		2	0	Frit	2x		Richard, bur. '83 as 'aged gent.'
John Baker tanner		2	1	Frit	2		bur. '73, bonds for John Dane
William Colbrooke		1	5	Cra			carp. *of Milk*, m. '44, bur 1704
Tho. Batherst		6	5	Cra	4x		packcarrier, *of Willsley*
Henry Bourner		1	1	Frit			poor, carpenter, bur. 1706
William Clarke	2	2	8	Ben	4		moved from Bid. '67/8
John Ford		1	7	Cra	1x		broadweaver, m. '59
Georg Weller		14	4	Cra	2x		tailor *of Goldford*, bur 1705
Alex Couchman			10	Cra	2x		broadw. *of Hess W. or Goldford*
Cetle		3	4	Hawk	4	=	Humphrey Kettle, m. (2nd) '70
Roger Jones		1	9	Frit	1x		m '63 , bur. '72
Joseph Murton		5	10	Cra	1x		m. '47, bur '89, *of Milkhouse*

Source: Thomas Smith's inventory, CKS PRC 11/33/220
Names in italics are of Cranbrook districts: *Chittenden Quarter, Milkhouse, Colliers Green, Goldford, Willsley and Hesseldens Wood*

and Umanden both paid tax on three hearths, and Wood was actually owed £8 by another Cranbrook butcher, Matthew Couchman, suggesting that his business was both wholesale and retail; the overseers assessed him on £10 rental value for his house, £25 for his lands. Stephen Smith, no doubt related to Thomas Smith of the inventory above, moved to Staplehurst soon after 1682, when he married into the premier butcher family of Munn of Benenden and Cranbrook, which had several members involved in the trade over generations.[9] All these men dealt with a great variety of people in the course of their everyday lives, and clearly had to be able to bear the cost of credit in the process.

Other retailers died with bills similarly unpaid. William Caffinch, the Staplehurst yeoman/ripyer, owed William Meckett for saddletrees; John Grant, the Hawkhurst miller, owed Phineas Pankhurst, innkeeper, for tobacco; and Stephen White of Goudhurst owed Goodman Smith for wine. Mary Harding, the widow of a brewer, owed for malt (including £3 in Canterbury and £8 in Wye), as did two millers, a hammerman, a mercer, a tanner, a clothier, a carpenter, and a carrier; the first three were probably buying wholesale. Local suppliers included the maltster, Thomas Hunt of Benenden, who provided £3-worth of malt to Walter Jones the mercer and £4-worth to Thomas Hodges the tanner, both from Benenden; and William Greenwell of Frittenden, who supplied £2-worth to Richard Haffenden, a clothier/yeoman, and £2-worth to Thomas Reynolds, a carpenter, both of Biddenden. These sundry debts begin to give a flavour of the 'tangled webs of economic and social dependency' mentioned by Muldrew.[10]

Wholesalers had to bear the considerable cost of credit at source. Peter Master, a Cranbrook mercer, died owing sums to a variety of London wholesalers, including £31 for grocery, £8 15s. for haberdashery, £6 13s. for hosiery, and £32 to three wholesalers for linen.[11] Stephen Leeds, a Benenden cordwainer, owed a Mr Lanes of London £30 for wine; the fact that he also owed for excise suggests that he retailed wine as well as shoes.[12] Sometimes middlemen, carriers like Samuel Yorkton of Cranbrook, transported such goods from London or the coast to the Wealden villages; when he died he owed £22 for unspecified wares, £39 16s. 6d. for linen, £6 10s. for grocery ware, £3 18s. for soap, £2 5s. for pots and glasses, and another £3 9s. for glasses, all to named individuals.[13] He also had outstanding bills for Richard Smith, the farrier, and for oats to John Courthop, Robert Taylor and Goodman Lansden. He died with his hotel bill unpaid, as he owed 'the Talbot in Southworke in London' 30s. Like Margaret Spufford's petty chapmen,[14] these carriers seem to have taken goods from wholesalers on credit and brought them to retailers in the Cranbrook area. Presumably, they then received payment from the retailer, took their profit, and paid the wholesalers the money due to them. John Prior, carrier of Biddenden, died with substantial debts, including £32 to a linendraper in London, £6 to one in Dover, and £4 for gloves and other wares in Maidstone. He also had to pay compensation to 'Esq. Vane' of Cranbrook 'in satisfaction of a looking glasse the said intestate brought for him from London as a Carrier and it was broke by an accident in bringing and for which he required the sum of £2'. Such were the hazards of the road at this time.[15]

Inevitably many died owing for agricultural items whether they were primarily husbandmen or pursuing other callings. The yeoman, Richard Turley of Hawkhurst, owed small sums to a wide variety of fellow-parishioners for oats, for a waggon, for straw, for pease, for wheat and for malt; indeed the inventory value of his estate was £27, but his debts and other commitments came to £61. His son, as administrator, paid John Elliott to keep ten sheep at a shilling a week for 16 weeks, presumably the period which elapsed before they could be sold to best advantage.[16] When the tanner, Edward Apsley, died, the yeoman Thomas Osmer looked after one of his cows and sold another. When the miller, Solomon Ware, died, Richard Finsett, husbandman, was owed £3 12s. for 'keeping his sheep, cattle and other work'. In fact Ware's inventory shows he had three cows, two steers, 40 sheep, 16 lambs and four oxen among his livestock alone.[17] A yeoman, John Thatcher, died owing a broadweaver for bagging hops for him, and the clothier, Alexander Osborne, was owed £2 for hop-poles by a yeoman. Shopkeepers and innholders like John Longley and Phineas Pankhurst died owing for hay and a mercer, Alexander Homsby, owed for sheep. Parishioners constantly relied on each other for goods and services, and lived off each other's credit.

Borrowing and Lending Money: Mortgages

More formal (specialty) lending and borrowing of money was important to those living in the Cranbrook area, and can be divided into three types. Mortgages tended to be for substantial sums, in which a formal agreement was drawn up for a loan at fixed interest and with property as collateral. Loans on specialty, in particular those on bond, involved a formal agreement for a loan, usually for a moderate sum at fixed interest, and enforceable by law but with no fixed repayment date.[18] Promissory notes were bills without security, used for small sums and for short-term loans. Such debts became void if they were unclaimed within the time-limit, as John Prior's very detailed probate account makes clear: 'the said debt is above seven yeares standing and therefore by the statute he is discharged', and again 'being above seven yeares standing he pleads the benefit of the statute and does refuse the payment thereof'.[19] Of the Cranbrook sample 44 per cent (103 of the 234) died with formal loans of one sort or another outstanding; on bond alone £9,505 was owed, representing approximately 40 per cent of the total sums owed.

Mortgages, like the two in the probate account of the Staplehurst yeoman, James Crump, who died owing interest of £12 on £100 over two years, and £3 on £50 over six months, were comparatively rare.[20] Useful insights, however, are provided by 11 contemporary wills. Samuel Bates, John Potter and Thomas Bayly, for instance, had each taken mortgages from family members, and done so at five per cent interest rather than six.[21] Thomas Irons, barber or gentleman of Biddenden, and Jarvice Morlen, yeoman of Benenden, provide a typical example of a mortgage to a friend, fellow churchwarden and social equal, in this case in a neighbouring parish.[22] John Leigh, gentleman and son of an eminent lawyer, who provided a £50 mortgage to Ann Fosten, widow of a Cranbrook innkeeper, also witnessed her will; there was clearly a closer link here than their apparently different social standing might suggest.[23] Finally, Jeremy Botting, who had lent to Jane Snoath, almost certainly provides an example of a purely business arrangement. Jane, widow of Henry Snoath, clothier, took out the mortgage herself, trusting that her four

27. The Probate Account of John Prior which shows that unsecured debts outstanding more than seven years became void 'by benefit of statute'. (PRC 2/41/73)

sons, aged 19, 15, 12 and 10 years, would pay off the sum owed and claim back the property in due course.[24]

Marriage Bonds

It was the custom of wealthier husbands in the Cranbrook area, often on the occasion of their second marriage and to young wives, formally to guarantee a certain sum to them when widowed. These marriage bonds were not loans so much as a form of life insurance (Table 9.6). Of the two sums which are not in round figures, that owed to Elizabeth, the wife of Josias Watts of Hawkhurst, was to include the value of his household goods, which came to approximately £73. The figure of £47 to be paid to Thomas Hodges' widow Sarah, was occasioned by her rather cheeky addition of interest to the original sum of £40 to cover the period 'since her marriage about the fourth day of November 1673' to his death 'in or about the month of May 1685'.

Table 9.6   *Marriage bonds from probate accounts, Cranbrook region, 1660-99*

parish	deceased / debtor	occupation	sum	to whom	charge / residue	
Frit	James Munn	gentleman	£500	2nd wife, Catherine	£351 /	£-299
Bid	Moses Lee	rector	£300	wife Elizabeth	£141 /	£-308
Hawk	Josias Watts		£273	wife Elizabeth	£311 /	£-17
Cra	Samuel Crampton	clothier	£200	wife Ellen	£230 /	£-5
Cra	John Webb	miller	£200	2nd wife Elizabeth	£165 /	£-58
Cra	Richard Kingswood	yeoman	£160	2nd wife, Charity	£21 /	£-181
Frit	Thomas Amery	clothier	£150	wife Mary	£171 /	£-9
Sta	Robert Kite	grocer	£150	wife Elizabeth	£252 /	£-1
Haw	Henry Batcheller		£100	2nd wife Catherine	£32 /	£-72
Ben	Thomas Dive	yeoman	£80	wife Rebecca	£344 /	£235
Bid	Edward Dunke		£80	wife Susanna	£79 /	£-20
Sta	Thomas Hughes	broadweaver	£60	wife Amy	£70 /	£-26
Ben	Walter Jones	mercer	£50	2nd wife Elizabeth	£68 /	£-14
Ben	Thomas Hodges	tanner	£47	2nd wife Sarah	£81 /	£-19
Sta	John Rolfe snr	clothier	£40	2nd wife Susan	£93 /	£-55
Haw	Thomas Mitten	husbandman	£30	wife Mary	£64 /	£-1

Note: Charge indicates the estimated value of the deceased's goods and chattels as provided by the inventory, and residue indicates the value left after debts had been paid.

The largest sum by far was for Catherine the wife of James Munn, yeoman and later gentleman of Frittenden, who had 'entered into a bond to Mr Thomas Boys and Thomas Morland in trust for her to lease her worth in case she survived him'.[25] She was Catherine Botting, daughter of Jeremy Botting, the 'banker' of the Cranbrook area. At the time of the marriage she was a spinster of 27 years, and James a widower with two children aged seven and ten. The second largest sum was committed by the Rector of Biddenden, Moses Lee, to his wife Elizabeth, widow of Mr Jonathan Rogers, at the time of their marriage in August 1661; in fact she was the wealthy partner. She outlived Moses by two years, and in her will she left gold pieces to her children by her first husband, adding the request to be buried at the latter's side. The £300 bond was therefore a worthwhile investment, on Moses' part, and in marked contrast to the £141 which he left as the value of his own goods and chattels when he died in 1681.[26]

Elizabeth, the second wife of John Webb, could have hoped to claim the £200 bond when he died in July 1683. In fact, because the value of his goods and chattels only came to £165, and his other debts amounted to £23, she only saw £142 of the sum agreed. Mary Amery, the widow of Thomas Amery, did comparatively better in that her husband left goods and chattels to the value of £171 and other debts amounting to £31; of the £150 which she was due to receive on his death, therefore, she capitalised to the tune of £140. The final column in Table 9.5 gives the truth of how little of the sum promised was actually available to the widow from the sale of goods and chattels; a minus figure means that she could not have received the full amount promised.[27]

Loans on Bond

Most bonds, however, were for loans of money borrowed for specific purposes in a formal way, with a legal record drawn up to verify the loan, and interest to be paid regularly to the lender on an annual basis until the loan was withdrawn. As has been said, such interest was at six per cent: William Tutt, clothier of Benenden, had typically borrowed £20 upon bond, and owed 36s. 'in interest at that time, one year and a half: £21 16s.'.[28] As with mortgages, however, the rate when borrowing from kin was normally five per cent; thus Golding Skinner of Frittenden owed his son-in-law 30s. on a debt of £30.[29] Such loans serviced both partners to the agreement; they provided a means by which cash could be raised, and a means of income via interest for the creditor. Despite some large loans on bond (Table 9.7) their average size was £29, with the median at £16 and the mode (most frequent loan) at £5.

Table 9.7   Debts on bond for loans of over £100, Cranbrook region, 1660-99

parish	deceased / debtor	occupation	sum	type of bond	charge / residue
Frit	Robert Freebody	gentleman	£320	loan from kin	£1996 / £689
Cra	Harman Sheafe	gentleman	£315	loan	£ 624 / £-215
Cra	Harman Sheafe	gentleman	£269	loan	£ 624 / £-215
Frit	Robert Freebody	gentleman	£158	loan from kin	£1996 / £689
Frit	John Munn	yeoman	£133	loan from kin	£ 648 / £207
Cra	Harman Sheafe	gentleman	£128	loan from kin	£ 624 / £-215
Bid	John Bishoppenden	yeoman	£124	loan from kin	£ 693 / £292
Cra	Robert Hovenden	clo / gent	£120	loan from kin	£ 88 / £-99
Cra	Thomas Goddard	clothier	£114	loan	£ 358 / £128
Cra	Richard Hope	joiner	£107	legacy to kin	£1501 / £647
Frit	Robert Freebody	gentleman	£106	loan	£1996 / £689
Cra	Richard Hope	joiner	£105	legacy to kin	£1501 / £647
Frit	Robert Freebody	gentleman	£105	loan (from kin)	£1996 / £689

At least six of the 11 cash loans of more than £100 known to have been taken out on bond during the period were loans from other family members; links for the other five have not been established. Robert Freebody borrowed the largest sum of all, from Mrs Mary Freebody junior, and another £157 10s. 'principal and interest' from Mr William Freebody (£150 at 5 per cent interest).[30] John Munn owed his sister-in-law, Frances Munn, £132 15s., and a lesser sum of £82 10s. to his sister Susan.[31] Harman Sheafe owed his sister, Mrs Merriam, £127 16s. 6d. John Bishoppenden had borrowed from his step-son, Stephen Chittenden, and Robert Hovenden from George Curtis, his son-in-law. Robert had borrowed a further £60 on bond from Robert Holden of Cranbrook, to whom he was also related by a marriage in the previous generation. The account of Robert Freebody specifically mentions that he died owing widow Beale £100 on bond and interest of £5, the implied five per cent interest strongly suggesting a loan within the family.[32] In addition to these six examples of family loans, Richard Hope, joiner of Cranbrook, exemplifies a novel form of kin-linked borrowing on bond. As executor for his father's will he controlled the legacies of £100 each which were to go to his two unmarried sisters; he seems to have contracted with them (hence the bond) to keep their legacies as lump sums for his own use and to pay them their annual interest after their coming of age.[33]

Harman Sheaf, gent., may have borrowed from within his family circle but his two largest debts, of £315 and £269, were to Stephen Pooke of Salehurst in Sussex and Mr Thomas Knight, citizen and linendraper of London.[34] The second of these was almost certainly a business loan rather than one within the family. That from Stephen Pooke might reflect a similarly business-like loan except that the sum involved suggests five per cent interest over a year on a loan of £300, and a kin link is possible.[35] Thomas Goddard owed Richard Caster and Stephen Ashbourne £113 10s. for a debt on bond, which also looks very much like a business arrangement.

Inventories, which provide information from the lenders' point of view, suggest that people made formal loans only occasionally, and possibly only one or two sums at a time. Sometimes probate inventories specify bond debts and name the debtor(s); Walter Jones, yeoman of Benenden, was owed a total of £95 by five people, the largest sum being £35 by his son-in-law. Solomon Ware, miller of Cranbrook, was owed £51 10s. on bond by the Buckland brothers, clothiers of Staplehurst, to one of whom his son was apprenticed at the time, and £20 by William Godden. As a retailer, John Delton, tallow-chandler of Cranbrook, was owed £55 on bills and bonds, and another £3 15s. 6½d. on book debts. Widows loaned regularly, as did some spinsters like Anne Beecher (£343); the wealthier clothiers, like Isaac Walter of Cranbrook, still had large sums owing to them (£585 on specialty and £92 on book), but inventories rarely itemise these debts.[36]

Probate accounts, which give the debtors' point of view, support the idea that many people loaned out money, but that they did so very selectively. They record 243 loans on bond; 182 (75 per cent) were from lenders mentioned only once, 12 twice, seven three times and only one more than three times, in his case 16 times. Among those who lent more than once were the Bates brothers, John and Samuel, both Quakers; of the four loans to their credit the largest was to John Rade, a relative by marriage (£15 18s., implying 6 per cent interest), two were to James Allay, tailor of Cranbrook (£6 and £5), and one to Robert Kite, the grocer of Staplehurst (£20), who borrowed from other known Quakers.[37] The implication that people lent and borrowed within the Quaker community is inescapable. Richard Burden, a Benenden yeoman, lent to three different individuals, all of whom were related to him by marriage. Among multiple lenders this pattern of lending to kin tends to be the norm, with Thomas Roads lending twice, probably three times, to family. Stephen Sharpey and William Moyse each lent twice to family and once to a fellow member of the vestry group; and others like Stephen Rade, John Love and Sarah

Hodges lent to a member of the family and to one of the vestry group. Religious persuasion, family and parish administration all provide common links here.

Such links cannot be established in every case. Many creditors do not figure in the reconstitution of the Cranbrook parishes because they originate from further afield; others are well-known individuals from the seven parishes, but no obvious point of contact reveals itself. Of those for whom a link can be identified, however, between a half and two-thirds have a kin-relationship.[38] These loans tend to include many of the larger sums mentioned in the probate accounts. Because kin-relationships can easily elude the researcher, this proportion was probably even higher. For instance, there is no immediate indication of a relationship between the carrier Samuel Yorkton, and the clothier Alexander Osborne from whom he had borrowed £20 on bond, but the reconstitution shows that each had married a Harding sister from Biddenden.[39] Similarly John Cryer, yeoman of Benenden, owed three separate sums to William Moyse, tanner of Benenden, as well as £101 in arrears of rent;[40] they were both linked by marriages to the influential Sharpe family.

Two further probate accounts give a feel for the local network within which formal loans were arranged. Anthony Gibbon, acting as 'accountant' for his brother Thomas, clothier of Hawkhurst, clarified relationships by referring to 'my sister Slowman' and 'my brother Bathurst' and 'my brother's widow'. Most of his creditors were family (Table 9.8). By contrast, John Burr of Benenden, a yeoman farmer of moderate means living in a two-hearth house in 1664, and leaving goods, chattels and credits to the tune of £164, died leaving 11 outstanding debts on bond of which only one can be securely linked to kin (Table 9.9).[41] In four cases the link with his creditors is involvement in the administrative group within the parish; such inter-relationships can be identified in nearly a fifth of all cases of borrowing on bond.

Table 9.8 *Sums owed on bond by Thomas Gibbon, clothier of Hawkhurst, 1663*

creditor	sum owed	link	via ...
to [brother] Bathurst	£51 10s.	brother-in-law	by Mary Gibbon
to [sister] Slowman	£50 0s.	brother-in-law	by Ann Gibbon
to Elizabeth Gibbon	£40 0s.	wife of	
to Thomas Domincike	£35 6s.	kinship	by Anne Gibbon
to John Colvill	£33 1s.	link not known	
to John Medhurst	£24 5s.	link not known	
to Stephen Sharpey	£21 18s.	kinship	by William Gibbon
to John Read	£5 3s.	link not known	

Holderness and Spufford have both seen kinship as a major factor in borrowing and lending,[42] and the Cranbrook evidence greatly supports this view. This kinship factor also helps to explain why so many of the instances of borrowing on bond appear to be one-off arrangements as far as the lender was concerned. The evidence further suggests that, if more were known about these relationships, especially among the so-called vestry group, the proportion of kin would rise. On the other hand money was also lent on a purely business basis, as exemplified by the largest

Table 9.9   *Sums owed on bond by John Burr, yeoman of Benenden, 1677*

to Jeremy Botting	£31 17s.		business	
to John Lamkin	£23 10s.			kin (a)
to Jeremy Botting	}		business	
to Thomas Hunt	} £21 4s.			vestry
to Samuel Kent	}			link not known (b)
to Nathaniel Chittenden	£10 10s. 6d.			link not known
to Mr Stephen Sharpey	£10		vestry	
to Mr John Sharpey	£6 18s.		vestry	
to Stephen Rade	£6 14s.		vestry	
to Mr Peter Henden	£5 14s.		vestry	
to Mr William Silke	£5 9s.		business	

Notes: (a) his 2nd wife was Mary Lamkin   (b) John Kent was the parish clerk

of John Burr's loans, £30 from Jeremy Botting, and such loans may make up as much as 20 per cent of cases. They include those where the lender appears to be a businessman, sometimes living beyond the immediate area, like 'Mr Throughton, grocer of Maidstone' who makes several appearances, as well as all but one of the loans arranged by Jeremy Botting.

The Professional Lender of Money on Bond

Jeremy Botting stands out uniquely as a professional lender of money on bond in the Cranbrook area at this period. His family had made impressive marriages in the previous generation,[43] and he had married Katherine Potter in 1652, thereby allying himself with several other influential families; he settled in the upper end of the town of Cranbrook where he pursued his trade as a cordwainer. There is a strong impression of dissent among some family members, but Jeremy himself appears in every way to have been a conformist: he was married in the Anglican church, was churchwarden in 1659 and 1660, and in his own will he entrusted his soul to Almighty God in the usual fashion; his only child to be born after 1660 was baptised.[44]

Jeremy Botting is mentioned by name 16 times in probate accounts which thereby hint at the extensive loan network which he had built up, covering five of the seven parishes in and around Cranbrook (Table 9.10). They are but a drop in the ocean, however, when compared with the £2,032 total for loans owing to him on bond as stated by his probate inventory.[45] Six per cent interest on such a vast sum would yield him £122 annually, enabling him and his family to live in comfort. His will shows that he anticipated leaving his children legacies totalling £1,500, and reinforces the impression of a man of considerable wealth.

The largest of these 16 loans was made to a relative by marriage. Elizabeth Evernden, widow of the Cranbrook clothier, John Evernden, was Jeremy's wife's sister, and she had also borrowed from other family members including her sister

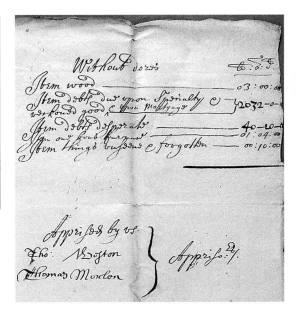

28. The opening lines of the Probate Inventory of Jeremy Botting show that he had an unusual amount of ready cash (£57 11s. 6d.) in his purse; and the closing lines of the same inventory which show that he was owed a total of £2,032 for 'debts due upon Specialty and reckoned good'. (CKS PRC 11/51/83)

Table 9.10   Jeremy Botting: loans on bond, 1668-85

Nathaniel Fosten	Cranbrook	victualler	1668	debt on bond	£11	2s.	0d.
John Cryer	Benenden	yeoman	1670	debt on bond	£10	3s.	6d.
John Colman	Cranbrook	blacksmith	1676	debt on bond	£ 5	1s.	6d.
John Henden	Benenden	gentleman	1676	debt on bond	£10	9s.	0d.
Elizabeth Russell	Frittenden		1676	debt on bond [a]	£ 7	10s.	0d.
John Burr	Benenden	yeoman	1678	debt on bond + int.	£31	17s.	0d.
John Burr	Benenden	yeoman	1678	debt on bond [b]	£ 7	1s.	4d.
Richard Haffenden	Biddenden	clo. /yeo.	1680	debt on bond	£10	6s.	0d.
Henry Parkes	Cranbrook	weaver	1680	debt on bond	£ 5	4s.	0d.
Henry Cruttenden	Cranbrook	blacksmith	1680	debt on bond	£ 5	0s.	0d.
Elizabeth Everden	Cranbrook	widow	1682	debt on bond + int.	£54	10s.	0d.
Arthur Gibbon	Cranbrook	victualler	1682	debt on bond [c]	£41	5s.	0d.
Richard Hope	Cranbrook	joiner	1683	debt on bond + int.	£16	11s.	6d.
Richard Bigge	Benenden	yeoman	1683	debt on bond + int.	£30	16s.	6d.
William Caffinch	Staplehurst	ripyer/yeo.	1683	debt on bond [d]	£35	16s.	0d.
Robert Kite	Staplehurst	grocer	1685	debt on bond + int.	£21	11s.	0d.

Notes   [a] in part of a just debt of £10 due to him upon bond
[b] owed jointly to Jeremy Botting, Samuel Kent & Thomas Hunt, in all £21 4s.
[c] in discharge of a judgement
[d] for a debt due upon two small bonds

Michel, widow of Humphrey Bryant. The most likely explanation of Elizabeth's need for these loans is that she was making provision for her three unmarried daughters, Sarah (24), Michel (22) and Katherine (19), now that her eldest daughter, Elizabeth, had married back into the Potter family. She was clearly in difficulties at her death as she owed back rent to Lady Baker (of £32 for each of two half years) and to Mr Francis Elvy (for £6 and £8).[46]

The relationship between Jeremy Botting and the other 15 clients indicated in Table 9.10 seems to have been a business one. Nathaniel Fosten and Arthur Gibbon, both of Cranbrook, were victuallers, and Robert Kite of Staplehurst was a grocer. Nowhere is there any evidence here of a kinship or social link. All three of them died unable to cover their debts with the value of their goods, chattels and sums owing to them; presumably they had over-stretched themselves in an attempt to carry stock.[47] Nathaniel Fosten was paying Hearth Tax on four hearths and two hearths, presumably one of which was the shop. He had also borrowed £14 on bond from Robert Robotham of Cranbrook and 50s. from a Mr Thatcher of Maidstone. Arthur Gibbon was landlord of the *George Inn* at Cranbrook which he rented from Robert Hovenden, gent. He owed another £126 which he had borrowed on bond from three other people. Robert Kite was also deeply in debt to a number of creditors; he owed nearly £150 on bond to eight other men apart from his debt to Jeremy Botting. All this cash may well have supported his business; it also had to support his involvement as a leading Quaker in the area; his house, on which he was assessed for six hearths, was used as a Quaker meeting place before 1680 (pages 188-90).

Some of those listed as borrowing from Jeremy Botting have already been mentioned: Richard Hope has been seen employing sharp practice to secure his sisters' money; John Burr and John Cryer were both in severe financial difficulties at the time of their deaths. The circumstances of Richard Bigge, John Henden and Richard Haffenden parallel those of Burr and Cryer in that they were all leading men of the vestries of Benenden or Biddenden, all had loans out from other creditors, and were part of a peer group of friends within which intermarriage was commonplace and who lent money on bond to each other. It appears that when the going really got tough they had to turn to a more business-like money-lender, albeit a parish administrator like themselves.

John Colman, blacksmith, Henry Cruttenden, blacksmith, and Henry Parkes, weaver, belonged to a rather different social and economic grouping from the men mentioned above. They each borrowed £5, the smallest sum on which it was normal to arrange a bond, and they all lived in Cranbrook. John Colman was not a wealthy man; his goods, chattels and debts owing to him totalled £18 6s. 8d., and his widow had to find an extra £24 10s. 11d. to settle his debts and pay for his funeral and probate. Henry Cruttenden's finances were in a chaotic state, and it took well over a year for his wife Margaret to bring them to probate. Her account lists 43 separate payments to be made, the vast majority of which were small debts owing to local people; the £5 owing to Jeremy Botting was the only sum borrowed on bond. Henry Parkes died young of smallpox in 1680; his relative, Elizabeth Petman, dealt with his affairs. She was his principal creditor, to whom he owed £11 19s. on bond and another debt of £23 6s., and she became guardian to his daughter.[48]

The professional lender on bond would benefit from the services of a scribe and lawyer, and in Jeremy Botting's case that man was Thomas Curtis, gentleman and attorney-at-law of Biddenden, whom he later appointed overseer of his will. Between them they ran what was in effect a small local banking business. While Jeremy Botting lived in a four-hearth house in Cranbrook Town borough, Thomas Curtis lived more modestly in a two-hearth house, paying his local assessments on land valued at £9 per annum. He was one of the most prolific of will-witnesses, a fact no doubt brought about by his presence, in a professional capacity, when the wills were being drawn up (page 152).

Part of an administrator's responsibility was to sell off the deceased's personal estate to meet the debts which he owed; this practice is made explicit when John Jennings was paid 15s. 'for his trouble in selling the deceased's goods for five days', and when Mr Charlton was paid 2s. 'for the use of the house where the deceased's goods were kept before they could be sold'.[49]

In 87 of the 234 Cranbrook area accounts (37 per cent) the value of the inventory failed to meet the deceased's debts. Contemporary Cranbrook wills show people providing for the sale of real estate to meet their debts; William Silcock, for instance, gave his 'beloved wife ... authority to sell all that my messuage called Cruthole ... and money therefrom to meet my debts and legacies'.[50] If there were no real estate, however, emergency measures had to be taken. The probate account of the Staplehurst grocer Robert Kite, shows how this was done in some detail.[51] He had ten outstanding loans on bond when he died in 1685. Two of these his accountants paid in full, including the one to Jeremy Botting. They also paid his rent in full. Eight debts were only partially met, indicated by the phrase 'in discharge of a greater debt', as 'to Samuel Bates of Cranbrook, in discharge of a loan on bond of £20, the sum of £12 5s.'.[52] They paid Robert Chapman to visit some of the creditors 'living in divers places in the country' and negotiate with them, but such negotiation was not always successful. He did not find all the creditors, and his negotiating skills fell down with Samuel Howsegoe of Tenterden, who brought charges against the accountants who were constrained to hire 'Mr John Lambe of Maidstone, Attorney, for his advice and attendance several times upon Counsell in suits against them'. Somehow, therefore, the accountant had to negotiate lower sums than those owed in order to allow creditors some share in the deceased's capital after the sale of his goods.

Chapter 10

The Nonconformist Factor

Introduction

Nonconformity as a factor in inter-relationships has presented itself on many occasions over the preceding chapters, and these strands need to be brought together. Before doing so, however, we need to establish the context in which people's religious preferences were constrained.

Cranbrook and its environs, long a centre of Puritan dissent,[1] continued to harbour many who found themselves at odds with the demands of the re-established Church; they were to experience major fluctuations in the religious climate during our period. In 1660 the Act for Confirming and Restoring of Ministers heralded the official re-establishment of the Anglican Church; in 1662 the Act for the Uniformity of Public Prayers required ministers to accept the format of that Church and of its worship.[2] All parishioners were to attend the Anglican Church on Sundays; not to do so made one a nonconformist subject to fine and imprisonment. In 1672 the Declaration of Indulgence lifted penalties except for Roman Catholics, and licensed individuals to hold non-Anglican meetings in specified places; this licensing reveals the names of the leading nonconformist preachers and their centres at that time. Within the year Parliament revoked the Indulgence; penalties resumed for those who failed to attend Anglican services or who were found attending illicit meetings.[3] In 1687 James II issued his own short-lived Declaration of Indulgence which even encompassed Roman Catholics, and in 1689, in the aftermath of the 'Glorious Revolution', the Act of Toleration provided nonconformists with the legislated freedom to develop their form of worship without too much interference from authority.[4]

In the Cranbrook area the displacement of local pastors who refused to accept the Acts of 1660 and 1662 by the newly appointed Anglican clergy appears to have been achieved without rancour in almost every case. This is despite the fact that those new men who took over benefices from popular predecessors may well have faced considerable resentment on the part of many of their supposed flock. But those who were ejected were not rabble-rousers; they came from backgrounds similar to those who supplanted them. Thus Daniel Poyntell, the popular Cromwellian minister at Staplehurst, was married in 1653 to Mary, daughter of Ninion Butcher, a wealthy author and gentleman with business interests in London; her family featured in the Heralds' Visitations, and her brother was taxed on houses with four, five and 11 hearths. Poyntell stayed on in Staplehurst, where he had an enthusiastic following, and was even allowed to preach in the church there for a while by permission of the Archbishop.[5] A popular and impressive man, he was joined there by the ex-minister of Benenden, Joseph Osborne, whose ancestral home, Loddenden, was in Staplehurst, and whose father was assessed there on six hearths. We are told that Osborne 'Liv'd in Friendship with all the Publick Ministers of the Places where he dwelt', and had been under pressure from Sir John Henden's family to conform and stay on at Benenden.[6] Even Ephraim Bothell, who was pilloried in the registers as 'defiling the bed of his spiritual Father. Since XVth June this Church of Hawkhurst hath been his concubine 16[5]9 – 1662', stayed on in Hawkhurst; later he conformed and became vicar of Chiddingly in Sussex (1667). Economically and socially he did not match the other two; he appeared as a 'desperate debtor' in 1665.[7]

Table 10.1   *Replacement of nonconforming ministers, Cranbrook region, 1660/62*

Parish	non-conformist minister	date of: entry	ejection	new Anglican incumbent
Benenden	Joseph Osborne*	20 July 1658	1662	Nicholas Moneyman
Biddenden	William Horner	20 May 1645	1660	Moses Lee
Cranbrook	Willm. Goodridge	20 June 1654	1662	John Cooper
Frittenden	[Robert Clarke ----------------no change-------------------Robert Clarke]			
Goudhurst	Edward Bright	by May 1646	1660	Edward Thurman
Hawkhurst	Ephraim Bothell	by Aug. 1651	1662	Jonathan Pleydell
Staplehurst	Daniel Poyntell	by Nov. 1653	1662	Stephen Sowton

Note: * variously Usborne or Osborne.

In due course George Hawe, the minister from Tenterden (1655-62), Samuel French, the minister from Town Malling (1657-60), and Francis Cornwall, sometime vicar of Marden, also gravitated to Staplehurst, which, according to Calamy, 'with Cranbrook and Tenterden enjoyed a considerable degree of public liberty which continued even to the time of the Indulgence'.[8] In the map of the Compton Census returns (page 43) nonconformists make up roughly one in three of the population of Staplehurst and its close associate Frittenden, and of Cranbrook; the proportions for Biddenden, Benenden, Hawkhurst and Goudhurst are between one in eight and one in ten. The last four parishes, and especially Goudhurst, were also involved in the clothing industry, and all the parishes shared the Wealden insularity, so neither of these suggested sources of nonconformity can stand alone. Maybe charismatic personalities (Fletcher in the 16th century, Poyntell now) influenced the high proportions in Staplehurst, Frittenden and Cranbrook.

A full appreciation of the inter-relationship of these men with each other, with their flocks and with the established church, is complicated by the fact that several groupings had developed during the 1640s and 1650s.[9] They were distinguished from each other mainly as Presbyterians, Congregationalists, Independents, Baptists (General or Arminian rather than Particular or Calvinist), and Quakers (Friends).

After 1660/2 these congregations showed themselves, to a greater or lesser extent, antipathetic to the practices of the Anglican church. Some leaders encouraged maintenance of communion with the Church of England 'with a design to show their charity towards that church', attending morning services while, like Adam Martindale, holding their own conventicles in the evenings.[10] In the Cranbrook area such men tended to be Presbyterians or Congregationalists; one is not surprised to find them and their adherents mentioned in the baptismal, marriage or burial registers while at the same time they were occasionally fined for attending illicit religious meetings. More separatist were Baptists, who were unlikely to figure in the parish baptismal registers, but did appear for marriage and burial. Most exclusive of all were the Quakers who eschewed the registers almost entirely and had their own burial ground. For clarity's sake these groupings are best treated separately.

Presbyterians, Independents and Congregationalists

There were Congregationalists at Goudhurst in the 1660s, and the 1669 return of conventicles records that at Cranbrook 'Mr Evenden and Mr Starr were the prechers as Independents and their hearers numbered between 200 and 300 people'.[11] Then the 1672 Declaration of Indulgence clarified the situation in our parishes by naming preachers and places, and linking them to particular nonconformist sects (although not always reliably).[12] In August of that year Daniel Poyntell, who may have returned for a while to his father's estate in Chislehurst where he was assessed on six hearths in 1664, was licensed to preach as a Presbyterian at Peter Burren's house in Staplehurst. At the same time in Cranbrook licence for Presbyterian worship was granted to Robert Trail in the home of William Love, packcarrier, at Baker's Cross,[13] and the dowager Lady Roberts obtained a licence for Thomas Brand to preach in her private chapel at Glassenbury.

The circumstances of these preachers and of the men whose houses provided meeting-places make it clear that they spanned the dividing line between those willing to accommodate Anglican services and those less happy to do so. Poyntell's children were registered 'born' in 1650s, as was appropriate at that time, but his daughter Frances was 'baptized' in March 1660, some months before the formal requirement. His 'host', Peter Burren, was a clothier (sometimes 'gentleman') who paid tax on eight hearths; each of his children (five between 1668-78) was duly baptised in the parish church at Staplehurst.

Unlike Peter Burren, William Love was not a wealthy man. He was taxed on three hearths in 1664, and at his death in December 1678 he left goods and chattels to the value of £141, out of which he owed a half-year's tax (3s.), tithes to the 'parson of Tenterden' (17s. 4d.) and the 'parson of Cranbrook' (5s.), a sesse of 12s. to the Overseers of the Poor, 3s. toward the repair of the highways, and £26 5s. rent to the heirs of Sir John Baker. There was enough left of his personal estate to distribute £18 14s. to each of his four children and twice that sum to his wife.[14] His two older daughters were naturally registered as 'born' in the 1650s, whereas

29. Shepherds, the property of the Sheafe family in Cranbrook Town itself, displays a fashionable late 17th-century brick frontage placed on a much older house, and exemplifies the wealth of the family.

his daughter Jeanne was baptised before dying in infancy (1660s), as did several other children. His two younger children, Mary and William, do not figure in the registers at all, but are revealed by his probate account; they were born in the 1660s but were not baptised.

Table 10.2 provides a list of the nonconformists from the seven parishes who were fined by the justices at the Quarter Sessions in 1673. The few who do not figure in the reconstitution may have been in service in the area or short-term visitors; more likely, they had escaped notice altogether because of their non-attendance at Anglican services. Most are known to the reconstitution, and did have some or all of their children baptised in the Anglican church. The clothier Thomas Boys, on the other hand, who was fined for attending a conventicle in 1675,[15] had at least two sons (both mentioned in Jeremy Botting's will), but in the registers there is only mention of the burial of his daughter. Also fined were Thomas Cruttenden and Ezechiel Chart, apothecaries; the former only features in the registers at the burial of his children and his wife; Ezechiel Chart does not feature at all, nor does Richard Read, yeoman, at whose house the meeting was held. While most, therefore, maintained some link with the established church despite their attendance at nonconformist conventicles, a few escaped such contact altogether.

After the death of 'the learned Mr Poyntell' (as he was called) in 1674 Thomas Brand moved to Staplehurst and took over the leadership of the Presbyterian church there; one suspects Lady Roberts' influence. He in turn was succeeded in 1684 by Samuel French whose burial was recorded in the Anglican register there in 1694. He is shown as paying on six hearths in 'an empty house' in Strood in

Table 10.2   *Nonconformists fined at Quarter Sessions, 1673*

Name	parish	fine	HT	comments if known in reconstitution
Thomas Moyse	Ben.	10s		tanner, chwd. '83-4, all children bapt. '68-81;
William Hartredge	Goud.	20s	1	nothing else known, died 1693;
John Mills, gent	Bid.	20s	4	gentleman, vestryman;
John Rose	Cra.	10s	3	saddler; children all 'born' 1654-64;
Robert Brissenden	Frit.	10s		all children bapt. '69-90, chwdn 1675-7;
James Bayly	Cra.	10s		tallow-chandler, ch. bapt. '66-70, then not;
Francis Cornwall	Sta.	10s	6	ex-vicar of Marden; Baptist preacher '72' (a);
Abraham Chapman	Sta.	10s	4	yeoman; all children baptised, 1663-1679;
James Holden	Hawk.	10s	3	children baptised from 1661-1674;
Robert Keele	Sta.	10s	?	
Samuel Bates	Cra.	40s		not in HT or reconst; Quaker meetings at his house;
Robert Delton	Cra.	40s	3	oversaw Rob. Hayward's will, not in register;
Thomas Brattle	Goud.	10s	4	all children baptised, 1664-73;
Thomas Coombes	Sta.	40s		tailor re. Q/S, not in reconstitution;
Richard Fo[r]ster	Frit	40s	7	if the innkeeper of Bid., 5 ch. bapt. '64-68;
William Bates	Cra.	40s	1	husbandman, children bapt. 1665-70;
Thomas Baseden	Cra.	10s	9	clothier, some child. bapt. '63-67, not all?
Thomas Robert	Cra.	10s	?	
Walter Viney	Sta	10s	2	butcher, 2nd of 3 marr.; child. bapt. 1670-87;
Ellen Young	Ben.	10s	?	
Samuel Fuller	Sta.	10s	6	gentleman; funerary inscription in church;
Thomas Fuller	Sta.	10s	?	presumably kin of the above;
Ann Cheebensende	Sta.	40s	?	
Stephen Weller	Cra.	10s	3	clothier; 1664, baptism; 1666 birth!
George Eastenden	Bid.	10s	?	
James Osborne	Bid.	10s	6	children all 'born' 1661-76; (b)
George Woolball	Sta.	10s	?	

Note: (a) Overseer of poor 1662, Churchwarden 1664; 4 children bapt. '63-73;
(b) In March 1662 James Osborne was paid 8s. 6d. by the Biddenden churchwardens to bring the new book of common prayer from Canterbury!

Kent in 1664, to which he again refers in his will 30 years later, when he asks his loving wife to sell 'my house in Stroud, Kent, now or formerly occupied by George Boys'. Meanwhile Lady Roberts brought a succession of Presbyterian ministers to Cranbrook, including Mr Edmund Trench (1672-83) who became her son-in-law in 1675; he moved to Brenchley in 1684 but returned in 1688, and died the following year.[16] Five of his children by Lady Roberts' daughter Bridget are recorded in the burial register at Cranbrook, one as an infant, but none was registered as baptised in the Anglican church. They could have been baptised in her private chapel.

In 1691 Comfort Starr, who had been curate in Carlisle from 1656 to his ejection in 1660, became the pastor of a Congregational church with 'some serious Christians of the poorer sort' who had ' struggled hard to keep up a meeting of 4 or 500 people' at Goudhurst.[17] Mention of the Goudhurst dissenters as 'the poorer sort' reminds us that, although the nonconformists named so far have been largely from the upper echelons of society, nonconformist assemblies encompassed all groupings.[18]

Baptists

The Baptist church in the area owed its origins to William Jeffery of Penshurst, who began preaching in 1640 at Richard Kingsnorth's house in Staplehurst called Spilshill.[19] There in 1644 William Jeffery converted the rector, Christopher Blackwood, and the then vicar of Marden, Francis Cornwall, to the Baptist cause.[20] By 1648 George Hammond, a tailor, and James Blackmore had become joint pastors of a Baptist group at Biddenden; in that same year Hammond founded a congregation in Cranbrook,[21] and as late as 1669 he was reported as illicitly teaching a very numerous conventicle there.[22]

The pattern of George Hammond's family, which is recorded in the Biddenden registers, shows some ambivalence in his attitude to the Anglican church, but more evident disassociation than that noted above with Presbyterians. His first child was christened (1647), the second died at birth, the third and fourth were 'born' (1651 and 1654); then, by another wife, his fifth child was christened (1658) but his sixth (1659) was 'born'. In 1663 his consistent dissent was recognised when he was gaoled for not frequenting the Church, whereas others were simply bound over.[23] In his will, in which he calls himself 'yeoman of Cranbrook', he committed his soul to the hands of Almighty God in typical Anglican fashion while requiring payment of '£40 to the then trustees of the Congregation of Baptists in Biddenden with whom I now walk, being a just debt of mine due'.[24] His association with the Anglican church was therefore minimal. His activities also straddled parish boundaries because nonconformist groups were not confined to the geographical limits of the Anglican parishes.

In April 1672 Nicholas and Theophilus Beach, John Weller, Richard Gunn and others had been fined sums ranging from 1s. 8d. to £3 8s. for being present at 'an assembly holden in the dwelling house of Susan Garret, widow, at Milkhouse in the parish of Cranbrook, under colour of exercising Religion in other manner than according to the Liturgy and practise of the Church of England'. The composition of this group (six broadweavers, a clothier, a mason, a butcher, a brazier, a cutler, two shoemakers, a tallow-chandler, two gardeners, two single women and a widow) underlines the fact that, although Baptist adherents might have had wealthy patrons, they themselves came from all walks of life.[25]

When it came to the Declaration of Indulgence later in 1672, Theophilus Beach's house in Cranbrook was licensed for Baptist meetings, and Richard Gunn was licensed to preach there. Theophilus was the son of Nicholas Beach, a prosperous yeoman who paid tax on six hearths; born in 1647, he was a tanner by trade. Apart from his birth, Theophilus does not figure in the registers at all; in his father's will dated 1683, which has a standard 'Anglican' ring about it, he was left £5 'unless he try to void my will; then only 5s', and named joint executor. His wife, Elizabeth, was buried in 1697, and we know from the funerary inscription set up to her in the church at Cranbrook that they 'left issue' five sons and five daughters, but not one of them figures in the registers. One of the sons, Theophilus, did marry in the Anglican church, in 1699; his bride was Hannah, 25-year-old daughter of Francis Cornwall, 'of Marden', who had been one of the first to be converted to the Baptist cause.[26]

Mention of Richard Gunn and John Weller, indicted with Nicholas and Theophilus Beach in 1672, brings us to another aspect of the Baptist church in the area: the way in which they worked together for their mutual advantage, and formed a community within the community. Richard Gunn, licensed to preach in Beach's house, was not a wealthy man; a shoemaker by trade, he lived in a two-hearth house in the town on which he was exempt from paying tax. John Weller, indicted with him, was also a shoemaker; he paid on three hearths in the town, and his will shows that he had considerable property occupied by others. When he came to write that will (1681) he asked Nathaniel Bennett and William Worsley, both well-known Baptists, to witness it, together with Jeffery Austin, who is not known. Subsequently, Nicholas Beach appraised his goods and chattels together with the same William Worsley, who also appraised the goods of Nicholas Beach himself (1683) and witnessed the will of George Hammond (1680). There was clearly a tight community here.[27] The third appraiser, Thomas Merriall, was a relative of Nicholas Beach by marriage and, at the time, a nonconformist; his four daughters and a son, aged 17, 12, seven, five and two, were baptised 'en bloc' in April 1685, suggesting that by then he had reverted to the Anglican cause.

We have already seen that John Bailey, husbandman of Staplehurst, even went so far as to seek guardians among his Baptist brethren in preference to his own wife (page 104); such an attitude, however, appears exceptional. When John Chandler asked William Jeffery to be guardian to his son, it was probably not the result of common religious feeling, because his children were all baptised in the Anglican church. In fact William Jeffery was the boy's uncle by marriage to Phoebe Chandler, and the link was as much kin as religion. On the other hand there is ample evidence that religious affiliations could lead to marriage alliances, as illustrated by the Beach-Cornwall marriage above. In this connection the Kingsnorth family of Staplehurst and Frittenden provide a singular example.

Richard Kingsnorth, one of the first to be won over to the Baptist cause by William Jeffery, mentions three daughters and five sons in his will proved 1673. One of his daughters married the ageing William Jeffery in 1670, and in 1672 he was himself licensed to preach in Staplehurst and three of his sons were similarly licensed for Charing, Frittenden, Lenham and Smarden.[28] While they maintained their adherence to the Baptist cause, Richard, James and John Kingsnorth all had their marriages recorded in the Anglican registers. Of their seven children mentioned in the Staplehurst register between 1654 and 1667 not one has a baptism ascribed; all have their births recorded well after it was normal to record baptisms, and many other children escaped registration altogether. The Kingsnorths were assiduous writers of wills, in almost every case underlining their nonconformist credentials by eschewing all mention of the customary preamble, with its '*In the name of God, Amen*', and commendation of their '*soul to Almighty God*'. Table 10.3 sheds some light on the extent to which these co-religionists supported each other in taking inventories and witnessing wills, and shows that in many cases their religious links were cemented by kinship.

Table 10.3   *Baptist inter-relationships: appraisers and will-witnesses, 1668-90*

		Inventories		
	deceased	appraisers 1	2	(3) + (4)
1668	Christopher Bourne	Leonard Hickmott	*Henry Snoath*	*Thomas & Henry Kingsnorth*
1673	*Richard Kingsnorth*	*Francis Cornwall*	*Henry Snoath*	
1683	*Anna Kingsnorth*	*Francis Cornwall*	John Robens	
1684	*Thomas Kingsnorth*	*Francis Cornwall*	Samuel Pattenson	
1684	*William Jeffery*	*Francis Cornwall*	Samuel Pattenson	
1690	*John Kingsnorth*	John Cooper	*Robert Edmett*	

		Wills		
	testators	witnesses 1	2	3 + (4)
1673	*Richard Kingsnorth*	Robert Adman, scri	*John Buss*	<u>*William Jeffery*</u>
1680	*Anna Kingsnorth*	John Buckwell	Ann Buckwell	Peter Whetcombe
1682	*Thomas Kingsnorth*	Steven Linke	*Sarah Vously*	Samuel Pattenson
1683	*William Jeffery*	Thomas Russell	John Buckhall	<u>*Thomas Kingsnorth*</u>
1685	*John Kingsnorth*	<u>*John Kingsnorth*</u>	Mary Abday	John & Elizabeth Cooper

Key: *Known Baptist sympathisers in italics*   <u>Known kinship link underlined</u>
Note: Sarah Vously, from Biddenden, baptised 1664, was probably in service.

For two Kingsnorths and Henry Snoath to have joined in the appraisal of Christopher Bourne's goods and chattels in Biddenden in 1668 suggests that there should be a Baptist link here. Christopher Bourne married (2nd) Elizabeth Buss in 1655, which also hints at a Baptist link, and he was the son of Freegift Bourne, a name redolent of a Puritan background. Henry Snoath, clothier of Staplehurst, had at least eight children between 1657 and 1675, not one of whom was baptised in the Anglican church; the births of the last four were noted in a spare space in its register at a later date. John Robbins was a relative by marriage to Hanna Kingsnorth. The children of John Buss continued to be 'born' after 1662, but John and Ann Buckwell had their children baptised, as did Thomas Russell. Samuel Pattenson, if he was the yeoman of Biddenden, was totally loyal to the Anglican communion. John and Elizabeth Cooper were registered as married in Biddenden in 1665; later, Richard Kingsnorth the younger appointed his loving friend John Cooper of Headcorn, yeoman, together with Robert Edmett of Biddenden, yeoman, overseers of his will in 1695. The probability is that the Coopers, and Robert Edmett, whose children appear in the Anglican register as 'born' in 1676 and 1680, were Baptists.

The evidence from wills, and from the recording of births rather than baptisms, shows that adherence to the Baptist church ran in families, and spread from one generation to the next. There is also some evidence of Baptists choosing to marry Baptists. Those whom we have met supporting the Baptist church in the area were, for the most part, men of substance. The Kingsnorths were mainly yeoman farmers, as were Nicholas Beach and Richard Read; apothecaries tended to prosper, Thomas Boys was a clothier and, as a tanner, Theophilus Beach was no doubt comparatively wealthy. These were the people who backed the church financially and materially, so one would expect them to be of a higher social standing than the bulk of their adherents. Among all these men, Richard Gunn, the licensed preacher, and John Weller, shoemaker, could be regarded as the only poor ones, and they not seriously so.

Other familiar names also received official recognition in 1672: thus Francis Cornwall was licensed to preach in Marden where he had been the vicar in the 1640s, and James Blackmore, last met in Biddenden, to preach in Tenterden. Richard Kingsnorth senior continued to hold meetings at his house, Spilsill Court, until he died in June 1673. This property then passed to the Osborne family, and Joseph Osborne, the pastor ejected from Benenden in 1662, who had been licensed to preach as an Independent in Brighton in 1672, came over from Tenterden where he had been living for a while and took over the Baptist centre at Spilsill. A chapel was built there against the north wall in 1689, and Osborne stayed on in Staplehurst until his death at the age of 84, in 1715.[29]

The Baptist Register of Births for Cranbrook runs from 1682 and indicates the vitality of the Baptist church as an organisation.[30] In parishes where it had yet to establish its own registers, the births (not baptisms) of at least some Baptist children were recorded in the Anglican registers. In Cranbrook the Anglican registers do not record such births, but do record some marriages and, as a matter of course, burials. It is difficult to establish how numerous Baptists were at this time. Between 1682 and 1701 only 15 births were recorded in the Baptist register; if they were the only ones born in the area, they represent only three per cent of the 519 who were recorded as born or baptised in the two Cranbrook churches.

Quakers

When George Fox, the great proselytiser of the Quaker cause, visited Cranbrook in 1655, he recorded 'a great meeting ... and many were turned to the Lord that day. ... Thomas Howsigoe, an Independent preacher, who lived near Cranbrook, was convinced, and became a faithful minister for the Lord Jesus'.[31] Subsequently Fox recorded his return to Kent in 1663: 'We went to Ashford where we had a quiet and a very blessed meeting; and on First-day we had a very good and peaceable one at Cranbrook. Then we went to Tenterden.'[32] These two visits, eight years apart, created and confirmed the presence of Quakers in the Weald.

Thomas Housegoe had been rector of Brightling in Sussex, but was converted to the Baptist cause only to leave in 1655 to become a Friend.[33] He, or his son, also Thomas, a Staplehurst clothier, appears as a trustee for the Quaker burial ground which was first established in 1658 at Ball Field in Cranbrook. His fellow trustees were John Colvill, clothier of Cranbrook, George Girdler, farmer of Tenterden, and James Wiggens, farmer of Sutton Valence. At the same time Stephen Bennett, yeoman of Staplehurst, gave farmland and buildings at Appledore worth £100 for poor Friends. The presence of the Quaker burial ground caused sufficient hostility among the townsfolk for it to be wrested back by the original owner in 1672.[34] The following year another burial ground was opened in a less contentious location at Courtstile in Cranbrook to cater for Quakers 'inhabbitting in the p~shes of Cranbrook, Staplehurst, Sutton Valence, Tenterden, Goodhurst and places adjacent ...'. This they bought from the Cranbrook clothier, John Colvill, and appointed as trustees: Thomas Nash and John Bennett, clothiers of Cranbrook; John Greensted (Grinsted), clothier of Staplehurst; James Wicken (Wiggens), yeoman of Sutton Valence; Thomas West, blacksmith of Tenterden; and John Hawkins, broadweaver of Goodhurst.[35]

From 1655 to 1680 the Wealden Quakers met in the homes of Friends: John Bennett's house 'a mile out of Cranbrook', or those of Richard or Samuel Bates, both Cranbrook shoemakers, or Robert Kite, mercer, and Thomas Housegoe, both of Staplehurst. Their organisation functioned across the parish boundaries, and rapidly gained support. In 1662 William Kilburn reported, 'Meetings of Quakers and Anabaptists have long been held at or near Cranbrook and lately many strangers have been amongst them and there are meetings in private places at night. At one meeting 150 Quakers stood silently, quaking and trembling two hours ...'.[36] The following year a warrant was issued for the arrest of Samuel Bates of Cranbrook and his wife Maria, together with a number of people from Goodhurst, who had used Bates' house for public meetings. This cross-parish organisation continued even after 1680, in which year a little house was purchased, again from John Colvill, in the High Street at Cranbrook for use as a Meeting House. Table 10.4 provides a list of the trustees, and highlights their anonymity as men who now avoided anything to do with the established church.[37]

John Colvill is typical in this respect. A wealthy man, assessed on seven hearths, he had married into the Courthope family in 1654, in Cranbrook church, before

---

Table 10.4   *Local trustees of the Quaker meeting house, Cranbrook, 1680*

Parish	trustee/purchaser	sum	
Benenden	George Courthope, millwright	10s. 0d.	not in registers
	Robert Courthope, clothier	£2 10s. 0d.	not in registers
Cranbrook	Thomas Nash, clothier	£3 0s. 0d.	not in registers, but [a]
	John Bennett, clothier	£4 0s. 0d.	in registers pre-1658 only
	John Afford, mercer	£5 0s. 0d.	marr. '74, a bapt '75; [a] & [b]
	Nathaniel Rowe, broadweaver	5s. 0d.	in registers pre-1653 only
	John Bates, cordwainer	£3 0s. 0d.	not in registers, but [a]
	John Turner, clothier	£2 0s. 0d.	not in registers
	Robert Lilly, cheesemonger	16s. 0d.	not in registers
	Thomas Spice, clothworker	5s. 0d.	not in registers, but [c]
Hawkhurst	Jeremy Vine, husbandman	10s. 0d.	not in registers
Goodhurst	John Hawkins	2s. 6d.	in registers pre-1657 only

Sources: Quaker Sufferings Book, CKS N/FQZ/1 and Draper (1993)
Notes: [a] John Bates, cordwainer, of Cranbrook and latterly of Goodhurst, by his will (CKS PRC 17/77/420) written 1690, left £5 to poor Friends via John Afford and Thomas Nash, and his orphaned daughters were provided for by the monthly meeting.   [b] John Afford's shop was frequently raided; he was helped by Nicholas Bishop to keep his stock, 1683.   [c] Thomas Spice is mentioned in will of his father, Richard, 1675, as 'sawyer', whereas his brothers Richard and John are both 'linenweavers'. The will omits any mention of soul or Almighty God

George Fox's arrival. Then the registers go silent, and none of his children is recorded. His own burial passed unrecorded as well. On the other hand in 1676 his son, John Colvill jnr, married in the Anglican church in Cranbrook, and in turn his son, also John, was duly baptised in the same church. In much the same way, John Bennett, assessed on four hearths, had his marriage recorded in 1656, but the registers go silent for him and his family after 1658. Thomas Nash, also assessed on four hearths, escaped the registers altogether, whereas his son, Stephen, had all his children baptised. The Staplehurst mercer, Robert Kite, had three children registered before the establishment of the Friends in the area; he died *c.*1683, but his burial is not recorded in the registers. The likelihood is that, as with the others mentioned above, he was buried in the Quaker burial ground. His son Abraham, however, used the Anglican church to the full, having ten children baptised at Staplehurst between 1679 and 1700.

There are strong hints here that families in the second generation were less zealous for the Quaker cause than the original converts, and this attitude is confirmed by the comment on early Quakerism in Kent, probably written about 1676: 'many called, but few chosen to stand the battel'.[38] Certainly Quakers and their families paid dearly for their fervour both in cash and in suffering. The Kent Sufferings Book 1655-1759 gives totals of Friends who were affected by persecution, and it is clear that despite the presence of men of influence, meetings in the house in Cranbrook were severely disrupted especially during the persecution of the early 1680s.[39] In 11 of the 35 years between 1660 and 1689, numbers of those who suffered for their avoidance of Anglican worship reached double figures, and the highest figures, 35 in 1660 and 29 in 1683, give an indication of the minimum strength of numbers of Quakers in the region as a whole, but centred on Cranbrook itself.[40]

Because Friends figure so little in the reconstitution there is bound to be a limit to the conclusions one can draw about their inter-relationships. They did call upon their brethren at important moments and for important duties; thus the Staplehurst yeoman, Stephen Bennett, called upon fellow Quakers, Thomas Scoones, bricklayer, and Robert Kite, mercer, to be overseers of his will (page 149) and Robert witnessed the will of John Bennett. James Allay was a Cranbrook tailor who turned to John and Samuel Bates when he wanted to borrow on bond.[41] All three were Friends. Quakers did intermarry, but because of their exclusiveness, and their reluctance to write wills, there is little evidence one way or the other. Many of those whom we have met shared links with the broadcloth industry but yeomen, husbandmen, a mercer, a blacksmith and several shoemakers also feature among leading Quakers; many of them were wealthy and became the trustees and purchasers of Friends' real-estate; the rank and file supporters, like Thomas Avard of Goudhurst or Henry Start 'lame and poor, on charity', and Thomas Skilton of Cranbrook, broadweaver, were so poor that others had to pay their fines.[42]

That subsequent generations did not adhere to the Quaker cause with the dedication of their parents should not surprise us; indeed, first generation Quakers showed extraordinary resilience in staying loyal to their beliefs despite occasionally ferocious persecution. At least 20 local Quakers from all walks of life (bricklayers, broadweavers, cordwainers, tailors, yeomen and clothiers) were imprisoned in Maidstone for several weeks in 1660 for refusing to swear the required oath, and by 1666 the action of preaching secured Thomas Relfe 60 days in gaol. William Wacher, tailor of Cranbrook, had been imprisoned for a month (1660) for refusing to promise good behaviour after he was caught pinning lines on the church door accusing Presbyterians who attended services there of hypocrisy; he and his wife were in gaol again for three months in 1666.

The 1670 Conventicle Act encouraged informers by offering them part of any fine imposed, and fines henceforth seem to have become more common than imprisonment. Samuel Bates and Robert Kite, for instance, were each fined £20 for allowing meetings at their houses (1675), and they both suffered appropriation of their goods; Kite's shop had literally been put under surveillance.[43] There is also a graphic description of a raid carried out in 1684 on John Afford's shop in Cranbrook by the constable, the borseholder and one each of the churchwardens and overseers of the poor. After failing to gain entry by the door they 'violently wrested open the hatch against which John Afford stood and let in the whole gange'. They took £30-worth of cloth and moved on to the house of Thomas Lilly, carpenter, where they broke down the door and removed £6-worth of beds and bedding before raiding the houses of Thomas Nash and John Turner, both clothiers. In such raids the parish officials often had the support of troops from the trained bands, and we are led to believe that they would customarily appropriate goods of greater value than the stated fines.

We are told that after the attack on Afford's shop 'officers began to be sum what mor sensible of their errur in breaking doores'. Certainly not every officer of the parishes was equally industrious in hounding his dissenting neighbours. The Sufferings Book notes with regret that some constables who were Presbyterians appropriated goods from Friends, whereas Jonah Fuller, a Cranbrook clothier, when he was constable of Cranbrook hundred, 'was a man of a tender spirit' who 'went his way without medling with them neither would act anything to ye ruine of any during his office'; he was fined £5 by the justices for not doing his duty, as was Richard Webb, gentleman of Frittenden, although he also was 'no professor'.[44]

Refusal to bear arms was one occasion for Quakers to fall foul of the law, and another reason for raids on more affluent Friends like John Colvill, John Bennet and John Afford of Cranbrook and George Courthope of Benenden. Refusal to pay tithes to the vicar or rector was another crime for which Quakers suffered repeated depredations. In 1660 John Colvill had 25 sheep (value £12) removed to cover a tithe of 40s., Edward Couchman two cows (value £13) for a tithe of 4s. Indeed John Colvill languished in Maidstone Gaol from 1670 to 1673 for refusing to pay tithes.

The intensity of such persecution varied according to the attitude of the Anglican minister. Giles Hinton, rector of Biddenden, for instance, certainly hounded the husbandman James Stone for not paying his tithes. There is record of Stone's imprisonment in 1683 and 1686, and of annual raids on his cereal crops and animals every year from 1689 to the turn of the century. Charles Buck, vicar of Cranbrook, could be similarly demanding; in 1687 Jeremiah Warner and four others, including John Bates who had actually moved to Goudhurst seven years before, were sent to gaol for failure to pay their dues. Jeremy Vine and James Allay also regularly lost goods to Charles Buck in the 1690s.

Nonconformists and Exclusivity

Despite the evidence that co-religionists worked together to their mutual advantage it would be wrong to conclude that they formed an exclusive web of inter-relationships. Thomas Burren, for instance, a Staplehurst clothier, had his children duly baptised in the Anglican church but asked two Baptists, Richard Kingsnorth and the schoolmaster Thomas Smith, to be overseers of his will. Thomas Burren was married to Thomas Smith's sister, so the kinship link would appear to have outweighed the pull of conflicting religious leanings.[45]

In the preamble to their wills both Elizabeth Stiver, widow, and Samuel French, the Presbyterian preacher in Staplehurst, omitted mention of their souls; both had as two of their three witnesses Elizabeth Earl and William Lingfield; Elizabeth Stiver left bequests to the Presbyterian Samuel French and to John Webb (related to Lingfield). Yet William Lingfield also witnessed the will of Walter Viney who quite happily committed his soul to Almighty God and had every one of the ten children baptised in the Anglican church. The case of Aaron Bowyer's will is even more intriguing. He was a barber-surgeon of Cranbrook who, to judge by the lack of any bequest of his soul to Almighty God, and the dearth of baptisms for his children, had marked nonconformist leanings; John Weller, the Baptist noted above, was a witness to his will; yet Aaron appointed the Anglican vicar of Cranbrook, Charles Buck, to oversee that will.[46]

Nonconformists were not averse to taking part in parish activities, nor were they prevented from so doing despite the 1673 Test Act which required all office-holders to be Anglicans.[47] Stevenson has shown that, at this period, highly cohesive and tightly-knit groups like Baptists and Quakers were involved in day-to-day parish life in Huntingdonshire, Cambridgeshire and Bedfordshire, witnessing and writing the wills of non-sectaries even while being persecuted at the hands of the Anglican Church and the judiciary, and Munby has done the same for Hertfordshire.[48] In Cranbrook itself some with strong nonconformist tendencies took on parish offices; they became surveyors of the highways, but progressed no further. In 1669 Richard Spice, broadweaver, nonconformist and possible Quaker, and John Bennett, clothier and leading Quaker, held this office (and no further office) together with Robert Robotham, who went on to be churchwarden and constable, and Richard Vinicombe, who continued to sign churchwardens' accounts but did not have his children baptised. The following year saw Thomas Nash, a Quaker trustee, appointed surveyor; he held no further office. John Afford, surveyor in 1674, was overseer of the poor in 1677; yet the Quaker Sufferings Book shows him being fined for attendance at Quaker meetings throughout the 1670s and 1680s, and his shop repeatedly raided for imposts in cash or kind. Nonconformity, and the avoidance of Anglican services which went with the more extreme forms of nonconformity, were therefore no bar to appointment to the less prestigious parish offices. Indeed, with the evidence that some with a nonconformist disposition worked in a charitable way for the community, it is not so surprising to find that nonconformists acted as overseers of the poor.

Eric Carlson had wondered whether some churchwardens may have 'concealed the ecclesiastical eccentricities and deviations of their neighbours' because they were themselves 'people of religious convictions which put them on or beyond the margins of the national church'.[49] Cranbrook provides the answer. Josias Colvill, brother of the leading Quaker John Colvill, was surveyor in 1665, churchwarden in 1671 and 1672, and constable in 1683; he died in 1687. As churchwarden he may well have found it difficult to persecute his family and their friends. More telling, Nicholas Beach, father of the leading Baptist Theophilus and fined for attending unlawful conventicles, was himself churchwarden in 1673 and 1674, and constable in 1682; he died in 1683. The Quaker Sufferings Book actually shows Nicholas Beach, as constable in 1682, raiding John Colvill's house for a fine of 40s., and Edward Beach, borsholder in the same year, raiding the house of George Courthope in Benenden for 20s.; it comments that they were punctilious about not overcharging.[50] The answer to Carlson's question, therefore, is that nonconformists did take office alongside their Anglican brethren, and did protect their kin and neighbours.

Table 10.5 *Nonconformist overseers and churchwardens, Staplehurst, 1660-75*

	Overseer	Churchwarden	Affiliation	ref. page:
Francis Cornwall	1662	1664	Baptist	184
Peter Burren		1666, 1667	Congregational	181
Richard Kingsnorth	1666		Baptist	184
John Kingsnorth	1670		Baptist	185
Robert Kite	1674		Quaker	190
Henry Snoath	1675		Baptist	186
John Bennett	1675		Quaker	190

Note: A Thomas Housegoe was churchwarden in 1667 and 1668, but he was not the Thomas Housegoe who was among the first Quakers (page 187); he died in 1664. The relationship between the two is not known, but the churchwarden had his children baptised in the 1660s and 1670s, and died in 1675.

The Cranbrook picture is no isolated aberration. In Staplehurst, that parish of strong dissent, the picture of nonconformist involvement in parish offices is remarkable, as shown in Table 10.5. Peter Burren was a wealthy clothier/gentleman whose children were all baptised (1668-78) but whose house was licensed for Presbyterian teaching in 1672; he was a close friend of Daniel Poyntell. Even more remarkable is the appointment of Francis Cornwall, known Baptist preacher, as overseer of the poor and churchwarden in the early 1660s. Here was an acknowledged leader of a nonconformist church holding the senior administrative offices in an Anglican parish.

Maybe a fitting conclusion to this section on nonconformist relationships is provided by Thomas Goddard, clothier of Cranbrook. He made his will on 31 December 1663,[51] and was buried 3 January 1664. He was a bachelor, who left goods and chattels to the value of £357 18s. 11d., of which £128 14s. 8d. was left after payment of necessary expenses, debts and legacies.[52] In the will, he leaves his soul to Almighty God in standard Anglican fashion, but his principal legatee was the leading Quaker John Colvill, to whom he left a substantial proportion of his real estate in Benenden with the proviso that he pay out '£5 yearly to John Weller, son of John Weller of Cranbrook, at 25s. per quarter, and to my mother-in-law [properly 'step-mother'] his now wife, £50'. This John Weller was almost certainly the poor thatcher who lived as a conformist with his wife and four children in a one-hearth cottage on which he was exempt from paying tax, rather than the Baptist shoemaker of the same name. Weller also received Goddard's best wearing apparel, while the poor widows of Cranbrook benefited under the will from a windfall of 5s. each (total £10). Several other legatees appear to have been conformists.

The conformist Thomas Goddard had chosen a Quaker, John Colvill, to be executor of his will not because he was a Quaker but because he had married Thomas' step-mother, Anne Goddard née Courthope. In fact the man who actually administered the estate was another legatee, Thomas Knight, clothier of Cranbrook, who was to receive Goddard's house and lands in Goudhurst, and the sum of £20; Colvill could well have been in prison at the time of the probate, which took nearly five years. Thomas Knight was almost certainly a Baptist; at the time of the bequest he was still a bachelor, but he went on to marry Barbara Wenman, who was also mentioned in Goddard's will. Another legatee was John Courthope, clothier and gentleman of Cranbrook, who was no doubt related to the testator through his step-mother. Some Courthopes, like George and Robert, were dissenters, while some, like Henry Courthope, led Trained Bands of troops against the dissenters with marked ferocity.[53]

This short history encapsulates many of the themes covered above and in earlier chapters. There is evidence of nonconformist interaction, but sometimes the dissenters are Quakers, sometimes Baptists; some were not dissenters at all. It is clear that kinship links played an important part. It is less easy to determine whether the influence of kinship outweighed that of religion, or whether occupation was the real key because most of the protagonists were clothiers. There is also a strong hint of friendship, between the two bachelors and Barbara Wenman, and charity in the bequests to John Weller and to the poor widows. It provides a salutary warning, if any such warning should still be necessary, that, in commenting on village societies in the late 17th century, it would be wrong to be prescriptive.

Bibliography

Abbott, M., *Life Cycles in England 1560-1720, cradle to grave* (1996)

Adair, R., *Courtship, illegitimacy and marriage in early modern England* (1996)

Archer, I., *The Diary Of Isaac Archer, see* Storey, M. (1993)

Arkell, T., 'Printed Instructions for administering the Hearth Tax', in Schurer, K. and Arkell, T. (eds.), *Surveying The People* (1992a)

Arkell, T., 'A Method for Estimating Population Totals from the Compton Census Returns', in Schurer, K. and Arkell, T. (eds.), *Surveying The People* (1992b)

Arkell, T., 'An Examination of the Poll Taxes of the later Seventeenth Century, the Marriage Duty Act and Gregory King', in Schurer, K. and Arkell, T. (eds.), *Surveying The People* (1992c)

Arkell, T., 'Interpreting Probate Inventories', in Arkell, T., Evans, N. and Goose, N., (eds.), *When Death Do Us Part: understanding and interpreting the probate records of early modern England* (2000)

Arkell, T., 'Identifying regional variations from the hearth tax', *The Local Historian*, 33, 3 (2003)

Ashurst, D., 'St Mary's Church, Worsborough, South Yorkshire', *Local Population Studies*, 55 (1995)

Assheton, Nicholas' diary, *see* Raines, F. R. (ed.)

Barley, M.W., *The English Farmhouse and Cottage* (1961)

Bedells, J., 'The Gentry of Huntingdonshire', *Local Population Studies*, 44 (1990)

Ben-Amos, I.K., *Adolesecence and Youth in Early Modern England* (1994)

Berry, B.M. and Schofield, R.S., 'Age at Baptism in pre-industrial England', *Population Studies*, 25 (1971)

Berry, W. (ed.), *Pedigrees of the Families in the County of Kent* (1830)

Boulton, J., 'The Marriage Duty Act and Parochial registration in London, 1695- 1706', in Schurer, K. and Arkell, T. (eds.), *Surveying The People* (1992)

Bowden, P.J., 'Agricultural Prices, Wages, Farm Profits, Rents', Ch.13 of Thirsk, J., *The Agrarian History of England and Wales* V, 2 (1985)

Bower, J., 'Probate Accounts as a source for Kentish Early Modern Economic and Social History', *Archaeologia Cantiana*, 109 (1991)

Bower, J., 'The Kent Yeoman in the seventeenth century', *Archaeologia Cantiana*, 114 (1994)

Bower, J., 'Introduction to Probate Accounts', in Spufford, P. (ed.), *Index to the Probate Accounts of England and Wales* (1999)

Boys, J., *General View of the Agriculture of the County of Kent* (1813)

Brandon, P., *The Kent and Sussex Weald* (2003)

Brown, W.N., 'The receipt of poor relief and family situation: Aldenham, Hertfordshire 1630-90', in Smith, R.M. (ed.), *Land, Kinship and Life-Cycle* (1984)

Calamy (1802), *see* Palmer, Samuel, edition of 1802

Calamy (1934), *see* Matthews, A.G., edition of 1934

Carlson, E., Introduction to *Ely Consistory Probate Records* (1994)

Carlson, E., 'The origins, function, and status of the office of churchwarden, with particular reference to the diocese of Ely', in Spufford, M. (ed.), *The World of Rural Dissenters 1520-1725* (1995)

Chalklin, C.W., *The Compton Census of 1676: the dioceses of Canterbury and Rochester*, Kent Records, 17 (1960)

Chalklin, C.W., 'The Rural Economy of a Kentish Wealden Parish 1650-1750', *The Agricultural History Review*, 10 (1962)

Chalklin, C.W., *Seventeenth-century Kent: a Social and Economic History* (1965)

Chambers, J.D., note on E.A. Wrigley's 'Population and History', in *Local Population Studies*, 3 (1969)

Chambers, R., *The Strict Baptist Chapels of England, Vol 3, The Chapels of Kent* (1950s)

Chartres, J.A., 'Carrying in England in the Seventeenth Century: Myth and Reality', *Economic History Review*, 30 (1977)

Chartres J. and Hey, D. (eds.), *English Rural Society 1500-1800* (1990)

Clay, C., 'Landlords and Estate Management in England', Ch. 14 of Thirsk, J., *The Agrarian History of England and Wales*, V,2 (1985)

Collinson, P., 'Cranbrook and the Fletchers: Popular and Unpopular Religion in the Kentish Weald', in Brooks, P.N. (ed.), *Reformation: Principle and Practice* (1980)

Collinson, P., *Godly People: Essays on English Protestantism and Puritanism* (1983)

Copeman, W.S.C., *The Worshipful Society of Apothecaries of London: A History, 1617-1967* (1980)

Cowper, H.S., *Loddenden and the Usbornes of Loddenden, The story of a Kentish Homestead* (1914)

Cowper, J. M., *Canterbury Marriage Licences*, Vol. 2 (1619-1660), Vol. 3 (1661-1676), and Vol. 4 (1677-1700) (1892-4).

Cox, N.C. and Cox, J.J., 'Probate 1500-1800: a System in Transition', in Arkell, T.,

Evans, N. and Goose, N. (eds.), *When Death Do Us Part: understanding and interpreting the probate records of early modern England* (2000)

Crawford, P. ''The sucking child': Adult attitudes to child care in the first year of life in seventeenth-century England', *Continuity and Change* 1, 1 (1986)

Creighton, C., *History of Epidemics in Britain* (1891/4)

Cressy, D., *Birth, Marriage and Death: Ritual, Religion, and the Life-Cycle in Tudor and Stuart England* (1997)

de la Bedoyere, G. (ed.), *The Diary of John Evelyn* (1995)

de Launay, J., *Cranbrook, Kent: Wills 1396-1640* (1984)

Drake, M., 'An Elementary Exercise in Parish Register Demography', *Economic History Review*, 14 (1962)

Draper, G., 'The first hundred years of Quakerism in Kent'; part 1, *Archaeologia Cantiana*, 112 (1993) and part 2, 115 (1995)

Dyer, A., 'Seasonality of Baptisms: an Urban Approach', *Local Population Studies*, 27 (1981)

Dyer, A., 'Epidemics of Measles in a Seventeenth-century English Town', *Local Population Studies*, 34 (1985)

Edwards, P., 'Farm and Family: Administering the Estate of William Poore, a Hampshire Downland Farmer, 1593-9', *Southern History* (1994)

Erickson, A.L., 'An Introduction to Probate Accounts', in Martin, G.H. and Spufford, P. (eds.), *The Records of the Nation, The British Record Society* (1990)

Erickson, A.L., *Women and property in early modern England* (1995) .

Erickson, A.L., 'Using Probate Accounts', in Arkell, T., Evans, N. and Goose, N. (eds.), *When Death Do Us Part: understanding and interpreting the probate records of early modern England* (2000)

Evans, N., 'Occupations and Status of Male Testators in Cambridgeshire, 1551-1750', in Arkell, T., Evans, N. and Goose, N. (eds.), *When Death Do Us Part: understanding and interpreting the probate records of early modern England* (2000)

Eveleigh, Rev.. C., 'Letters relating to the condition of the church in Kent, 1678-1690', *Archaeologia Cantiana*, 21 (1895)

Evelyn, John's diary, *see* de la Bedoyere, G. (ed.)

Everitt, A., 'Social Mobility in Early Modern England', *Past and Present*, 33 (1966)

Everitt, A., 'Nonconformity in Country Parishes', in Thirsk, J. (ed.), *Land, Church and People, Essays presented to H.P.R. Finberg* (1970)

Everitt, A., *The Community of Kent and the Great Rebellion 1640-1660* (1973)

Everitt, A., *Continuity and Colonization—the Evolution of Kentish Settlement* (1986)

Eversley, D.E.C., 'Exploitation of Anglican Parish Registers by Aggregative Analysis', in Wrigley, E.A. (ed.), *An Introduction to English Historical Demography* (1966)

Finlay, R., 'Distance to church and registration experience', *Local Population Studies*, 24 (1980)

Fox, G., *A Journal of the Life, Travels, Sufferings, Christian Experiences and Labour of Love of George Fox*, 2 volumes (8th edition, 1891)

French, H.R., 'The search for the 'middle sort of people' in England, 1600-1800', *Historical Journal*, 43 (2000)

Furley, R., *A History of the Weald of Kent* (1874)

G. (? Jacob Giles), *The Compleat Parish Officer* (1734)

Goody, J., Thirsk, J. and Thompson, E.P. (eds.), *Family and inheritance, Rural society in western Europe, 1200-1800* (1976)

Goose, N. and Evans, N., 'Wills as an historical source', in Arkell, T., Evans, N. and Goose, N., *When Death Do Us Part* (2000)

Gough, Richard, *The History of Myddle*, Hey D. (ed.) (1981)

Hainsworth, D.R., 'The estate steward and his world in later Stuart England', in *Stewards, Lords and People* (1992)

Hair, P.E., 'Bridal pregnancy in rural England in earlier centuries', *Population Studies*, 20, 2 (1966)

Harleian Society, *see* Visitation of Kent

Harrington, D. (ed.), Pearson S. and Rose, S., *Kent Hearth Tax Assessment, Lady Day 1664* (2000)

Harris, R., *Weald and Downland Open Air Museum Guidebook* (1998)

Haslewood, Rev.. F., *The Parish of Benenden, Kent* (1889)

Hasted, E., *The History and Topographical Survey of Kent*, reprint of 2nd edition 1797-1801 (1972)

Hey, D., *An English Rural Community: Myddle under the Tudors and Stuarts* (1974)

Hill, C., *The World Turned Upside Down: Radical Ideas during the English Revolution* (1972)

Hindle, S., 'Power, Poor Relief, and Social Relations in Holland Fen, *c.*1600-1800', in *The Historical Journal*, 41, 1 (1998)

Hindle, S., 'The Growth of Social Stability in Restoration England', in *The European Legacy*, Vol. 5, No. 4 (2000)

Hindle, S., 'Dependency, Shame and Belonging: Badging the Deserving Poor, *c*.1550-1750', in *Cultural and Social History* (2004)

Holderness, B.A., 'Credit in English rural society before the nineteenth century, with special reference to the period 1650 to 1720', in *Agricultural History Review*, 24 (1976)

Holderness, B.A., 'Widows in pre-industrial society: an essay upon their economic functions', in Smith, R.M. (ed.), *Land, Kinship and Life-Cycle* (1984)

Houlbrooke, R.A., *The English Family, 1450-1700* (1984)

Howe, P., 'Identifying nonconformity in late seventeenth-century St Albans', *Local Population Studies*, 68 (2002)

Hume, R., in Yates, N., Hume, R. and Hastings, P., *Religion and Society in Kent, 1640-1914* (1994)

Jackson, S. and Laxton, P., 'Of such as are of riper years? A note on age at Baptism', *Local Population Studies*, 18 (1977)

Johnston, J.A., 'Probate Inventories and Wills of a Worcestershire Parish, 1676-1775', *Midland History*, 1 (1971)

Josselin, Ralph's diary, *see* Macfarlane, A. (1991)

Kussmaul, A., *Servants in Husbandry in Early Modern England* (1981)

Landau, N., *The Justices of the Peace, 1679-1760* (1984)

Lansberry, H.C.F. (ed.), *The Government and Politics of Kent, 1640-1914* (2001)

Laslett, P., 'The Gentry of Kent in 1640', in *Cambridge History Journal*, 9, ii (1948)

Laslett P., 'Mean Household Size in England since the Sixteenth Century', in Laslett, P. and Wall, R. (eds.), *Household and Family in Past Time* (1972)

Laslett, P., 'Long-term trends in bastardy in England', in *Family life and illicit love in earlier generations: Essays in historical sociology* (1977a)

Laslett, P., 'Clayworth and Cogenhoe', in *Family life and illicit love in earlier generations: Essays in historical sociology* (1977b)

Laslett, P., *The World we have Lost—Further Explored*, 3rd edition (1983)

Laslett, P., 'Natural and Political Observations on the Population of late Seventeenth-century England: reflections on the work of Gregory King and John Graunt', in Schurer, K. and Arkell, T. (eds.), *Surveying The People* (1992)

Levine, D. and Wrightson, K., *The Making of an Industrial Society: Whickham 1560-1765* (1991)

Macfarlane, A., *The Family Life of Ralph Josselin, a seventeenth-century clergyman: an essay in Historical Anthropology* (1970)

Macfarlane, A., with Harrison, S. and Jardine, C., *Reconstructing Historical Communities* (1977)

Macfarlane, A., *The Origins of English Individualism: The Family, Property and Social Transition* (1978)

Macfarlane, A., *Marriage and Love in England, 1300-1840* (1986)

Macfarlane, A. (ed.), *The Diary of Ralph Josselin, 1616-1683* (1991)

Maguire, L.J., *Cranbrook Baptist Church* (1995)

Marsh, C., 'In the Name of God? Will-making and Faith in Early Modern England', in Martin, G.H. and Spufford, P., *The Records of the Nation* (1990)

Matthews, A.G., *Calamy revised, being a revision of Edmund Calamy's Account of the Ministers and Others ejected and silenced 1660-2* (1934)

Morant, V., 'The Settlement of Protestant Refugees in Maidstone', *Economic History Review*, 4 (1951)

Morant, V.E., 'On Smuggling Fullers Earth', *Archaeologia Cantiana*, 99 (1983)

Morehouse, H.J. (ed.), *Adam Eyre, A Dyurnall, or Catalogue of All my Accions and Expences from the 1st of January, 1647,* Surtees Society, 65 (1877)

Muldrew, C., *The Economy of Obligation; the Culture of Credit and Social Relations in Early Modern England* (1998)

Munby, L., *The Common People are not Nothing: Conflict in Religion and Politics in Hertfordshire 1575-1780* (1995)

Nuttall, G., 'Dissenting Churches in Kent pre-1700', *Journal of Ecclesiastical History*, 14 (1963)

Ogilby, J., *Britannia, Volume the First, or an Illustration of the Kingdom of England and Dominion of Wales* (1685)

Olsen, P., *The Story of Glassenbury, 1272-1999* (2001)

Outhwaite, R.B., 'Age at Marriage in England from the Late Seventeenth to the Nineteenth Century', *Transactions of the Royal Historical Society*, 23 (1972)

Oxley, D., "The seat of death and terror': urbanization, stunting and smallpox', *Economic History Review*, 56, 4 (2003)

Palmer, S., *The nonconformist's memorial, being an account of the lives, sufferings and printed works of the two thousand ministers ejected from the Church of England, chiefly by the Act of Uniformity, Aug. 24, 1662, originally written by Edmund Calamy, D.D.,* II (1802)

Pearson, S., *The Medieval Houses of Kent: an historical analysis* (1994)

Pearson, S., 'Introduction', in Harrington, D. (ed.), *Kent Hearth Tax Assessment, Lady Day 1664* (2000)

Petrie, S., 'The Religion of Sir Roger Twysden (1597-1672): A case study in gentry piety in seventeenth-century England', *Archaeologia Cantiana*, 124 (2004)

Pile, C.C R., *Dissenting Congregations in Cranbrook* (1953)

Pile, C.C.R., *Cranbrook Broadcloth and the Clothiers* (1981)

Pollock, L.A., *Forgotten Children, Parent-child relations from 1500 to 1900* (1983)

Poole, A., 'Baptismal delay: some implications from the parish registers of Cranbrook and surrounding parishes in the Kentish Weald', *Local Population Studies*, 65 (2000)

Poole, A., 'Kinship and other social and economic links as a basis for personal relationships in the Cranbrook region of Kent, 1660-1700', Roehampton PhD thesis (2002)

Poole, A., 'Debt in the Cranbrook region in the late seventeenth century', *Archaeologia Cantiana*, 123 (2003)

Poole, A., 'Welfare provision in seventeenth-century Kent; a look at Biddenden and neighbouring parishes', *Archaeologia Cantiana* 125 (2005)

Raines, F.R. (ed.), *The Journal of Nicholas Assheton of Downham*, Chetham Society, old series, 14 (1848)

Razzell, P., 'The growth of population in eighteenth-century England: A critical reappraisal', *Genealogists' Magazine* 25; 4 (1995); 5 (1996)

Razzell, P., 'Evaluating the same-name technique as a way of measuring burial register reliability in England', *Local Population Studies*, 64 (2000)

Reynolds, G., 'Infant mortality and sex ratios at baptism as shown by reconstruction of Willingham, a parish at the edge of the Fens in Cambridgeshire', *Local Population Studies*, 22 (1979)

Russell, D., *Cranbrook Congregational Church, a short history* (1993)

Sachse, W.L. (ed.), *The Diary of Roger Lowe of Ashton-in-Makerfield, Lancashire, 1663-74* (1938)

Schofield, R., answer to a query in *Local Population Studies*, 9 (1972)

Schofield, R., 'An Anatomy of an Epidemic: Colyton, November 1645 to November 1646', in Slack, P. (ed.), *The Plague Reconsidered; a new look at its origins and effects in sixteenth- and seventeenth-century England* (1977)

Sharpe, J.A., *Early Modern England: a Social History 1550-1760* (1987)

Sharpe, P., 'The total reconstitution method: a tool for class-specific study?', *Local Population Studies*, 44 (1990)

Sharpe, P., *Population and Society in an East Devon Parish: reproducing Colyton 1540-1840* (2002)

Short, B.M., 'The South-East: Kent, Surrey and Sussex', Ch. 9 of Thirsk, J., *The Agrarian History of England and Wales*, V, 2 (1985)

Silverthorne, E. (ed.), *The Deposition Book of Richard Wyatt, JP, 1767-1776*, Surrey Record Society, 30 (1978)

Slack, P., *Poverty and Policy in Tudor and Stuart England* (1988)

Slater, M., *Family Life in the Seventeenth Century: The Verneys of Claydon House* (1984)

Smellie, K.B., *A History of Local Government* (1968)

Snell, K.D.M., 'Parish Registration and the study of labour mobility', *Local Population Studies*, 33 (1984)

Souden, D., 'Movers and stayers in family reconstitution population', *Local Population Studies*, 33 (1984)

Spufford, M., 'The Significance of the Cambridgeshire Hearth Tax', in *Proceedings of the Cambridge Antiquarian Society*, 55 (1962)

Spufford, M., 'The dissenting churches in Cambridgeshire from 1660-1700', *Proceedings of the Cambridge Antiquarian Society*, 61 (1968)

Spufford, M., *Contrasting Communities, English Villagers in the Sixteenth and Seventeenth Centuries* (1974)

Spufford, M., 'Peasant inheritance customs and land distribution in Cambridgeshire from the sixteenth to the eighteenth centuries', in Goody, J., Thirsk, J. and Thompson, E.P. (eds.), *Family and inheritance, Rural society in western Europe, 1200-1800* (1976)

Spufford, M., *The Great Reclothing of Rural England: Petty Chapmen and their Wares in the Seventeenth Century* (1984)

Spufford, M., 'The limitations of the probate inventory', in Chartres, J., and Hey, D. (eds.), *English Rural Society 1500-1800* (1990)

Spufford, M. (ed.), *The World of Rural Dissenters 1520-1725* (1995)

Spufford, M., 'The scope of Local History, and the Potential of the Hearth Tax Returns', Phillimore Lecture to the British Association for Local History, June 2000, in *The Local Historian*, 30, 4 (2000)

Spufford, M. and Went, J., *Poverty Portrayed* (1995)

Spufford, M. and Takahashi, M., 'Families, Will Witnesses, and Economic Structure in the Fens and on the Chalk: Sixteenth- and Seventeenth-Century Willingham and Chippenham', *Albion*, 28, 3 (1996)

Spufford, P. (ed.), *Index to the Probate Accounts of England and Wales* (1999)

Spufford, P., 'Long-Term Rural Credit in Sixteenth- and Seventeenth-century England: the Evidence of Probate Accounts', in Arkell, T., Evans, N. and Goose, N. (eds.), *When Death Do Us Part: understanding and interpreting the probate records of early modern England* (2000)

Spurr, J., *English Puritanism 1603-1689* (1998)

Stapleton, B., 'Family strategies: patterns of inheritance in Odiham, Hampshire, 1525-1850', *Continuity and Change*, 14 (1999)

Steel, D.J. (ed.), *National Index of Parish Registers* (1968)

Stevenson, B., 'The Economic and Social Status of Protestant Sectarians in Huntingdonshire, Cambridgeshire and Bedfordshire (1650-1725)', Cambridge PhD thesis (1990)

Stevenson, B., 'The social and economic status of post-restoration dissenters, 1660-1725', in Spufford, M. (ed.), *The World of Rural Dissenters 1520-1725* (1995a)

Stevenson, B., 'The social integration of post-restoration dissenters, 1660-1725', in Spufford, M. (ed.), *The World of Rural Dissenters 1520-1725* (1995b)

Stone, L., 'Social Mobility in England, 1500-1700', *Past and Present*, 33 (1966)

Stone, L., *The Family, Sex and Marriage in England 1500-1800* (1977)

Storey, M. (ed.), *Two East Anglian Diaries, 1641-1729* (1993)

Takahashi, M., 'The Number of Wills Proved in the Sixteenth and Seventeenth Centuries', in Martin, G.H. and Spufford, P., *The Records of the Nation* (1990)

Tarbutt, W., 'The Cloth Trade in Cranbrook', *Archaeologia Cantiana*, 9 (1874)

Tarver, A., 'Understanding Probate Accounts and their Generation in the Post-Restoration Diocese of Lichfield and Coventry to 1700', in Arkell, T., Evans, N. and Goose, N. (eds.), *When Death Do Us Part: understanding and interpreting the probate records of early modern England* (2000)

Tate, W.E., *The Parish Chest*, 3rd edn. (1969)

Taylor, A.H.., 'Municipal records of Tenterden', *Archaeologia Cantiana* 32 (1917)

Thirsk, J., 'Industries in the Countryside', in Fisher, F. J. (ed.), *Essays in the Economic and Social History of Tudor and Stuart England* (1961)

Thirsk, J. (ed.), *The Agrarian History of England and Wales*, V, 1640-1750 (1983-5)

Thomas, H.B., 'Birchley and the Randolphs of Biddenden', *Archaeologia Cantiana* 68 (1954)

Todd, B.J., 'Demographic determinism and female agency: the remarrying widow reconsidered ... again', *Continuity and Change*, 9, 3 (1994)

Venn, J. and Venn, J.A., *Alumni Cantabrigiensis* (1922)

Visitation of the County of Kent, 1663-68, Harleian Society 54.

Wales, T., 'Poverty, poor relief and life-cycle: some evidence from seventeenth-century Norfolk', in Smith, R.M. (ed.), *Land, Kinship and Life-Cycle* (1984)

Watkinson, J., 'Congregational Churches in Kent', from *Articles published in the Kentish Express* (1911-12)

Weatherill, L., 'Probate Inventories and Consumer Behaviour in England 1660-1760', in Martin, G.H. and Spufford, P., *The Records of the Nation* (1990)

Weatherill, L., *Consumer behaviour and material culture in Britain, 1660-1760*, 2nd ed. (1996)

West, F., 'Infant mortality in the East Fen parishes of Leake and Wrangle', *Local Population Studies*, 13 (1974)

Whatmore, Rev.. L.E., *Recusancy in Kent, Studies and Documents* (1973)

Whiteman, A., *The Compton Census of 1676: a critical edition*, The British Academy Records of Social and Economic History, New Series X (1986)

Whiteman, A., 'The Compton Census of 1676', in Schurer, K. and Arkell, T. (eds.), *Surveying The People* (1992)

Woodruff, Rev.. C.E., 'Letters relating to the condition of the Church in Kent, 1678-1690', *Archaeologia Cantiana*, 21 (1895)

Woodward, D., 'The impact of the Commonwealth Act on Yorkshire parish registers', *Local Population Studies*, 14 (1975)

Wrightson, K., *English Society 1580-1680* (1982)

Wrightson, K., 'Kinship in an English village, Terling, Essex, 1500-1700', in Smith, R.M. (ed.), *Land, Kinship and Life-Cycle* (1984)

Wrightson, K. and Levine, D. *Poverty and piety in an English village, Terling, Essex, 1525-1700* (1979)

Wrigley, E.A., 'Family Reconstitution', in Wrigley, E.A. (ed.), *An Introduction to English Historical Demography* (1966a)

Wrigley, E.A., 'Family Limitation in Pre-Industrial England', *Economic History Review*, 2nd ser., 19 (1966b)

Wrigley, E.A., 'Marriage, fertility and population growth in eighteenth-century England', in Outhwaite, R.B. (ed.), *Marriage and Society; Studies in the Social History of Marriage* (1981)

Wrigley, E.A. and Schofield, R.S., *The Population History of England 1541-1871; A Reconstruction*, paperback edition (1989)

Wrigley, E.A., Davies, R.S., Oeppen, T.E. and Schofield, R.S., *English Population History from Family Reconstitution, 1580-1837* (1997)

Zell, M., 'Population and Family Structure in the Sixteenth-century Weald', *Archaeologia Cantiana*, 100 (1984)

Zell, M., *Industry in the Countryside; Wealden society in the sixteenth century* (1994)

Zell, M., 'Credit in the pre-industrial English woollen industry', *Economic History Review*, 49, 4 (1996)

Zeuner, D., *The Bayleaf Medieval Farmstead* (1990)

Notes

Abbreviations

CKS   Centre for Kentish Studies, Maidstone, Kent
KMI   Kent Monumental Inscriptions
PRC   Parish Record Collection
PRO   Public Record Office
VCH   Victoria County History

Introduction

[1] Spufford M. (1974), 57.
[2] Poole (2002).
[3] Spufford M. (2000), 2.
[4] Harrington (2000).
[5] Wrigley (1966b); Macfarlane (1977).
[6] Sharpe (1990), 50. She has since done so (2002).
[7] Hey (1974), 45.

Chapter 1: The Sources

[1] Tate (1969) 46-7.
[2] Woodward (1975) 25.
[3] Tate (1969) 48; Boulton (1992) 230.
[4] Sharpe (1990) 50.
[5] Souden (1984) 11ff.
[6] Boulton (1992) 223.
[7] Steel, D.J. (1968) 28-30.
[8] Ashurst (1995) 46-57.
[9] Benenden, Biddenden, Cranbrook, Goudhurst and Staplehurst, for which transcriptions already existed.
[10] Wrigley & Schofield (1989) 16-21.
[11] Wrigley (1966a).
[12] CKS P152/1/1.
[13] quoted in CKS PRC 2/40/185 (1684).
[14] quoted in CKS PRC 17/77/201 (1688).
[15] in Berry & Schofield (1971) 455-8, re-used by Wrigley & Schofield (1989) 96 and Wrigley, Davies, Oeppen & Schofield (1997) 53, 110-11, 229-30, 309, see Poole (2000), 13; (2002) 18-20.
[16] e.g. Woodward (1975) 30; Jackson & Laxton (1977) 31; Razzell (1995) 137-42; (1996) 182-8; (2000) 9.
[17] Cressy (1997) 180-3.
[18] Wrightson & Levine (1979) 165.
[19] Berry & Schofield (1971) 454.
[20] Drake (1962) 427-8.
[21] Sharpe (2002) 19; Drake estimated 15 per cent for his Yorkshire parishes (1962) 428.
[22] Cowper (1894).
[23] Whiteman (1986); Whiteman (1992); Nuttall (1963) 14 .

[24] Spufford M. (1968) esp. 292-3 for discussion.
[25] Chalklin (1960) 155.
[26] Whiteman (1986) xli; xliv.
[27] Harrington (2000).
[28] Clarification courtesy of Elizabeth Parkinson, March 2002.
[29] Arkell (1992a) 39-40; (2003) 148-9.
[30] Pearson in Harrington (2000) xxiii ff; maps I & 13, and Appendix VII, 461ff.
[31] Harleian Society (1906).
[32] Bedells (1990) 30-1.
[33] Wrightson & Levine (1979) 93.
[34] Takahashi (1990) 209; see also Spufford M. (1976) 170-1; Carlson (1994) xxivff.; Evans (2000) 183-4.
[35] CKS PRC 17/71/16 to 17/79/457; a further 123, proved at the Prerogative Court at Canterbury, are in the PRO at Kew.
[36] Compare Erickson (1995) 204-5, 20 per cent for widows in the 17th century.
[37] Spufford M. (1974) 37; Goose & Evans (2000) 60; CKS 17/73/158 (1670/1) will of James Willard has yeoman, 11/33/270 (1671) his inventory has labourer!
[38] Macfarlane (1970) 64.
[39] Spufford M. (1974) 325-44; Carlson (1994) xxxvi-xlvi ; Marsh (1990) 216ff.
[40] See esp. Spufford M. (1990); Weatherill (1990) 252ff.; Arkell (2000) 77ff.; Cox & Cox (2000) 14ff.
[41] CKS PRC 11/17/12 to 11/61/157.
[42] See esp. Erickson (1990) 273ff. and (2000) 103ff.; Spufford P. (1999) and (2000) 213ff.; Bower (1991); Edwards (1994); Tarver (2000) 229ff.
[43] CKS PRC mainly 1/8/90 to 2/42/158; Spufford P. (1999); Erickson (2000) 104.
[44] Erickson (2000) 110-4.
[45] Benenden, CKS P20 5/1 (1663-); Biddenden, P26 5/1 (1660-); Cranbrook, P100 5/1 (1588-); Frittenden, P152 5/1 (1665-); Staplehurst, 347 5/1 (1665-).
[46] Biddenden, CKS P26/12/1 (1652-); Cranbrook, P100/12/1 (1672-); Goudhurst, P157/11/1 (1675-); Staplehurst, P347/12/2-5 (1657-).
[47] CKS Q/S 231/9-15, 232/16-25.
[48] Tate (1969) 198-205.
[49] CKS P152/13/1.
[50] CKS P152/13/2.
[51] CKS P152/14/1.
[52] CKS P347/25/5.
[53] CKS N/FQZ/1.
[54] Macfarlane (1977) 135.

Chapter 2: The Cranbrook Region

[1] In general see Harris (1998); Brandon (2003).
[2] Thirsk (1961), Chalklin (1962).
[3] Everitt (1986) 121-4.
[4] Brandon (2003) xvi, 153-60.
[5] Hasted (1972) VII 91, also 173.
[6] Ogilby (1685); Chalklin (1965) 164-5.
[7] Chartres (1977) 81-2.
[8] CKS PRC 2/41/73 (1687) debt to innkeeper at Farningham, £7 for horsemeat.
[9] Barley (1961) 26ff.; Pearson (1994) 141ff. and (2000) lxiii-xcix; Chalklin (1665) 236ff.
[10] Pearson (2000) lxv.
[11] Barley (1961) 59-63; Chalklin (1965) 211, 253.
[12] Pearson (2000) lxxvii; CKS PRC 11/33/270 (1671); Spufford M. (1962) 82.
[13] Evelyn, Diary (1995) passim; for parallels see Macfarlane (1970) 71ff.
[14] Poole (2002) 88-95 for more detail.
[15] Spufford & Went (1995) 6 ff.; Laslett (1992) 22.
[16] Zell (1984) 233, 257.
[17] Arkell (1992b) 99-102.
[18] Arkell (1992b) 98, 103-9.

[19] Chalklin (1965) 50 ff.
[20] CKS PRC 17/75/255 (1681).
[21] Chalklin (1965) 52.
[22] See also Hey (1974) 59-61.
[23] Chalklin (1965) 68 ff.
[24] Stede-Cripps marriage agreement, 1665; see CKS PRC 17/80/139 (1703), Bearsted (courtesy of Peter Spufford); contrast Wrightson & Levine (1979) 27; Bower (1994) 155.
[25] Boys (1813) 25.
[26] Chalklin (1962) 34-5; Zell (1994) 91-7.
[27] Short (1984) 292.
[28] Thirsk (1961) 79; Chalklin (1965) 233.
[29] *VCH Kent*, III, 325; Chalklin (1962) 35-6.
[30] Thirsk (1961) 70 (quoting Lande, 1634).
[31] CKS PRC 11/32/113 (1670); 11/33/230 (1671).
[32] Chalklin (1965) 46 ff.; Short (1984) 296.
[33] CKS PRC 2/35/164 (1672); 2/41/18 (1685).
[34] CKS PRC 1/11/80 (1666), fat ox, commuted to £5.
[35] Clay (1985) 202-3.
[36] Chalklin (1965) 60; Clay (1985) 209; Short (1985) 296.
[37] Short (1985) 270.
[38] Thirsk (1961) 79; Chalklin (1965) 10-11.
[39] CKS U78 P6 (1669); see U814 P8 for Peter Courthop Esq. , estate map 1636.
[40] Chalklin (1961) 29; Short (1985) 270.
[41] Chalklin (1961) 36; CKS PRC 17/77/71 (1682), permission for 2000 loads.
[42] Chalklin (1961) 44; Short (1985) 271.
[43] Short (1985) 271.
[44] Harris (1998) 22-3; Zeuner (1990) 22.
[45] Thirsk (1961) 70-88.
[46] Morant (1983) 73-99; Pearson (1994) 138-41.
[47] Tarbutt (1874) xcvi-c; Pile (1981) 1-20; Zell (1994) 153-227; (1996) 667-91. Philpot, *Villare Cantiacum* (1667).
[48] Everitt (1973) 56.
[49] Zell (1994) 164ff.
[50] See e.g. CKS PRC 11/23/18 (1664).
[51] Eveleigh (1895) 184; Pile (1981) 21.
[52] Brandon (2003) 153-60.
[53] See Furley (1874) II, 576.
[54] Wrightson & Levine (1979) 22-3.
[55] Arkell (2000) 79.
[56] He was a clothier with a farm: CKS PRC 2/39/49 (1680).
[57] CKS PRC 17/78/463 (1695).
[58] Kussmaul (1981) 31, 70.
[59] Spufford M. (1962) 80-93; (1974) 36-45; (1990) 45-79.
[60] Erickson (2000) 116.
[61] Macfarlane (1970) 77; Pearson (2000) lxix-xcix.
[62] Pearson (2000) Table 3, lx-lxi.
[63] Short (1985) 308.
[64] Pearson (2000) Table 1, xxx.
[65] Pearson (2000) xliii-xlv.
[66] See Spufford M. & Went (1995) 52 for a parallel.
[67] Zell (1996) 671.
[68] But see Hill (1972) 357.
[69] Matthews' Calamy (1934) xii; *VCH Kent II* (1926) 100.
[70] Whiteman (1986) xxx, xxxi, 26, n. 114.
[71] Everitt (1970) 187-8; nonconformist percentages courtesy of Joanna Mackinder.

Chapter 3: Making the Family

[1] Stone (1977) 21-30.

2 Laslett (1983) 90 ff.
3 CKS PRC 17/78/43 (1691), 17/78/104 (1692).
4 Laslett (1983) 93ff; Stone (1977) 130.
5 Macfarlane (1970) 110-7, 126-43, 149-60.
6 Wrightson (1982) 48-50; (1984) 314; see Raines (1848).
7 Laslett (1972) 152; Wrightson (1982) 44.
8 Wrightson (1982) 45; see also Macfarlane (1978) 75-6; Wrightson & Levine (1979) 192ff.; Wrightson (1984) 313-332.
9 Wrightson (1982) 47
10 CKS PRC 17/75/121 (1680); 17/77/418 (1689/1690).
11 CKS PRC 17/72/175 (1664/1665).
12 Johnston (1971) 32.
13 Hey (1974) 203-4.
14 Hey (1974) 201; Stone (1977) 61.
15 Kussmaul (1981) 57-66; Macfarlane (1986) 92-4.
16 Macfarlane (1986) 142.
17 Houlbrooke (1984) 70ff.; Slater (1984) 60-3, 141-4; Adair (1996) 134-6; Cressy (1997)esp. 256.
18 CKS PRC 17/77/221 (1683/89); 17/71/266 (1661/62).
19 Cressy (1997) 237 ff. for a splendid variety of courtship narratives; see also Sachse (1938) on Roger Lowe, Morehouse (1877) on Adam Eyre.
20 Compare Stone (1977) 61; Wrightson (1984) 322-3.
21 Laslett (1983) 82ff; Hollingsworth used Cowper (1894) Vol II, 1619-1660.
22 Outhwaite (1972) 57, n.13.
23 Cressy (1997) 305.
24 Cressy (1997) 309.
25 Outhwaite (1972) 63.
26 Cressy (1997) 311 quoting Henri Misson (1719); Outhwaite (1972) 63-7.
27 Slater (1984) 64.
28 Evelyn (1995), 10 June 1647.
29 Dyer (1981) 26.
30 Adair (1996) 97.
31 Steel (1968) 147; Snell (1984) 30.
32 Wrigley (1966b) 94ff.
33 Dyer (1981) 30.
34 Adair (1996) 146 ff
35 Hair (1966) 233-43; Adair (1996) 94.
36 Wrightson & Levine (1979) 131.
37 Adair (1996) 92.
38 Adair (1996) 48-9; Laslett (1977a) 133-6.
39 Wrigley (1981) 158.

Chapter 4: Growth of the Family

1 Evelyn, diary, 18 October, 1660.
2 CKS PRC 2/37/120 (1678).
3 Stone (1977) 63 for an average between 24 and 30.
4 Wrigley (1966b) 87; Sharpe (2002) 174 acknowledges a problem.

	1600-29	1630-46	1647-59	1660-99	1700-19	1720-49	1750-69	1770-99	1800-24
females married	162	83	48	61	27	58	46	107	100
average per year	5.4	4.9	3.7	2.0	1.4	1.9	2.3	3.6	4.0
mean age 1st marriage	27.3	26.5	30.0	28.8	30.7	27.2	26.3	26.4	24.9

5 Souden (1984) 19.
6 Wrigley (1966b) 94.
7 Sharpe (2002) 189-197.
8 Chambers (1969) 21-23 quoting Creighton (1891-4); Schofield (1977) 119-21; Sharpe (2002) 92ff, 171.
9 But note Mary and Anthony Ridley of Goudhurst ('poor' at burial), with intervals of (8), 34, 28, 24 and 22 months!

10 Macfarlane (1970) 199ff; Storey (1993); de la Bedoyere (1995).
11 Evelyn, diary 1621-2.
12 Slater (1984) 31-34.
13 Sharpe (2002) 192ff for a similar pattern in Colyton.
14 Macfarlane (1986) 20-28.
15 Stone (1977) 105ff.
16 Slater (1984) 108-38, esp. 121-2.
17 Macfarlane (1970) 105ff; Pollock (1983) esp. 262-71.
18 Cressy (1997) 8, 10.
19 Wrightson (1982) 108ff; Houlbrooke (1984) 134ff; Laslett (1983) 119-20.
20 Schofield (1972) 49-50 for summary; Crawford (1986) 29.
21 Finlay (1980) 27; Wrigley & Schofield (1989) 97.
22 Pollock (1983) 51 for 15 per cent.
23 Wrigley, Davies, Oeppen & Schofield (1997) 102-3.
24 Chambers (1969) 21-23 quoting Creighton (1891-4).
25 Dyer (1985) 38; for the disease itself see Oxley (2003) 627/8.
26 Stone (1977) 159
27 Razzell (1996) 186-7.
28 Barley (1961) 258-9.
29 Crawford (1986) 30.
30 Archer, diary, 10 December 1670; she succeeded in the end.
31 Crawford (1986) 34-35.
32 Evelyn, diary, 1621-2; Macfarlane (1970) 83.
33 Crawford (1986) 31.
34 Archer, diary, 10 December 1682.
35 Evelyn, diary, 26 March 1664.
36 *The Times*, 9 September 1999, and again 11 September 2000: 'A baby aged two months was smothered to death by her mother as she slept next to her parents on a single mattress in hospital'.
37 Crawford (1986) 32.
38 Crawford (1986) 40.
39 Evelyn, diary 27 Jan. 1658; Archer, diary, July 1679.
40 Archer, diary, 30 Oct. 1675; Stone (1977) 79; Macfarlane (1970) 170.
41 Evelyn, diary, 15 Feb. 1658; Archer, diary, 31 Mar. 1670.
42 Storey (1993); see Macfarlane (1970) 171ff .
43 Storey (1993).
44 CKS PRC 17/78/182 (1678).
45 Stone (1977) 66.
47 CKS PRO 2/40/172 (1684).

Chapter 5: Preservation of the Family

1 Kussmaul (1981) 70; Ben-Amos (1994) 74, 81.
2 Stone (1977) 54-60.
3 Wrightson (1984) 327; 22 per cent of Tarling testators had no children.
4 Abbott (1996) 73. Wrigley, Davies, Oeppen & Schofield (1997).
5 Wrigley, Davies, Oeppen & Schofield (1997) 171-3, male median 12.9 months, female 19.4.
6 CKS PRC 17/74/111, 1676/7.
7 Laslett (1977b) 58; Stone (1977) 58-60; Macfarlane (1986) 235.
8 Holderness (1984) 428; Todd (1994) 421-50.
9 Holderness (1984) 430-1.
10 Gouge (1622) 582.
11 Wrightson (1984) 327; Macfarlane (1986) 232-3.
12 CKS PRC 17/76/148 (1684).
13 CKS PRC 17/78/163 (1687/92).
14 CKS PRC 17/71/495 (1661/2); 17/78/134 (1692).
15 CKS PRC 17/77/120 (1687/8); see 17/77/407 (1690).
16 CKS PRC 2/36/214 (1675); 2/36/216 (1675).

[17] CKS PRC 17/78/312 (1694).
[18] CKS PRC 17/73/376 (1675).
[19] CKS PRC 17/76/89 (1681/2).
[20] CKS PRC 2/40/185 (1684).
[21] CKS PRC 17/77/119 (1686/7).
[22] CKS PRC 17/78/299 (1694).
[23] CKS PRC 17/76/313 (1684/5).
[24] CKS PRC 17/76/141 (1682/4).
[25] CKS PRC 17/73/373 (1675).
[26] CKS PRC 17/77/209 (1687/8); 17/71/381 (1663/4).
[27] Most probate accounts show the deceased as intestate.
[28] CKS PRC 2/38/193 (1679); 2/39/150 (1681).
[29] CKS PRC 2/37/173 (1677).
[30] CKS PRC 1/10/106 (1664).
[31] CKS PRC 1/11/59 (1665).
[32] CKS PRC 2/36/213 (1675).
[33] CKS PRC 17/76/276 (1685/1686), 17/72/522 (1668/1669.
[34] CKS P20/25/2; Hume (1994) 91ff.
[35] Statute of Artificers 1563; Laslett (1983) 3.
[36] Ben-Amos (1994) 87.
[37] CKS PRC 17/74/285 (1677/1679), 17/71/495 (1661) and 17/72/467 (1668).
[38] CKS PCR 17/75/242 (1679/1682); Josselin, 14 April 1660, 10 November 1668.
[39] Information courtesy of Cliff Webb; 14 apprentices identified, median age 16.
[40] CKS PRC 17/77/404 (1688/90).
[41] Wrightson (1984) 328-9.
[42] CKS PRC 17/77/271 (1677/89).
[43] CKS PRC 17/77/374 (1690/1).
[44] CKS PRC 17/75/400 (1683).
[45] CKS PRC 17/78/176 (1692).
[46] CKS PRC 17/72/254 (1661/6).
[47] CKS PRC 17/77/286 (1689).
[48] CKS PRC 17/72/345 (1667).

Chapter 6: The 'chiefer sort'

[1] Laslett (1983), 32-3; (1992) 12-13.
[2] French (2000) 277-293.
[3] Wrightson (1982) 23; Stone (1966) 16-55; Everitt (1966) 56-73.
[4] Hainsworth (1992) 6-10.
[5] Hasted (1972) VII, 94, 100-101; Olsen (2001) 38.
[6] CKS PRC 2/35/79 (1671).
[7] Harleian 54: 139-40; Berry (1830) 177-8, 216.
[8] Haslewood (1889) 175-7; Hasted (1972) VII, 175.
[9] Whatmore (1973), 25.
[10] CKS PRC 2/36/156 (1676) and several others.
[11] Chalklin (1965) 210; Landau (1984) 23-38.
[12] Landau (1984) 218.
[13] G. (1734) 43, 57, 82; CKS 100/5/1 26 December 1670.
[14] Hasted (1972) I, 253-58.
[15] Landau (1984) 170 (map), 388 (table).
[16] CKS P26/12/1 for annual signatures.
[17] Sharpe (1987) 190, quoting £1500 over seven or eight years.
[18] CKS PRC 1/10/25 (1664); Hasted VII 148.
[19] Everitt (1973) 33-34.
[20] Everitt (1966) 60-1; Landau (1984) 297.
[21] Chalklin (1965) 194.
[22] Laslett (1992) 12-3; Arkell (1992c) 146-7.
[23] Zell (1996) 687-91.
[24] Frittenden does not figure in Zell's list, and Goudhurst's records are inadequate.

25 Compare Stapleton (1999) 387.
26 Zell (1994) 220-7.
27 Zell (1994) 225.
28 See also Stone (1966) 33-36.
29 Chalklin (1965) 194; Stone (1966) 34-5.
30 Stone (1966) 54; French (2000) 292.
31 de Launay 1984) 617.
32 CKS PRC 17/71/359 (1662); 11/20/111 (1662).
33 CKS PRC 17/73/412 (1676); 11/38/189 (1676).
34 Harleian Society (1906); Petrie (2004) 137-62.
35 Laslett (1948) 157, 160.
36 CKS PRC 17/72/95, 1661/4.
37 CKS PRC 17/73/315 1674/5.
38 KMI 3: 307, 308 & 317; Harleian 54: 137-8; Thomas (1954) 62-71.
39 See CKS PRC 17/73/234 (1673).
40 Cowper (1914).
41 Chalklin (1965) 210-11.
42 Tate (1969) 12; Josselin diary, passim.
43 Hasted (1972) VII, 141.
44 Woodruff (1895) 184-7.
45 Hasted (1972) VII, 133.
46 Smellie (1968) 13; Hindle (2000) 573.
47 CKS P100/5/1, 25 January 1685/6; see French (2000) 285; Hindle (1998) 78-80.
48 CKS PRC 2/37/46 (1676); 2/37/121 (1678); 17/77/221 (1683/9).
49 CKS PRC 17/75/426 (1683); 17/77/271 (1677/89); 17/73/376 (1675); 17/74/411 (1679).
50 CKS PRC 17/72/539 (1669/70); 17/75/255 (1681); 17/78/176 (1692).
51 Stone (1977) 130.
52 CKS PRC 17/72/253 (1667).
53 CKS PRC 17/72/402 (1665/8).
54 CKS PRC 17/72/340 (1665/7).

Chapter 7: The 'other inhabitants'
1   French (2000a) 277-293; (2000b) 66-99.
2   CKS PRC 17/74/400 (1678/1680).
3   CKS PRC 17/71/447 (1663).
4   CKS P26/5/1 (1667), and P20/5/1 & P26/12/1 passim; compare Chalklin (1965) 251; Thirsk (1985) V, 2, 35.
5   CKS PRC 2/36/261 (1675); 2/35/106 (1672).
6   CKS PRC 2/38/114 (1679).
7   Laslett (1977b) 62.
8   CKS PRC 2/36/216 (1675).
9   CKS PRC 1/9/156 (1663); 2/40/124 (1683); 2/40/169 (1684).
10 See Sharpe (1987) 191ff.; Copeman (1980) 16-22.
11 CKS PRC 1/10/86 (1664).
12 CKS PRC 2/42/148 (1699); 1/14/76 (1669) 2/38/19 (1679).
13 CKS P26/12/1, Biddenden Overseers' accounts for this and much to follow.
14 CKS PRC 2/39/89 (1680).
15 CKS PRC 2/36/71 (1657); 1/13/148 (1669).
16 Tate (1969) 191-8.
17 CKS P100/13/1; P152/13/1; Q/SO E2 (1679).
18 CKS P152/13/2.
19 From 1692 additions subject to JP's approval, see Hindle (2004) 9.
20 Laslett (1983) 32; (1992) 12; Slack (1988) 80-81.
21 Wales (1984) 352.
22 Wales (1984) 358 on Cawston, Norfolk, and Chalklin (1965) 255, for close parallels.
23 Compare Wales (1984), 385, n.66.
24 CKS P100/5/1.

[25] Harrington (2000); refer Arkell (2003) 151-3. See Poole (2005) for more details.
[26] Wales (1984) 385.
[27] CKS PRC 17/75/161.
[28] See also Sharpe (2002) 258.
[29] CKS QS 231/9-231/25, paralleling Colyton, Sharpe (2002) 253, 258.
[30] Wales (1984) 375.
[31] CKS P152/14/1.
[32] CKS PRC 2/40/94 (1683).
[33] CKS PRC 2/36/203 (1675).
[34] Tate (1969) 221-226.
[35] CKS PRC 17/72/543 (1670); Sharpe (2002) 266.
[36] Brown (1984) 420.
[37] As did the rector of Myddle, see Gough (1981) 41.
[38] CKS PRC 17/72/165 (1687).

Chapter 8: Support across Village Societies
[1] Houlbrooke (1984) 86.
[2] Thomas Hutton, pewterer of Cranbrook, moved to Canterbury in 1664.
[3] Cowper (1892) I, iii-iv.
[4] Wrightson (1984) 330.
[5] CKS PRC 17/75/420 (1684); 17/77/22 (1687).
[6] CKS PRC 17/77/271 (1677/89); 17/78/239 (1691/4).
[7] CKS PRC 17/73/229 (1672/3); 17/72/539 (1669/70).
[8] CKS PRC 17/75/242 (1679/82).
[9] CKS PRC 17/77/374 (1690/1); 17/77/419 (1689/90).
[10] CKS PRC 17/72/253 (1661/6).
[11] CKS PRC 1/12/56 (1667).
[12] Calamy (1802) 2: 325.
[13] CKS PRC 17/71/229 (1662).
[14] Marsh (1990) 233.
[15] Spufford & Takahashi (1996) 381, 393-4, ref. Willingham, Cambridgeshire.
[16] CKS PRC 17/74/216 (1678).
[17] CKS PRC 17/73/229 (1672/3).
[18] CKS P154/13/1, 5 March 1690.
[19] CKS PRC 17/73/340 (1674).
[20] CKS PRC 17/75/394 (1684); see Clay (1985) 231ff.
[21] CKS PRC 17/73/158 (1670/1).
[22] CKS PRC 17/77/230 (1688); 17/78/134 (1692).
[23] CKS PRC 17/76/470 (1687).
[24] CKS PRC 17/76/108 (1684).
[25] CKS PRC 17/76/428 (1681/6).
[26] CKS PRC 17/72/340 (1665/7).
[27] CKS PRC 17/78/159 (1690/2).
[28] Marsh (1990) 221, 242; see 228-30 for delay in copying up wills.
[29] CKS PRC 17/78/436 (1695).
[30] Howe (2002)16.
[31] CKS PRC 2/42/152 (1699).
[32] CKS N/FQz/1, 394.
[33] CKS PRC 2/35/216 (1673).
[34] CKS P152/1/1.
[35] CKS PRC 1/11/102 (1667).
[36] Landau (1984) 228ff.; Silverthorne (1978) for table of fees.
[37] See also Hey (1974) 190ff.
[38] Cox & Cox (2000) 29-30; see Arkell (2000) 72-102.
[39] CKS PRC 2/42/152 (1699).
[40] CKS PRC 20/13/343 (1685).
[41] CKS PRC 1/10/106 (1664).

Chapter 9: Borrowing and Lending Money

1   Holderness (1976) 98.
2   Spufford, P. (2000) 227.
3   Bower (1994) 160.
4   Holderness (1976) 101.
5   Spufford, P. (2000) 215.
6   CKS PRC 2/36/213 (1675).
7   CKS PRC 2/41/183 (1690).
8   CKS PRC 11/33/220 (1671).
9   Compare Hey (1974) 143; Stapleton (1999) 390-1.
10 Muldrew (1998) 97.
11 CKS PCC 1/14/76, 1669.
12 CKS PCC 1/14/72, 1669.
13 CKS PCC 1/12/98, 1667.
14 Spufford, M. (1984) 80.
15 CKS PRC 2/41/73 (1687).
16 CKS PRC 2/41/18 (1685).
17 CKS PRC 11/20/126 (1662).
18 See Muldrew (1998) 109ff.
19 CKS PRC 2/41/73 (1687).
20 CKS PRC 1/10/25 (1664). Spufford, P. (2000) 220 for 6 per cent interest, Usury Act of 1651, confirmed 1660.
21 CKS PRC 17/77/420 (1690), 17/72/263 (1666), 17/77/371 (1687/91).
22 CKS PRC 17/77/271 (1677/89).
23 CKS PRC 17/71/421 (1663).
24 CKS PRC 17/77/177 (1687/8).
25 CKS PRC 2/42/8 (1691).
26 CKS PRC 2/40/55 (1682).
27 CKS PRC 2/41/88 (1686); 2/40/87 (1683).
28 CKS PRC 2/36/251(1675).
29 CKS PRC 1/11/80 (1666).
30 CKS PRC 2/41/50 (1687).
31 CKS PRC 1/15/48 (1670).
32 CKS PRC 2/35/106 (1672); 1/8/103 (1662).
33 CKS PRC 17/73/326 (1674); 20/13/333 (1683).
34 CKS PRC 19/3/142 (1667).
35 de Launay (1984) 523/638/648.
36 Holderness (1984) 435; CKS PRC 11/19/123 (1662); 11/20/126 (1662); 11/32/83 (1670); 11/33/29 (1671); 11/35/211 (1673).
37 CKS PRC 2/38/66 (1678); 2/36/6 (1674); 20/13/343 (1685).
38 Holderness (1984) 441 for 40 per cent kin in Lincolnshire.
39 CKS PRS 1/12/98 (1667).
40 CKS PRC 1/14/30 (1669/70).
41 CKS PRC 1/11/30 (1665); 2/37/121 (1678)
42 Holderness (1984) 441; Spufford, P. (2000) 223-4.
43 de Launay (1984) 523 (Sheaf family).
44 CKS PRC 17/73/234 (Jonas 1673); CKS PRC 17/76/100 (Jeremy 1684).
45 CKS PRC 11/51/83 (1687).
46 CKS PRC 2/40/25 (1682).
47 CKS PRC 1/13/44 (1668); 2/40/33 (1682).
48 CKS PRC 2/37/28 (1676); 2/40/107 (1683); 2/39/89 (1680).
49 CKS PRC 2/42/122 (1696); 2/42/150 (1699); Edwards (1994) 21-43.
50 CKS PRC 17/73/409 (1674).
51 CKS PRC 20/13/343 (1685).
52 CKS PRC 1/13/4 (1669) for payment at 6s. 8d. in the pound for non-bonded debts.

Chapter 10: The Nonconformist Factor

1   Collinson (1980) 176.

[2] Evelyn, Diary, 17 Aug. 1662.

[3] Evelyn, Diary, 27 April 1673.

[4] Spurr (1998) 149.

[5] Calamy (1802) II 336.

[6] Calamy (1802) II 320; (1934) 374-5.

[7] CKS PRC 1/11/72 (1665).

[8] Calamy (1802) II 333; (1934) 214; Nuttall (1963) 188.

[9] Nuttall (1963) 182-3.

[10] Spurr (1998) 133, 135.

[11] Watkinson (1911-2) 52.

[12] Spurr (1998) 143.

[13] Pile (1953) 11.

[14] CKS PRC 2/38/154 (1679).

[15] Russell (1993) 1.

[16] Calamy (1802) II 449-456.

[17] Calamy (1802) I 378; Nuttall (1963) 187.

[18] Spufford M. (1995) 1-4, 18-19.

[19] ref. Chambers (1950s) III, 5; by 1653 the congregation numbered 84.

[20] Nuttall (1963) 185.

[21] Maguire (1995).

[22] Nuttall (1963) 186.

[23] CKS Q/S 231/9/43.

[24] CKS PRC 17/75/262 (1680/1).

[25] Maguire (1995); Pile (1953) 11; Chalklin (1965) 226-7.

[26] Inscriptions in Cranbrook church.

[27] CKS PRC 17/75/438 (1681/83); 11/47/194 (1683).

[28] Nuttall (1963) 186.

[29] Nuttall (1963) 182, 186; Chambers (1950s) III, 5.

[30] Maguire (1995).

[31] Fox (1891) I, 227 and 229.

[32] Fox (1891) II, 2.

[33] Nuttall (1963) 183-4

[34] Draper (1993) 326-8.

[35] Pile (1953) 7, conveyance July 1673.

[36] Pile (1953) 6.

[37] Draper (1993) 326-8.

[38] Draper (1995) 10, 18.

[39] CKS N/FQZ/1 35-51, 392-8; Draper (1993) 328-30.

[40] Draper (1995) 3.

[41] CKS PRC 2/36/6 (1674).

[42] CKS N/FQZ/1 32, 50.

[43] CKS N/FQZ/1 34.

[44] CKS N/FQZ/1 33-34.

[45] CKS PRC 17/77/63 (1687), 17/75/208 (1680/1); see also Hey (1974) 217.

[46] CKS PRC 17/75/32 (1680).

[47] Sharpe (2002) 49, 220.

[48] Stevenson (1990) 339; see also 1995a & 1995b; Munby (1995) 33-7.

[49] Carlson (1995) 200, prefigured by Spufford, M. (1968) 266.

[50] CKS N/FQZ/1 306.

[51] CKS PRC 17/72/568 (1663/4).

[52] CKS PRC 1/13/49 (1668).

[53] CKS N/FQZ/1 50.

Index of Parishioners named in the Text

General Index